WHERE IS THE GOD OF JUSTICE?

WHERE IS THE GOD OF JUSTICE?

BIBLICAL PERSPECTIVES ON SUFFERING

WARREN MCWILLIAMS

Copyright © 2005 by Hendrickson Publishers, Inc.
P. O. Box 3473
Peabody, Massachusetts 01961-3473

ISBN-13: 978-1-56563-571-5
ISBN-10: 1-56563-571-X

Printed in the United States of America

Second Printing – June 2006

Cover Art: Julius Schnorr von Carolsfeld (1794–1872). Image depicts Lot and his family leaving Sodom as the city burns in the background; Lot's wife looks back. "*Lot fliehet aus Sodom.*" From *Die Bibel in Bildern* published in 1853. Image appears courtesy of the Digital Image Archive, Pitts Theology Library, Candler School of Theology, Emory University. Used with permission.

Library of Congress Cataloging-in-Publication Data

McWilliams, Warren, 1946–
   Where is the God of justice? : biblical perspectives on suffering /
Warren McWilliams.
     p. cm.
   Includes bibliographical (p.) references and indexes.
   ISBN-13: 978-1-56563-571-5 (alk. paper)
   ISBN-10: 1-56563-571-X (alk. paper)
   1. Suffering–Biblical teaching. I. Title.
   BS680.S854M385 2006
   233–dc22
                         2005027800

For Patty

CONTENTS

PREFACE

The author of Ecclesiastes writes "Of making many books there is no end" (Eccl 12:12), and the reader might wonder why another book on suffering is needed.[1] If you have bothered to pick up this book and read this far, you probably have wondered about why your friends or your relatives have suffered. Or, perhaps you have suffered. I am convinced that dealing with suffering is the biggest problem, theological and practical, faced by most Christians.

More books on suffering are needed as long as people continue to suffer, and as they struggle with the meaning of suffering for their lives. For Christians the issue of suffering relates directly to God's character. How can a good, loving God allow suffering in his world? The title of this work comes from Malachi 2:17. "Where is the God of justice?" was a query raised by post-exilic Jews perplexed by their lack of prosperity after rebuilding the temple in Jerusalem. Some Bible scholars suggest that for these people the question was more sarcastic than sincere, but I choose it as the title of this study because it could be asked by genuine seekers for truth.[2] To borrow a phrase from Peter Kreeft, this work is for those who have "wept and wondered."[3]

What kind of book is this? I would classify this work more as a theology of suffering than a traditional theodicy. This book focuses on the question of God's justice, and it highlights the Bible more than philosophical argumentation. In short, this work focuses on biblical perspectives on suffering. In an earlier study, I organized biblical teachings along canonical categories, with chapters on blocks of material such as suffering in the Pentateuch (the first five books of the Bible), suffering in the prophets, and suffering in the gospels.[4] My approach this time is more thematic or theological, offering biblical perspectives on the many types of suffering.

Some books on the Christian view of suffering tend to be abstract, stressing theoretical and philosophical perspectives. Here I will focus on concrete experiences of suffering, at times adopting the perspective of the womb to the tomb, or the entire span of human life. As Shirley Guthrie comments, "Against all attempts to explain evil away in one way or another, Christian faith is uncompromisingly realistic."[5] One way to reinforce our awareness of the realism of our faith is to look carefully at specific forms of suffering. Part Two will highlight several cases of suffering, including animal suffering, an issue not always treated in books such as this one. Except for the suffering of God, I will not highlight suffering that is voluntarily assumed, such as martyrdom or the monastic vow of poverty.

Before you and I tackle these diverse forms of suffering in Part Two, in Part One I will focus our attention on a few perennial questions. Even here, however, I will be as practical and concrete as possible. For instance, questions such as "Does God cause tornadoes?" become very important for the survivors of such disasters as earthquakes, tornadoes, and floods.

This book is intended for anyone who has ever suffered or for anyone who tries to help suffering people. Pastors and church staff members might find some help for their ministries here, but I also hope concerned lay people will also find these chapters accessible and helpful. My stance is more exploratory than dogmatic. I would never claim to have figured out why suffering happens, but I hope this book will suggest ways Christians can think about the issue of suffering and respond creatively. Readers interested in going deeper into the discussion will, I hope, look at the sources mentioned in my notes and highlighted in the bibliography. My overall theological stance is evangelical, but I hope that Christians from across the theological spectrum will find this book stimulating.

I have presented some of the ideas in this book in sermons and in the classroom over the years. Earlier versions of the chapters on tornadoes and animal suffering were presented to regional meetings of the American Academy of Religion.

I want to thank Shirley Decker-Lucke at Hendrickson Publishers for working with me on this book. My thanks also to the anonymous outside reader who offered constructive criticisms of several chapters.

I dedicate this book to my wife, Patty. For over thirty-five years she has encouraged me in my roles as husband, father, teacher, and minister. Although I am the trained, professional theologian in our family, she handles adversity with more courage and hopefulness than I do. For several years I have told students and church audiences that she is a better Christian than I am. Those who know the two of us well will heartily agree. Patty epitomizes the stance of reverent creativity I mention in the last chapter. Our daughters, Amy and Karen, also inspire me to be a better Christian and to think more clearly about life's important issues. University Baptist Church continues to be a community of compassion and comfort for me and others who struggle with discerning God's presence in our lives. My colleagues at Oklahoma Baptist University, especially my co-workers in the Joe L. Ingram School of Christian Service, challenge me to be a better teacher and scholar through their discipline and creativity.

Warren McWilliams
Joe L. Ingram School of Christian Service
Oklahoma Baptist University
Shawnee, Oklahoma

INTRODUCTION: IS GOD JUST?

Is God just? Can we trust God? Christians affirm the goodness of God, but our life experiences often seem to contradict this basic affirmation of our faith. A quick review of recent news in my town and state reveals a lengthy catalogue of human suffering. The obituaries in my morning newspaper report deaths due to car wrecks, house fires, and terminal illness. Many are poor and homeless. Native Americans and other minority groups continue to combat discrimination in the workplace. In the late spring the state of Oklahoma often lives up to its nickname, "tornado alley."

Some suffering is considered newsworthy by the news media, but chronic suffering, such as gender discrimination or a long battle with a debilitating disease, might never make the headlines. For example, the bombing of the federal building in Oklahoma City in 1995 and the terrorist attacks on the World Trade Center and the Pentagon on September 11, 2001, continue to attract attention in Oklahoma and around the world. But a young single mother who struggles to finish her education, work outside the home, and to care for her small child is almost invisible to most people.

The biblical writers often affirm God's justice. The Psalmist describes God as a "lover of justice" (Ps 99:4). Isaiah reports God saying: "For I the Lord love justice" (Isa 61:8). God is just, yet many people suffer. Why? In the post-exilic period some Jews had become cynical about God's justice and posed the question that is the title of this work: "Where is the God of justice?" (Mal 2:17). Although that question could be asked by a believer struggling with her suffering, one evangelical scholar suggests Malachi's audience had moved close to denying the existence of God.[1] Christians who suffer today still wrestle with the perennial question, "Is God just?" As believers, they know the Bible affirms the goodness of God, yet their experience of suffering seems to contradict their theology. Their suffering prompts questions about the meaning of life in general and the nature of God in particular. How does their belief in the God revealed supremely in Jesus relate to life in the real world?[2]

In this book I will develop a biblically based theology of suffering. Rather than focus on the view of suffering in a specific biblical book, such as Malachi, I will draw insights from throughout the Bible that will assist us as we encounter suffering throughout human life.[3]

TOWARD A THEOLOGY OF SUFFERING

What is suffering? How should we describe or define suffering? Why is suffering a problem for Christians? Questions such as these dominate Christian responses to pain, evil, and suffering.

In this section I will contrast two general Christian approaches to questions about God, evil, and suffering. These approaches are not mutually exclusive, but their starting points and methods differ significantly. The first approach could be labeled the theodicy approach. The term "theodicy" comes from the Greek words for God (*theos*) and justice (*dike*). Theodicy could refer either to the question "Is God just?" or to attempts to answer that question. In this book I will be more concerned with theodicy in the former sense of the question, "Is God just?" I will not focus much attention on theodicy in the second sense, or theodicy as an attempt to answer the question, "Is God Just?" using philosophical methods. Theodicy as the examination of possible answers to questions of God's justice is an approach often followed by philosophers, philosophers of religion, and Christian apologists. Reason and logic are primary tools in this first approach.

Some biblical scholars use the term "theodicy" in reference to God's relation to evil and suffering. They do not mean the philosophical endeavor to justify God. For example, Old Testament scholar Walter Brueggemann suggests that, "In Israel . . . what is called theodicy is not explanation but protest."[4]

The second approach could be called a theology of suffering. This approach draws on the classic understanding of theology as faith seeking understanding. This second approach generally is more sensitive to practical concerns about suffering. This book generally falls within the theology of suffering category.[5] I will not ignore reason or logic, but a theology of suffering approach takes the insights of the Bible as significant and essential for addressing the question, "Is God

| **Is God just?** |

just?" Reason is not ignored in this approach, but the focus will be on faith seeking understanding of the biblical teaching.

Theodicy

Although I will develop a theology of suffering, a brief review of some of the insights of the theodicy approach will help set the stage for the rest of the book. In the theodicy approach, one traditional strategy is to describe the intellectual problem thoughtful Christians encounter as a trilemma. That is, Christians try to juggle three questions or issues.[6]

1) Is God willing to prevent evil but unable to do that? If so, then God is impotent.

2) Is God able to stop evil but unwilling? If so, then God is malevolent.

3) If God is both willing and able to prevent evil, why is there evil?

Christian theologians and philosophers have worked for centuries on this intellectual puzzle. We will look at some of these issues in Part One, but our primary focus will not be philosophy of religion. These "intellectual" issues are crucial to an overall Christian response to suffering, but my focus will be more on the practical side of the problem of suffering.[7] Kenneth Surin has helpfully classified theodicies into two categories, those with a more theoretical emphasis and those with a more practical emphasis.[8] My work would be closer to Surin's second category, since some writers in that category are doing theology of suffering more than philosophical theodicy.

Another standard strategy for Christians is to distinguish two types of evil or suffering, moral and natural.[9] First, moral evil or suffering consists of events due primarily to human activity. In other words, a free, moral being makes decisions that lead to suffering. Traditionally called sin, this moral suffering includes racial discrimination, child abuse, slavery, and other forms of sinful activity. Langdon Gilkey's gripping account of his experiences in a Japanese internment camp during World War II is a striking example of moral evil.[10] Sometimes the sinner causes suffering for himself, but at other times the sinner's actions causes pain for another person.

Second, natural evil or suffering results from the forces of nature. This type of evil is illustrated by tornadoes, hurricanes, floods, diseases, and other "natural" disasters. The chapter on tornadoes in Part One will deal in more depth with natural evil.

Christians who follow the theodicy approach in the narrower sense of rational solutions to the problem of evil have proposed numerous explanations for human suffering. Some of these views have strong biblical support, and I will return to some of them in later chapters. Princeton theologian Daniel Migliore has summarized some of these proposals, highlighting three views that have been prominent in Christian tradition. First, some Christians appeal to mystery, acknowledging that they will never know why people suffer. Second, suffering might be due to divine punishment for sin or divine chastisement. Third, human suffering might be "an opportunity for spiritual growth."[11]

Migliore also highlights four contemporary approaches to theodicy. First, protest theodicy points to those who express anger at

God for their suffering. Second, theodicy from the vantage point of process theology stresses that God's power operates more as persuasion than as coercion, allowing for evil to happen. Third, a person-making theodicy stresses that people can become more mature through their suffering. Fourth, liberation theologies emphasize the need for praxis in response to suffering. Praxis refers to the active struggle for justice and freedom against oppressive social structures.

Theodicy in the sense of a logical, philosophical response to the problem of God's relation to evil has a long history.[12] The field has experienced considerable ferment in recent years, with some thinkers rejecting the attempt to do theodicy in the classic sense of defending or justifying God.[13]

Our Goal: A Theology of Suffering

Although some valuable insights can be gleaned from the more logical, philosophical theodicy approach, the approach in this book is closer to a theology of suffering. I write as a Christian who has struggled with the issue of evil and suffering, and I will assume a faith seeking understanding stance. Questions about God's justice and goodness will be addressed seriously, but I will not attempt to develop a detailed Christian apologetic for God's goodness. Christians can draw insights from the Bible that will help them deal with the suffering in their lives.

A theology of suffering intersects with several other fields of study. Several years ago Lucien Richard reviewed the theologies of suffering offered by a wide range of Roman Catholic and Protestant theologians.[14] In terms of systematic theology, the theology of suffering would be a sub-topic in the discussion of God's providence. Christian systematic theologians have often discussed evil, theodicy, and related subjects under the umbrella of God's care and concern for his creation.[15] A theology of suffering could also fall under the rubric of pastoral or practical theology. Paul Fiddes, for instance, devotes significant attention to suffering in the context of his discussion of a pastoral doctrine of the Trinity.[16]

FROM WOMB TO TOMB

Although the distinction between the theodicy approach to suffering and a theology of suffering is not absolute, a theology of suffering is the main focus of this book. Part Two will address specific examples of suffering in a loosely chronological scheme. Scholars from many disciplines have increasingly recognized the significance of a "womb to tomb" perspective when addressing questions of theodicy. Such a perspective encompasses the many stages that make up the typical human life span. For example, Lewis Sherrill's classic *The Struggle of the Soul* traced the distinctive spiritual crises of each stage of human development.[17] Later, Gail Sheehy popularized much psychological research in *Passages: Predictable Crises of Adult Life*.[18] Much earlier William Shakespeare used a scheme of seven ages for humanity in *As You Like It*.[19]

Paying attention to the human life cycle should help us see how Christians can respond to suffering in ordinary life. Theologians who share an interest in narrative, or story, theology can identify with a theology of suffering organized in a womb to tomb manner.[20] Jürgen Moltmann, for instance, addresses the beginning and ending of life.[21] Some Christians have found a narrative approach more helpful for dealing with their own suffering. Rather than deal topically with God's power and other theological topics, they reflect theologically via narrative. For instance, David Keck reflects on his mother's Alzheimer's disease, and John Goldingay reports on how he and his wife responded to his wife's multiple sclerosis.[22]

Although I will not follow a strictly chronological, developmental pattern, in Part Two I will highlight specific cases of suffering. Some cases are more typical of certain stages of life. For instance, the struggle with infertility is more typical of younger married couples. The concern with aging is typical of older people and those who relate to them. Other types of suffering, such as illness, discrimination, and violence, appear throughout the life span.

Following a loosely developmental plan of organization also reminds us that not all suffering occurs in a crisis situation. We often think of suffering as the result of a car wreck, a hurricane, or a murder. Some examples of suffering discussed in Part Two, such as racial discrimination and poverty, will remind us that some suffering is chronic or long term.

C. S. Lewis: A Case Study in Christian Suffering

Many readers will be familiar with the story of C. S. Lewis, who provides a helpful case study in how a Christian responds to suffering. Lewis is one of the most famous Christian authors in the twentieth century, having written novels such as *The Lion, the Witch and the Wardrobe*, works of popular theology, and scholarly volumes on English literature. He presented his life story, up to his conversion to Christianity as an adult, in *Surprised by Joy*. In his early life he had experienced several forms of suffering. His mother died of cancer while he was a child, and he had a distant relationship with his father. He had some traumatic experiences at boarding schools, and he

How does suffering change from womb to tomb?

was later wounded while serving in World War I. His brother, Warren, was an alcoholic, and Lewis observed the devastation of World War II while teaching at Oxford University.[23]

An Intellectual Approach

Lewis's experience with suffering can be studied profitably by comparing two books he wrote on the subject. In 1940 he wrote *The Problem of Pain*, still one of the best studies available. Lewis had thought it best to publish the book anonymously, since he thought he could not live up to his own principles.[24] He suggested that the main purpose of his book was to tackle "the intellectual problem raised by suffering"; he would not presume to tell others how to handle their own pain.[25]

In this book Lewis worked as a Christian apologist, attempting to explain how a good and powerful God could allow suffering to afflict humans. On the subject of divine omnipotence, for instance, Lewis clarified that God could not do the logically impossible. God would not do nonsense, but this was not a genuine limitation on divine power.[26] To explain God's goodness, Lewis used four analogies to illustrate God's love. Moving from the lowest form of love to the highest, Lewis identified the love of an artist for his creation, the love of a man for an animal, a father's love for a son, and a man's love for a woman.[27]

Lewis developed his apologetic argument with chapters on human sin, heaven, hell, and animal pain. Throughout the book, Lewis intended to present mainstream, orthodox Christian teaching. He admitted that in the chapters on animal suffering and heaven he was more speculative.[28]

Lewis's *Problem of Pain* was well received. Indeed, the director of religious programs at the British Broadcasting Corporation (BBC) soon wrote Lewis to invite him to do a series of radio addresses. Lewis reluctantly agreed, and those addresses were eventually collected in the volume entitled *Mere Christianity*.[29] This book remains a favorite among Lewis's admirers.

Although *The Problem of Pain* was popular and led him into further apologetic writing, some readers feel the tone of this book is too academic or theoretical for them.[30] Even though Lewis had experienced much suffering earlier, and he was writing during the early stages of World War II, some readers do not find the book emotionally engaging.

An Emotional Approach

A radically different tone appears in Lewis's later book on suffering, *A Grief Observed*. In this book Lewis agonizes over his wife's death, and he is at times very angry at God. What has happened in between the two books? To summarize a long, complicated story, Lewis had experienced the death of his wife, Joy. Lewis had been a confirmed bachelor, living with his brother at the Kilns, while he taught English literature at Oxford University and then Cambridge University. Some readers may be familiar with some of the story through the movie *Shadowlands*, which is based loosely on these events. Joy died of cancer, and Lewis's faith in God was shaken severely.

Lewis recorded his grief over Joy's death in a remarkably candid way. Indeed, the book was first published under a pseudonym. Some Lewis scholars believe that Joy's death so shattered Lewis's faith that he never tried to defend Christianity again. One scholar claims that "Lewis is left with a deity of dubious moral character."[31]

Without going into the fine points of Lewis's interpretation, I acknowledge that he seems extremely angry at God in this book. In his grief, Lewis experienced the absence of God, not his comforting presence.[32] His anger at God's disappearance leads to a description of God as "The Cosmic Sadist."[33] He even compares God to a vivisectionist, someone who experiments on animals.[34] Lewis did not doubt God's existence, but he questioned God's goodness. "Not that I am (I think) in much danger of ceasing to believe in God. The real danger is of coming to believe such dreadful things about Him."[35]

How could a strong, mature Christian such as C. S. Lewis respond this way to the death of a loved one? In the 1993 movie *Shadowlands*, Anthony Hopkins portrays Lewis as a cool, rational academic delivering lectures on suffering, a subject he apparently does not understand very well. The movie, based on William Nicholson's play, stresses the discontinuity between the Lewis of *The Problem of Pain* (1940) and the author of *A Grief Observed* (1961).[36] Certainly some Christians have responded to grief, physical pain, or some other form of suffering by abandoning faith in God. Many Christians have been mad at God when their suffering was extreme and unbearable. Another, better approach to Lewis's experience will be presented in the next section.

The Stages of Suffering

The stark contrast between Lewis's two books on suffering makes more sense to me when I put that contrast in the context of recent thinking about the stages of suffering. A few decades ago psychologists such as Elizabeth Kubler-Ross popularized the notion of stages of grief. A grieving person, psychologists suggest, typically moves through a series of stages as she approaches resolution of the grief. In her pioneering work, Kubler-Ross identified five stages typically experienced by a terminally ill person: denial and isolation, anger, bargaining, depression, and acceptance. Not all dying people experience these stages uniformly, but awareness of the stages can help people who minister to the dying.[37] One of Lewis's biographers noted, "Lewis knew by instinct what is now a commonplace of bereavement counseling, that grief must be expressed and lived through."[38]

Some theologians have developed similar temporal schemes for suffering. Dorothee Soelle, for example, proposes three stages of suffering.[39] In the first stage the sufferer feels numb and isolated. She is mute or moaning. The sufferer is so overwhelmed by the suffering that she may become apathetic and give up hope for any significant change in her situation. Soelle's second stage focuses on the experience of lament or protest. Theological reflection can begin in this stage because the sufferer can at least start to talk about her pain. In the third stage the sufferer begins to use more rational language to describe what is happening to her, to experience solidarity with others, and to make plans for action.

Although I will not try to correlate Lewis's experience as recorded in *A Grief Observed* with these three stages of suffering, I am convinced that his angry outbursts at God fit this general pattern. Like any Christian grieving over the death of a spouse, Lewis was on an emotional roller coaster. His grief over Joy's death, like biblical laments, seems to fit into stage two of Soelle's scheme. Probably the most famous lament, "My God, my God, why have you forsaken me?" (Ps 22:1), is echoed by Lewis early in his book.[40] Job's complaints in the poetic middle section of the book that bears his name, the "confessions" of Jeremiah, and the testimony of sufferers across the centuries parallel Lewis's anger at God.

Lewis's faith in God was severely tested by Joy's death, but Lewis did not lose his faith. The last book he wrote for publication, *Letters to Malcolm: Chiefly on Prayer*, is a strong statement of his mature faith. His comments in *A Grief Observed* do not contradict his earlier confident apologetic in *The Problem of Pain*; rather, he emerges as a much more human, even vulnerable defender of the Christian faith.

Christians have responded in a variety of ways to suffering. In recent decades a trend labeled "protest theodicy" has highlighted the biblical laments.[41] Although Christians have developed many different theodicies across the centuries, protest theodicy highlights this central concern with the goodness or justice of God. Rather than questioning the existence of God in light of suffering, adherents of protest theodicy question the moral character of God. This kind of theodicy will not settle for easy answers and insists on the biblical precedence for debating with God. Abraham, for instance, challenges God to be just in his treatment of Sodom. A good God should not kill innocent people in that sinful town. "Shall not the Judge of all the earth do what is just?" (Gen 18:25). Abraham wants God to demonstrate his justice by protecting any innocent people in Sodom.

Lewis's response to Joy's death, reflected in *A Grief Observed*, demonstrates the intermingling of thought and emotion, especially in the second stage of suffering. Both in *A Grief Observed* and the earlier *The Problem of Pain* Lewis attempted to make sense of suffering. The earlier book is a carefully argued apologetic, but the second book reveals his personal agony over the loss of his spouse. One reason Lewis's grief was so intense was Joy had experienced a remission from her cancer. Lewis understood this remission as a miracle, and he was devastated when the cancer returned.

In *A Grief Observed* Lewis is aware of the delicate balance between thought and emotion in the grieving process. Feelings might even disguise themselves as thoughts.[42] Lewis believes he should be thinking, not feeling.[43] In *The Screwtape Letters* Lewis mentions the "law of Undulation," the emotional roller coaster humans experience in ordinary life.[44] These emotional ups and downs should not overwhelm our thinking. In *Mere Christianity* Lewis argues that emotions, not reason, are the real enemy of faith. Emotions can carry out "a sort of blitz on his belief."[45]

Even if we do not accept all of the details of Soelle's three stages of suffering, many sufferers would agree that they have experienced a process of reaction to their pain. The old saying "Time heals all wounds" may be trite, but it contains an element of truth. The

Hebrew prophet Habakkuk, for example, seems to move through a process of reflection and reaction to the news of the Babylonian threat to Judah. In his opening dialogue with God, Habakkuk is upset at the perversion of justice; the evil Babylonians will defeat God's people (1:2–4). By the end of the book, Habakkuk rejoices in the Lord in the midst of trouble (3:17–19). How long it took for Habakkuk to move "from worry to worship" is not mentioned, but, like Lewis's grief over Joy's death, his spiritual pilgrimage is clear.[46]

LIFE IS A RIDDLE

G. K. Chesterton reportedly compared three literary classics this way: "The Iliad is great because all life is a battle, the Odyssey because all life is a journey, the Book of Job because all life is a riddle."[47] For Christians who suffer the loss of a loved one or some other tragedy, life may be a riddle. Christians are puzzled: How can a good and just God allow such pain?

Friends and relatives of suffering people may be asked, "Do you have any answers to the problem of suffering?" Many Americans have adopted a problem-solving approach to life. When they identify a problem, such as a leaky faucet, they quickly seek an answer or a solution to the problem such as do-it-yourself plumbing or calling a professional. When I was in a junior high school algebra class, we had to work many math problems. Thankfully, the answers were in the back of the book. We could quickly learn if we had figured out the problem correctly. Such approaches do not always work with the so-called problem of suffering.

Biblical Perspectives on Suffering

The goal of this book is to reflect on biblical perspectives on suffering. The Bible, however, does not offer simple or simplistic answers to life's complex problems. After I had taught a conference on suffering at a church, one person commented, "I thought Warren would tell us why Debbie had her stroke." That person assumed that the Bible would give a specific answer to a case of suffering in the present century.

Although the Bible does not give us simple answers, it does help us discover answers that are better than some answers other sources offer. Careful reading of the Bible eliminates some popular views of suffering. For example, the Bible rejects the view that evil and suffering are the result of an eternal struggle between two equal forces. Although the Bible affirms the existence of the devil, it does not accept dualism. We will look at some other misleading answers in Part One, especially in the chapter on tornadoes.

What kind of answers to our suffering should we expect from the Bible? First, the Bible suggests that we can have partial answers in this life. Some scholars describe the biblical perspectives as "clues." Peter Kreeft, for example, helpfully analyzes clues from philosophers, artists, and the biblical prophets in his study of suffering.[48] D. A. Carson uses the image of puzzle pieces to illustrate what the Bible says about suffering.[49]

The Suffering of Job

Our experience may be like that of one of the most famous sufferers in the Bible, Job.[50] The readers of that book know early on that Job's suffering is a testing of his faith in God. Job, however, remains in the dark about the ultimate reason for his suffering throughout the story. Even though he has a meaningful encounter with God in the closing chapters of the book, God does not tell him about the discussion between God and Satan at the beginning of the book. Job's friends, of course, think they have the complete answers to his suffering, but they are wrong. Occasionally we may know the immediate cause of our suffering, but more often we are "in the dark." We look for answers and explanations, but rarely do we get the final word. The Apostle Paul described our limited knowledge this way: "For now we see in a mirror, dimly, but then we will see face to face. Now I know only in part; then I will know fully, even as I have been fully known" (1 Cor 13:12). Austin Farrer presents a helpful perspective: "No, God does not give us explanations; we do not comprehend the world, and we are not going to. It is, and it remains for us, a confused mystery of bright and dark. God does not give us explanations; he gives us a Son ... A Son is better than explanations."[51]

The Suffering of Jesus

Farrer's comment hints at a second type of answer we can expect from the Bible. Although both biblical testaments offer many examples of suffering, the story of Jesus should be central. Too many discussions of suffering have lingered on abstract treatments of divine omnipotence and goodness while neglecting Jesus.[52] Frank Tupper's magisterial study of providence hinges on the importance of Jesus: "Contextualized in

| How can a good God allow suffering? |

the history of Israel on the one side and in the ongoing history of the church on the other, *the Story of Jesus constitutes the definitive Story of God*, the story that says, 'God is love,' the story that tells the tale of what 'God is love' actually means."[53]

The story of Jesus is the climax of a larger story of God's dealings in human history. Even though we consider many stories of human suffering in this chapter, such as that of C. S. Lewis, we should never elevate those stories above the biblical story.

Neither Resignation, nor Understanding

What can we expect the Bible to tell us about suffering? Two examples will further illustrate the perspective I have gained from my study. The first example comes from the grief of John Claypool over the death of his daughter. Claypool preached on suffering regularly as his daughter's condition deteriorated and she eventually died of leukemia. About a month after her death he preached on Abraham and Isaac (Gen 22). He said he had considered three roads or responses to her death. The two he rejected were "the road of unquestioning resignation" and "the road of total intellectual understanding." The approach he recommended was to see his daughter as a gift from God; Claypool was grateful that he had ever been given her in the first place.[54]

My second example comes from John Henry Newman's hymn text, "Lead Kindly Light."

> Lead, kindly Light, amid the encircling gloom, Lead thou me on;
> The night is dark, and I am far from home; Lead thou me on!
> Keep thou my feet; I do not ask to see the distant scene:
> one step enough for me.[55]

Although many sufferers wish to have more knowledge or answers from God, I like Newman's willingness to receive guidance from God one step at a time. My personal goal in presenting this study of biblical perspectives on suffering is to help readers see a little more of the light the Bible sheds on our darkest moments.

PART ONE

BIBLICAL PERSPECTIVES ON PERENNIAL QUESTIONS

 **Chapter One**

IS SUFFERING A PUNISHMENT FOR SIN?

This chapter is the first of four chapters that deal with questions suffering people often ask. Sufferers often have many questions about their experience, and, if they are Christians, they frequently address these questions to God. Daniel Simundson addresses seven of these concerns in his valuable study, *Where Is God in My Suffering?*[1] In Part One of our study, we will focus on four questions. The question "Where is the God of justice?" (Mal 2:17) provides the umbrella or context for this book and will be addressed throughout our study. The four questions highlighted in Part One are representative of the concerns expressed by sufferers or by the people who try to help them with their suffering.

> **Do we suffer as punishment for sin?**

Sufferers in biblical times had no qualms about addressing questions to God. As we saw in the introductory chapter, they did not always receive full-fledged, complete answers to their questions. Habakkuk, for instance, was perplexed about the threat of a Babylonian invasion. Habakkuk understood the Hebrews to be God's chosen people, so how could God let a bad, pagan nation attack the good guys? God never gave the prophet a theoretical answer to his query, but God told him he needed to live by faith, not sight (Hab 2:4; 2 Cor 5:7). The Bible frequently records human questions and divine responses.

Even though my major concern in this book is to sketch out a theology of suffering rather than a traditional, philosophical theodicy, paying some attention to selected perennial questions will help set the stage for our later discussions. Christians, for example, often ask about God's role in relation to tornadoes and other natural disasters (chapter two). Some wonder if God experiences suffering or anguish when we suffer (chapter three). Christians wonder how long God will allow evil to flourish (chapter four).

WHOSE FAULT IS IT?

One of the most common responses to suffering is the blame game. Many people assume there is a close link between sin and suffering. If there is suffering, then someone has sinned. Often nicknamed the doctrine of retribution, this familiar response to suffering can be diagrammed this way:[2]

> good → success
> bad → suffering

Most Bible scholars have noticed the prominence of this theme in many biblical books, and retribution has been identified as the basic biblical view of suffering.[3] A full discussion of biblical teaching on retribution is beyond the scope of this book, but the popularity of retribution as an explanation for suffering in popular culture and some churches demands some attention.[4]

Jesus dealt with this theological perspective on two significant occasions. First, his disciples tried to figure out whose sin caused a man to be born blind. "Rabbi, who sinned, this man or his parents, that he was born blind?" (John 9:2). Here the disciples reflected a common Jewish view of that day: sin led to suffering, and pious living led to prosperity. Some of the rabbis believed that a person could commit a pre-natal sin, so the disciples were not being foolish to ask if the man could have caused his own blindness.[5]

Whose fault is suffering?

Jesus rejected the application of the doctrine of retribution to the blind man's situation. Sin and suffering do not always correlate. Because this man was blind, however, Jesus could perform a miracle, demonstrating God's power (John 9:3). Jesus did not linger on speculative questions such as the origin of suffering; he quickly moved to help the sufferer.

Likewise, Jesus rejected a retributive interpretation of two different situations (Luke 13:1–4). The slaughter of some Galileans by some of Pilate's men was not due to the Galileans being more sinful than other people. Also, the tower did not fall on eighteen people in Siloam because they deserved death.

Despite Jesus' criticism of the application of this doctrine of retribution in specific cases, it is still a major theme in the Bible. Retribution is an important topic, but it needs to be understood carefully in the context of other biblical themes.[6] My interpretation of its validity as a Christian response to suffering will involve several stages. I will look at the question "Is suffering a punishment for sin?" by starting with a general answer and then move on to more specific possible answers.[7]

A GENERAL ANSWER FOR A GENERAL QUESTION

Is suffering a consequence of sin? My general answer to this general question would be "yes." Actions do have consequences, and sin often results in suffering, either for the sinner or those affected by his actions. The story of the "fall" of Adam and Eve in Genesis 3 supports this positive general answer. Human sin has produced human suffering. Without going into the details of the specific punishments on Adam, Eve, and the serpent, the connection between sin and suffering seems clear. God creates a good world, but suffering enters human history after the original people sin. God announced the consequences of sin on the serpent, the woman, and the man (Gen 3:14–19). Surprisingly, the story of these original sinners is not cited often in the rest of the Bible as an explanation for human suffering. Based on this story, however, the idea that sin produces suffering is certain.

SPECIFIC ANSWERS FOR A SPECIFIC QUESTION

Although many Christians would agree that sin and suffering have some connection, they disagree with specific applications of the doctrine of retribution to suffering today. Several of my close friends have died of cancer. Their medical conditions seemed to have no correlation with their morality or relationship to God. No one at their funerals would have thought they deserved to die at a young age. Still, our basic conviction that God is just seems to give credibility to the notion of retribution.

> **Is *my* suffering a punishment for *my* sin?**

What does the Bible say about retribution? Does God punish us for our sins with disease, death, and other tragedies? I will look at three possible answers to a more specific form of the original question: Is *my* suffering a punishment for *my* sin? By adding the personal pronouns to the question, I am getting closer to the way most sufferers today formulate their concern. Is my suffering my fault? Do I deserve my pain?

Suffering Is a Punishment for Sin

The first answer to these more specific questions is still affirmative. Yes, my suffering is my fault. This view may be an instinctive response for some Christians based on their understanding of some Bible texts and an underlying conviction that God is just. This positive answer seems so logical that it often appears in popular culture. Lucy, a character in Charles Schulz's *Peanuts* comic strip, often expresses this positive view. When Charlie Brown's baseball team is losing another game, several of the characters express their opinions. Lucy's view is "If a person has bad luck, it's because he's done wrong, that's what I always say." When Linus gets a splinter in his finger, Lucy's explanation is the same: "That means you're being punished for something!" Like Job's friends, she demands that Linus confess his sin.

This first answer to the question about personal blame could be supported by selected biblical texts. For example, Moses warned the Hebrews "be sure your sin will find you out" (Num 32:23b). The Apostle Paul cautioned his readers that actions have consequences: "Do not be deceived; God is not mocked, for you reap whatever you sow" (Gal 6:7). Some people claim Jesus' support for the doctrine of retribution because of passages such as the story of the two builders that concludes the Sermon on the Mount (Matt 7:24–27). Their different approaches to home construction have different results.

Perhaps the most famous example of the "yes" answer to our question can be seen by the responses to suffering given by Job's friends. They insist on the direct link between Job's sin and his suffering. As long as he prospers, they assume he is good. When he suffers, they know he is actually a sinner with unconfessed sin. Eliphaz asks Job, "Think now, who that was innocent ever perished? Or where were the upright cut off?" (Job 4:7). Job's friends assume that all suffering is deserved; they leave no room for the category of innocent suffering or disproportionate suffering.

Suffering Is Not a Punishment for Sin

The second answer to the question "Is my suffering a punishment for my sin?" is negative. People who give the "no" answer insist that some suffering is clearly innocent. Or, at least some suffering is disproportionate to the amount of sin committed. Job, for instance, never rejects the doctrine of retribution promoted by his friends, but he argues that he does not deserve as much suffering as he receives. In chapter 31 Job identifies several sins he could have committed that should appropriately result in the tragedies he has already suffered. He does not claim sinless perfection, but he questions the justice of his suffering. He appeals to the justice of God to correct the wrongs he experiences (31:6).

The teachings of Jesus, mentioned at the beginning of this chapter, about the man born blind, the men killed by Pilate's men, and the tower of Siloam accident could support a negative answer to our question (John 9:1-3; Luke 13:1-4). These people do not get what they deserved; they experience injustice. Jesus also notes that his followers will, in some contexts, experience rejection and persecution (Matt 5:10-12), and the wicked, like the false prophets, will be popular (Luke 6:26).

Other texts that support a negative answer identify the prosperity of the wicked. In Psalm 73 the author begins by affirming the justice of God, but he becomes disturbed when he notices "the prosperity of the wicked" (73:3).[8] Sometimes the good suffer and the wicked prosper. The doctrine of retribution does not seem to fit the real world. The psalmist receives some consolation when he is reminded that the prosperity of the wicked is temporary (73:16-20).

Suffering Might Be a Punishment for Sin

The third answer to my question is a mediating one. *Maybe* my suffering is linked to my sin. Such an answer is not necessarily a cop out on a difficult subject. Again we need to acknowledge that human experience does not always fit easily into our doctrinal categories. The author of Ecclesiastes, for instance, raises a serious objection to the doctrine of retribution. He observes that piety and prosperity do not always correlate. "Again I saw that under the sun the race is not to the swift, nor the battle to the strong, nor bread to the wise, nor riches to the intelligent, nor favor to the skillful; but time and chance happen to them all" (Eccl 9:11). Although many Christians would not be as skeptical as the author of Ecclesiastes, they would acknowledge that the doctrine of retribution does not always work in their lives.

Jesus does not endorse the cynicism of Ecclesiastes, but he does note that life's experiences do not always meet our expectations about justice. Although God is just, he "makes his sun rise on the evil and on the good, and sends rain on the righteous and on the unrighteous" (Matt 5:45). When tornadoes devastated much of central Oklahoma in May 1999, they did not skip over the homes of all Christians and strike only the homes of unbelievers.

I often tell my college theology students that there are three possible answers to any difficult question: yes, no, and maybe. Our question, "Is my suffering a punishment for my sin?" can be answered these three ways. Some suffering can result from specific sins. For example, some types of food or drink can result

> **What, precisely, is retribution?**

in health problems. Some behaviors seem to have specific health consequences. Promiscuous sexual relationships, for example, might lead to sexually transmitted diseases or unwanted pregnancies.

We can dig a little deeper into our discussion by raising some more questions about the doctrine of retribution. I do not raise these issues to further muddy the waters but to help us think as clearly as possible about the relation of sin and suffering.

FURTHER EXPLORATIONS ON SIN AND SUFFERING

A quick glance at six more questions related to retribution will help us see both the value and the danger of this doctrine for understanding our suffering. These six questions overlap to some degree, but for the sake of analysis I will outline them separately.

First, is retribution individual or collective? In early Hebrew history retribution was understood in relation to groups. If the Hebrew nation was faithful to God, it would prosper. If the Hebrews rebelled against God, they would suffer. Leviticus 26 and Deuteronomy 28 illustrate the collective interpretation of retribution. This view is challenged by later prophets. Jeremiah and Ezekiel, writing in the context of the exile, both criticize the proverb about sour grapes (Jer 31:29-30; Ezek 18:2-4). Apparently the Hebrews had explained their captivity by blaming their ancestors. Their fathers had eaten sour grapes and the children experienced the consequences.

God replies to this sour grapes version of retribution by insisting they are in Babylon because of their sins. The wisdom literature, especially Proverbs, also stresses individual responsibility. What you do matters. For example, if you work hard you will get ahead, but if you are lazy you will be poor (Prov 6:6-11).

Second, is retribution material or spiritual? Some Bible texts emphasize the material rewards and punishments people receive. Deuteronomy 28 and Leviticus 26 mention long life, good health, and other forms of material prosperity for the faithful Hebrews. The book of Proverbs also used physical rewards and punishments as illustrations of retribution. Some texts stress more spiritual rewards, such as a strong relationship with God, inner peace, and forgiveness of sins. A disciple of Jesus would be "blessed" because of her strong relation with Jesus, but she might experience persecution in this life (Matt 5:10-12). The Apostle Paul identifies "peace with God" as one of the consequences of salvation, but Christians can also expect suffering (Rom 5:1-5).

Third, is retribution temporal or eternal? This question, closely related to the second one, highlights the timing of rewards and punishments. Some texts stress a this-worldly situation, but others look ahead to life after death in heaven and hell. At the risk of making a sweeping generalization, I suggest the Old Testament tends to stress temporal and material consequences, and the New Testament tends to stress eternal and spiritual results of actions in this life. A strong Christian might, for example, experience ridicule and persecution in this life but be with God in heaven for eternity. We will look at the topic of eschatology, or the study of last things, in chapter four. The New Testament has a stronger affirmation of the eschatological or eternal elimination of suffering than the Old Testament presents.

Fourth, is retribution a direct divine act or an indirect divine act? This question will be explored more in the next chapter, but a few comments can clarify the issue here. In some passages God says he will directly reward or punish (e.g., Lev 26:4, 6, 9, 11, 12, 16-20, 22). In other texts God seems to be in the background. God is still sovereign over his creation, but he has created a world in which actions seem to have "natural" consequences. The book of Proverbs, for example, does not always mention God's direct involvement in life. Laziness produces poverty, but God's role is more indirect than direct (Prov 6:6-11).

Fifth, is retribution a reversible formula? Job's friends seem to believe that the doctrine of retribution is reversible.[9] If good actions produce prosperity and bad deeds lead to trouble, then you can gauge a person's character by looking at his or her condition in life. A suffering person must be a sinner! Earlier we saw that the doctrine of retribution can be diagrammed this way:

good → success
bad → suffering

Job's friends assume the formula can also look like this:

good ← success
bad ← suffering

Job's experience and God's criticism of their theology suggests the danger of reversing this formula (Job 42:7). Many sufferers today, however, still tend to think God must be punishing them for something they have done wrong. They ask, "What have I done wrong? Why is God punishing me?" Some suffering may result from sin, but the retribution formula is not reversible.

Sixth, is retribution a comprehensive explanation or a helpful generalization? Again, Job's friends are the best illustration of this issue. Although scholars can distinguish some differences in the views expressed by Job's four friends, these friends tend to argue that retribution is a comprehensive explanation of suffering. In other words, all suffering is deserved. Most Christians see retribution as a helpful generalization. All things being equal, good people will get ahead, and bad people will be punished. Ecclesiastes' "time and chance" factor (9:11) reminds us that retribution allows for many exceptions.

FROM RETRIBUTION TO REDEMPTION

Our explorations so far into the doctrine of retribution may have puzzled or bewildered readers. How, exactly, is my suffering related to my sin? So far we have seen that a general answer is that sin and suffering are connected, at least in the general sense that the sin of Adam and Eve unleashed suffering into human history. When we personalized the question, "Is *my* suffering due to *my* sin?," then we looked at three possible answers, yes, no, and maybe. Adding the six additional questions pushed us even farther into a complicated discussion.

If we were talking one on one about your suffering or my suffering, we might see the relevance of a particular biblical text or theme. Prooftexting, lifting a biblical text out of its context to "prove" a point, is always dangerous in theological discussion. Serious biblical scholarship tries to avoid prooftexting. When, for instance, AIDS was first identified in the 1980s, many people insisted it was God's punishment on homosexuals. Pointing to passages that link sin and suffering, these Christians drew the conclusion that this disease was God's specific punishment for that sin. Other Christians soon responded that such an argument is an illegitimate use of Scripture, especially since non-homosexuals had contracted the disease through transfusions of infected blood. Arthur Ashe, a professional tennis player, contracted HIV through receiving such bad blood during surgery.[10] Recent authors on the Christian view of suffering avoid connecting AIDS with homosexuality.[11]

> **How do we respond to our suffering and the suffering of others?**

The Development of the Doctrine of Retribution

To help avoid the danger of prooftexting in our application of retribution to cases of suffering, it might help to consider the development of the doctrine of retribution in the Bible. Since we cannot identify the exact dates when some biblical books were written, developmental studies are always tentative. One valuable proposal, however, sketches out three stages in the Old Testament understanding of suffering.[12]

First, some believe that all sufferers are sinners. This view, held by Job's friends, insists that all suffering is deserved. If you are suffering, it is your fault. You need to confess your sins and seek God's forgiveness. Then your reconciliation with God can begin, and your suffering will disappear.

Second, some sufferers are saints. Using the word *saint* in the popular sense of a good person, this view is illustrated by people like Job. Job is not sinless, but he exemplifies what we usually call innocent suffering. He is being tested not punished.

Third, one sufferer is the savior. The best illustration of this stage is the Suffering Servant poems in Isaiah. Although sometimes the servant is identified as the nation Israel (Isa 41:8; 49:3), the servant is sometimes an individual who suffers on behalf of others. The Suffering Servant experiences both innocent and vicarious suffering:

> Surely he has borne our infirmities and carried our diseases; yet we accounted him stricken, struck down by God, and afflicted. But he was wounded for our transgressions, crushed for our iniquities; upon him was the punishment that made us whole, and by his bruises we are healed. (Isa 53:4–5)

Christians have traditionally identified this unnamed servant as Jesus. Jesus brings redemption through his sacrificial death on the cross, and the apostle Philip applies one of these Isaiah texts to Jesus in his conversation with the Ethiopian eunuch (Acts 8:32–35). Whether Isaiah intended his message to be messianic, Christians have seen in these texts an anticipation of Jesus' ministry and redemptive death.

Responding to Suffering

Not all suffering is the result of the sinner's actions. Some suffering is innocent. Jesus' suffering is both innocent and redemptive. Given these basic biblical truths, how do we respond to our suffering and the suffering of those around us?

First, when we suffer we need to ask ourselves if we are at fault. Rationalization is an easy trap to fall into when we are in any kind of trouble. Blaming someone else for my problems is easier than accepting personal responsibility. If I am suffering, my first step is to be honest with myself and honest with God. If my sin is causing my suffering, then I need to confess that sin to God and seek help with overcoming that sin.

Second, I need to see if my sin is causing suffering for others. Actions do have consequences, and my sins could be affecting other people as well as myself. I should attempt to be reconciled with that person and undo any of the suffering that I can (Matt 5:23-26). C. S. Lewis once noted that the majority of human suffering is due to human sin: "When souls become wicked they will certainly use this possibility to hurt one another; and this, perhaps, accounts for four-fifths of the sufferings of men."[13]

Third, we should avoid being judgmental about the sufferings of others. All too often Christians begin to think and talk like Job's comforters. We assume that the retribution formula is comprehensive and reversible, so another person's suffering is their fault. Christians who are deeply committed to justice, either God's justice or some human understanding of justice, often become judgmental of others. James reminded us that God alone is the true judge, and we should not judge others (James 4:12).

Several years ago a friend told me about a man dying of lung cancer. The dying man said that his cancer must be due to his chain smoking. Some Christians, strong advocates of divine retribution, might argue that the cancer was God's punishment for the man's sin of abusing his body. I would acknowledge the right of the dying man to see a connection between his sin, as he would name it, and his suffering. I do not think another person should try to make this connection for the dying man, since that expression comes close to the judgmental attitude James warned us about. God alone is judge. Some suffering is the result of sin, but God alone should announce the specific connection between sin and suffering.

 **Chapter Two**

DOES GOD CAUSE TORNADOES?

May 3, 1999 is a date that Oklahomans will long remember. Late that afternoon and into the night, several severe tornadoes destroyed homes, businesses, and churches, hurting many people and killing several others. The pictures of the devastation dominated television news and newspapers for days. Many compared the scenes of destruction to a war zone. The rebuilding of homes and businesses took months.

December 26, 2004, is another date that will long be remembered, especially by people in south Asia. On that date a massive earthquake caused tsunamis that killed over 180,000 people. Many nations and organizations rushed disaster relief to the area.

Christians respond in a variety of ways to events such as tornadoes and tsunamis. The Oklahoma tornadoes prompted one teenage girl to wonder out loud why God spared her church building but let the storms destroy her pastor's home. One local minister admitted that sometimes Christians do

> **Does God cause natural disasters?**

not have any answers. A denominational leader suggested that the best response would be to ask "What now?" rather than "Why?" about the tornadoes. Another church leader noted that no one in his congregation was questioning God about the tornadoes. Another pastor suggested that as long as the laws of physics are operative, tornadoes can happen, so do not blame God.[1]

In 1992 two of the most powerful hurricanes in U. S. history hit Florida (Andrew) and Hawaii (Iniki). More recently, a seemingly unending series of hurricanes devastated Florida and Haiti in 2004, and then Hurricanes Katrina and Rita hit the Gulf Coast in 2005. When such disasters occur, journalists tend to ask academic theologians: "Why does God allow disasters to happen?" Like the pastors and lay people responding to the Oklahoma tornadoes, answers differ. One might note that "the ways of God are mysterious." Another might appeal to natural law, suggesting that it produces the "greatest good for all." Another theologian might say that some good can come out of these tragic events, since the survivors can develop qualities such as patience and love.[2]

How should a Christian answer the question that titles this chapter? Does God cause tornadoes, hurricanes, floods, avalanches, and other natural disasters? Some Christians insist that tornadoes and hurricanes are forms of divine retribution; God sends them as punishment on sinners. For example, in his sermon on "The Cause and Cure of Earthquakes," John Wesley said these events were a sign of God's wrath against sin.[3] In a widely circulated pamphlet, Wesley interpreted the 1755 Lisbon earthquake as divine retribution.[4] In the previous chapter we saw that retribution is a typical Christian response to evil, and it can be applied to events such as tornadoes.

In this chapter we will look at several possible Christian views of the origin of tornadoes, hurricanes, and other natural disasters. All of these fit within the traditional category of "natural evil."[5] The topics of illness, disability, and birth defects are sometimes classified as natural evil, but they will be included in chapter six.

The topic of natural evil has been neglected in the last century, when the Holocaust and other forms of moral evil have received more attention.[6] Christians today often find it easier to understand the Holocaust and terrorism, because people sin by misusing their freedom and hurt other people. Although we are overwhelmed by the enormity of suffering caused by other humans, we continue to be puzzled by natural disasters. This chapter probably comes close to the category of "popular theodicy."[7] Although academic theologians may have neglected the topic of natural evil, many lay Christians and others have theological opinions about the subject. I will assume that most Christians take the relationship between God and tornadoes to be a relevant, if neglected topic.[8] Not everyone, however, would see the need to even raise this theological question.[9]

GIVING THE DEVIL HIS DUE

Some Christians argue that God is not to blame for hurricanes and tornadoes. Instead, they would insist that the primary agent behind these disasters is the devil. After reading the thoughts of the seminary theologians about Hurricane Andrew, one lay person wrote a letter to the editor proposing Lucifer as the cause of the hurricane. Lucifer rebelled against God, and God threw him down to earth, where he reigns now. According to the letter writer,

> God does not have complete control over planet earth, as revealed in the Lord's Prayer. Satan is using every means at his disposal including hurricanes, tornadoes, earthquakes, etc., to hurt man thereby hurting God. Does Satan have the power to control nature? You'd better believe it. We read in Job where Satan called down fire out of heaven and again where he spawned a great wind, probably a tornado. When nature rages out of control, you can bet Satan had a hand in it.[10]

This lay person's proposal would find a receptive hearing among many Christians. The Bible has a lot to say about God's superhuman enemies, such as the devil and demons. The Apostle Paul stresses that Christians are engaged in a spiritual war with these beings (Eph 6:10–20). In recent years American popular culture has seen a resurgence of interest in good and bad angels.[11]

Did the devil do it?

A full-scale discussion of the devil and the fallen angels is beyond the scope of this short chapter, but a few comments are necessary in relation to the topic of natural disasters. The letter writer correctly noted that some of Job's problems involved natural evil. A messenger told Job that the "fire of God fell from heaven," killing animals and humans (Job 1:16). Another messenger reported that "a great wind came across the desert" and destroyed a house, killing Job's children (Job 1:18–19). Since God had just allowed Satan to test Job's integrity, seeing Satan as the direct cause of these disasters is a natural interpretation.

Job's response to these disasters complicates the discussion. Job does not mention Satan as the cause of these evils; rather, he attributes all of his troubles to God's intervention. Having heard several reports of death and destruction, Job concludes, "the Lord gave, and the Lord has taken away." (Job 1:21). When his wife urges him to curse God, Job again points to God as the ultimate source of good and evil in life: "Shall we receive the good at the hand of God, and shall we not receive the bad?" (Job 2:10).

Job's references to the role of God in suffering brings us back to the original question: Does God cause tornadoes? Job would apparently answer, "Yes." The author of the book, however, informs readers that the immediate cause of natural disasters is Satan. Job is always in the dark about the actual circumstances of his suffering. As readers of the book of Job, however, we see that both God and Satan play roles.

Some Christians across the centuries have reconciled the roles of God and Satan by distinguishing God as the ultimate cause of everything that happens and other forces or personalities as the direct cause (e.g., Satan, natural forces, human freedom).[12] For example, the Bible twice records David's plan to take a census of the Israelites. In one account the inspiration or cause of the census is God (2 Sam 24:1). In the other account Satan prompts the census (1 Chr 21:1). A traditional explanation is that the author of 2 Samuel understands God as the ultimate cause of the event, and the author of 1 Chronicles sees Satan as the immediate, or proximate, cause.

The Danger of Dualism

If we grant that God might allow Satan to be the direct cause of suffering, we need to avoid the danger of dualism. Scholars use this term for a variety of viewpoints. For example, dualism can be used to describe the belief that there are two types of reality: material and spiritual. This use of dualism usually understands the material to be bad and the spiritual to be good. Several New Testament writers, especially John and Paul, respond to an early version of Gnosticism, which held to this version of dualism.

An emphasis on the power of the devil, however, can easily lead to another definition of dualism in which the devil and God are seen as two equally powerful divine beings engaged in an eternal struggle. Zoroastrianism is sometimes classified as a religious or cosmic dualism, with a good god and an evil god.[13] Christians do not hold to an eternal dualism, but we can affirm a provisional dualism, meaning that Satan does oppose God within the framework of history as we know it.[14] God is the sovereign creator and lord of the universe, but Satan continues to resist God's will. So, some Christians believe that Satan, not God, is the cause of tornadoes and hurricanes.[15] Other views, however, also have their advocates.

A FALLEN WORLD

Another possible answer to our question about God's relation to tornadoes would be that humans, not God, are the key factor. Human sin has created a fallen world, a world that is different from the paradise created by God.[16] Christians with this worldview usually point to the story of Adam and Eve as the clue to their position. When the original humans sinned, their action had consequences for the entire created world, not just themselves. The world as created by God was "very good" (Gen 1:31), but after the original sin the ground was cursed (3:17-18). The world is no longer the good world originally prepared by God for his people; the post-fall world is a fallen world, a world affected by the results of human sin. The Apostle Paul noted that all of

> **Does human sin cause natural disasters?**

creation is "groaning" until the end of time (Rom 8:18-25). Elizabeth Achtemeier wisely said, "Nothing is 'natural' anymore. That is, nothing is as God made it. Our scientists are not studying a 'natural' world; they are studying an unnatural one—a cosmos distorted and groaning in travail because of human sin."[17]

The impact of human sin on creation can be seen in many arenas. One complex issue is animal suffering, to which we will return in chapter thirteen. Another obvious example is the current ecological crisis. Several biblical authors note how the earth or the ground is affected by human sin. For example, Isaiah said the "earth mourns" and is polluted (Isa 24:4–5). Some Christians would suggest, then, that tornadoes and hurricanes are the indirect result of human sin. These are expressions of nature's "groaning" ever since the fall of Adam and Eve.[18] Sallie McFague argues that so-called natural disasters are "increasingly human-generated disasters, not entirely natural and certainly not from God."[19]

ACTS OF GOD

Events such as hurricanes, floods, and avalanches are often called "acts of God" in insurance policies. When Job experiences such tragedies, he interprets them as acts of God. He does not mention Satan or a fallen world as primary causes. Many Christians affirm the omnipotence and sovereignty of God over his creation, so they interpret God as the immediate or direct cause of all events, good and bad. To them, the creator of the world exercises control over natural forces, so whatever happens in the world must, somehow, be an act of God. To attribute these events to some other cause would be to dishonor God.

Not all Christians would agree with the "acts of God" approach to tornadoes. A few years ago, for instance, the governor of Arkansas refused to sign a disaster-relief bill passed by the state legislature because it described natural disasters as acts of God.[20] As a conservative Christian, he said such a category offended his conscience.

Monergism

The relation of God to natural disasters is a case study in a complicated, controversial theological discussion. At the risk of vastly oversimplifying a complex topic, I will contrast two views of God's sovereignty or relation to the world. One view, labeled monergism by theologians, stresses God's total and direct control over his creation. The word *monergism* comes from two Greek roots and literally means "one work." In this view God alone is powerful; God alone causes things to happen. This view would insist that tornadoes are the will of God.

Several Bible texts seem to support the monergistic view of God's relation to the world, including tornadoes and floods. For example, Isaiah reports, "I form light and create darkness, I make weal and create woe, I the Lord do all these things" (Isa 45:7). Amos writes, "Does disaster befall a city, unless the Lord has done it?" (Amos 3:6b). These texts, and several others, are used to support God's direct involvement in all events, the good and the bad.

> **How responsible is God?**

The monergistic view is also called pancausality or omnicausality. Both of these terms mean "all cause," suggesting that God is the only true cause of events. Critics of pancausality or omnicausality insist that monergists have taken texts such as Amos 3:6 out of context and have ignored other relevant texts.[21] For instance, a challenging case study is the hardening of Pharaoh's heart. Some texts suggest that God hardens the Pharaoh's heart (Exod 7:3), but others indicate that the Egyptian leader was already predisposed to keep the Israelites from leaving Egypt (Exod 7:14, 22).[22]

Anti-Monergism

Advocates of the second view of God's relation to natural disasters reflect a wide range of theological backgrounds. They are united, however, in critiquing monergism. John Sanders, for instance, advocates belief in God's general sovereignty over the world rather than specific sovereignty, or monergism.[23] Likewise, Donald Bloesch argues that omnicausality is a misunderstanding of divine omnipotence. "God's omnipotence does not mean that he is the direct or sole cause of all that happens; rather he is Lord over all that happens. It means that God is omnicompetent, capable of dealing with all circumstances, that nothing can ultimately defeat or thwart his plans for all his people."[24] Another critic insists that monergists have erred by drawing generalizations about divine actions from texts about specific historical events.[25] Georgia Harkness, who also rejects monergism, reminds us, however, that God is ultimately in charge of the world. Commenting on physical disasters she states, "In an ultimate sense we must call them, as the insurance policies do for prudential reasons, acts of God. If they are not, something else besides God controls our world. . . . [But] we cannot suppose that when the floods and tornadoes come, God deliberately sends them to smite their victims with the wrath of his displeasure."[26]

Is Suffering the Will of God?

Related to the issue of God's sovereignty over the physical world are several other traditional concerns. For example, many Christians ask if suffering, whether through natural disasters or moral evil, is the will of God.[27] Some Christians respond to suffering by making a distinction between the perfect will of God and the permissive will of God. God's perfect will includes the salvation of all people (1 Tim 2:4), but God's permissive will allows for human freedom. That is why some people are able to refuse the offer of salvation. In Christian history the debate about the exact nature of God's will often involved the followers of John Wesley and John Calvin. Wesleyans usually allowed for a distinction between God's perfect and permissive wills, but Calvinists usually insisted on God being directly in charge of history. Calvin said nothing happened by chance; everything was governed by God.[28]

God's Self-Limitation

Another factor related to God's sovereignty over nature is the issue of God's self-limitation or self-restraint.[29] Those who allow for a divine permissive will often insist that God has limited himself in order to create some flexibility in the universe. God voluntarily limits himself in the act of creation when he creates a reality separate from himself. In his relation to humans, for instance, God gives people the privilege and responsibility of having "dominion" over the created order (Gen 1:26; Ps 8:6–8). By limiting himself, God allows for human freedom and stewardship of the created world. One possibility, of course, is that humans might misuse that freedom and be bad stewards.

The theme of divine self-limitation may suggest that tragic events such as hurricanes and floods arise from the contingency of nature built into the world by God's design. Just as God gives humans some freedom, so God allows for some contingency in the rest of the natural order. Some Christians in the Calvinist tradition resist this understanding of God. They insist that God exercises complete control over all aspects of the world. As one critic put it, in monergism "God micromanages every detail."[30]

That God has limited himself does not mean that God is a finite being. Although some philosophers and theologians have tried to solve the overall problem of suffering by depicting God as limited or finite, the notion of a finite God is not the same as a self-limiting God.[31] A loving, omnipotent God could choose to limit himself voluntarily. As Georgia Harkness notes,

> A self-limited God is one who, in His infinite wisdom and goodness, has chosen to create a world of natural order and human freedom. In such a world, which He maintains with consistency and constancy of purpose, some events occur which are not in accordance with His will and which must be judged by both man and God to be evil circumstances requiring challenge and amelioration.[32]

A finite God, by definition, cannot do some things. In his bestselling book on suffering, Rabbi Harold Kushner proposes a God who is not omnipotent. Kushner wrote *When Bad Things Happen to Good People* after his teenage son died of progeria. In this work he concludes that God is not able to do everything.[33] God does not cause all evil, and he is limited by the laws of nature. "I recognize His limitations. He is limited in what He can do by laws of nature and by the evolution of human nature and human moral freedom. I no longer hold God responsible for illnesses, accidents, and natural disasters, because I realize that I gain little and I lose so much when I blame God for those things."[34] Kushner's theology is not deistic, since he insists on the love of God. A deistic God is uninvolved in the world and unmoved by human suffering. Kushner has, however, depicted a finite or limited God.[35]

One of the dangers of Kushner's theology or any belief in a limited God (rather than a self-limiting God) is "cosmic dualism."[36] Cosmic dualism envisions a world that is in part beyond God's control or influence. Once created, the world is subject equally to good and evil forces. In order to keep from blaming God for hurricanes and tornadoes, Kushner seems to exalt the power of chaotic natural forces.

A THEODICY FOR TORNADO ALLEY

Tornadoes are a fact of life in my part of the world. In fact, some meteorologists call Oklahoma "tornado alley" because of the prevalence of tornadoes each spring. Many Oklahomans, Christian or not, puzzle over theological issues in the aftermath of those tornadoes.

So, we are back to the original question, Does God cause tornadoes? My review of popular theodicies is not comprehensive, but perhaps I can formulate an answer in light of the options considered here.

God Does Not Cause Tornadoes, But . . .

My simple answer would be, "No." As an evangelical theologian, I believe in divine omnipotence and sovereignty, but I do not believe that God directly causes each tornado, directs its path, and determines who will be injured or killed by that tornado. I would agree with those Christians who describe a loving, all-powerful God who limits himself in order to allow freedom for humans and some contingency in the world. Like the governor of Arkansas, I would like to remove the "acts of God" language from insurance policies.

Is there a clear answer?

Although my basic answer to our question is negative, I would acknowledge that God can and has used the forces of nature to accomplish his will. For example, God sent ten plagues on the Egyptians to force the Pharaoh to let the Israelites leave. The seventh plague in particular, the hail and thunderstorms, fits the category of natural disasters (Exod 9:13–35). Also, God sent a storm at sea both to punish Jonah for his rebellion and to get his attention (Jonah 1:4). If God clearly revealed that a tornado, hurricane, or flood today was sent by him, then my answer to this chapter's question would be, "Yes." Normally, however, it seems that tornadoes and other natural disasters are not directly caused by God. God "sends rain on the just and the unjust" (Matt 5:45), and most tornadoes do not skip over God's people. God created a world in which bad things can happen, but he does not create tornadoes to destroy specific people and places.

We have barely scratched the surface on a number of complex theological issues in this chapter. Issues such as the will of God, miracles, and providence are all relevant to our study of suffering and would need consideration for a full-blown theodicy of natural disasters. Reaching a perspective on God's general relation to the world is essential to tackling specific forms of suffering in Part Two. For example, the question "Does God cause disabilities?" is parallel to the question about God's relation to tornadoes. Topics such as infertility, blindness, and birth defects require Christians to have a biblical understanding of God's relation to the world.

If we should not blame God as the direct cause of tornadoes, we should still recall that he made the kind of world in which bad things do happen. Job was not necessarily wrong to think of God as ultimately behind what was happening to him. In an earlier study, I concluded that "God is ultimately responsible for human suffering."[37] When one of my friends read that line, he became upset with me. He had experienced some tragedies in his life, but he did not blame God for them. After some further discussion, he realized that he and I were not that far apart in our views of God. The key word in my conclusion is "ultimately." I do not believe that God directly causes all natural disasters. Although God can use natural forces to punish the wicked or to catch the attention of others, just as he did during the plagues in Egypt, I believe he created a world with some contingency in it. He does not micromanage all events, even though he is aware of and concerned about all events (Matt 6:26-32).

If I believed that God is the direct cause of tornadoes, then, to be theologically consistent, I should criticize meteorologists and storm trackers, the kind of people popularized in the movie *Twister*, for trying to thwart the will of God. These people and the technology they use saved many lives in May 1999 in Oklahoma. Instead of criticizing them, however, I suggest that Christians should applaud advances in science and technology that help us to control the forces of nature. God granted us dominion over the created world. Wise stewardship of that responsibility would include the creative, humane use of technology. In the same way, people who build storm shelters or safe rooms in their homes are not sinning or trying to deter the will of God.

Chapter Three
DOES GOD SUFFER?

The suffering of Jews during World War II, what we now call the Holocaust or Shoah, is unimaginable to most people. Popular movies such as *Schindler's List* can, at best, give outsiders a glimpse of the horrors faced by Jews in the German concentration camps. One of the most eloquent statements by a Holocaust survivor is Elie Wiesel's *Night*. One scene, in which Wiesel depicts the execution of Jews, raises the question of God's relationship to human suffering. Three people, two men and a boy, are being hanged in front of a large crowd. Someone near Wiesel asks, "Where is God? Where is He?" As the three victims die a slow, agonizing death, the crowd watches. The same person asks again, "Where is God now?" and Wiesel answers to himself, "Where is He? Here He is—He is hanging here on this gallows. . . ."[1]

In the late twentieth century Christian theologians began to echo Wiesel's claims about divine suffering. In 1974 prominent German Christian theologian Jürgen Moltmann quoted Wiesel's depiction of the execution of Jews in his discussion of *The Crucified God*. Insisting that God suffers, Moltmann noted about Wiesel's horrifying experience: "To speak here of a God who could never suffer would make God a demon."[2] A decade later Ronald Goetz reported in a popular Christian magazine that what was once Christian heresy, divine suffering, was now "the new orthodoxy."[3] In another popular Christian magazine a scholar focused on the suffering of God as a natural consequence of God's love.[4] Joni Eareckson, a Christian who has been paralyzed for more than thirty years, entitled her memoirs *When*

> **Where is God?**

God Weeps: Why Our Sufferings Matter to the Almighty.[5] During the last few decades the notion that God suffers has been widely, but not universally, proclaimed among Christians.[6]

To my college students and to many Christians today, the answer to the question we will address in this chapter is simple or obvious. They know popular Christian songs about God weeping over human suffering. For example, contemporary Christian artist Eli composed "God Weeps Too," which stresses God empathizing with people such as a grieving widow. Shirley Erena Murray composed a contemporary hymn entitled "God Weeps." Many Christians today seem to agree that God suffers. God identifies with our pain. He feels what we are feeling when we suffer.

Can God suffer?

ONLY THE SUFFERING GOD CAN HELP

While Elie Wiesel suffered as a Jew in a German concentration camp, a Lutheran pastor was in another camp, arrested because he opposed Hitler. In his writings he also affirmed the suffering of God. Dietrich Bonhoeffer wrote:

> God lets himself be pushed out of the world on the cross. He is weak and powerless in the world, and that is precisely the way, the only way in which he is with us and helps us. . . . The Bible directs us to God's powerlessness and suffering; only the suffering God can help.[7]

Although scholars puzzle over the precise meaning of many of Bonhoeffer's fragmentary comments in his letters and papers, the concept of a suffering God has captured the imagination of many Christians in the last half of the twentieth century.

God Does Not Suffer

For much of Christian history, however, most Christians rejected the doctrine of divine suffering. Tracing a full history of this issue is beyond the scope of our brief study, but we need to see why most Christians throughout history rejected what seems so obvious to many believers today.[8]

Some scholars note that early Christian thought was influenced by Greek or Hellenistic philosophy. Some of these Hellenistic thinkers, especially the Stoics, stressed the *apatheia*, or indifference, of God. God was above or beyond emotions; emotions were, in their thinking, lower than reason. A God who felt pain would be inferior to a totally rational God.[9] Emotionlessness characterized God, and humans were to strive for a similar *apatheia*.

Another factor was the development of the *via negativa*, the way of negation, a key method for defining God's attributes. In medieval theology, some scholars stressed what God was not as a way of protecting God's majesty or transcendence. The divine attributes that have the prefix "in-" or "im-" reflect this approach to the doctrine of God. God is not finite or limited, so he is infinite. God does not change, so he is immutable. The majority view was that God was impassible, meaning he does not suffer.

An early debate about the Trinity demonstrates that not all Christians of previous generations understood God as impassible. Some early Christians argued that God did suffer, but they failed to distinguish carefully between the death of God the Son on the cross and the suffering of God the Father. These Christians have been labeled patripassianists (meaning the father suffered) or theopaschites (God suffered). The reaction against their fuzzy thinking was so strong that for centuries theologians were reluctant to affirm divine suffering.

God Does Suffer

If impassibility, or the view that God does not suffer, has been the consensus among theologians for centuries, then why do so many Christians today affirm divine suffering? Paul Fiddes, author of a major study on the issue, offers four reasons why Christians believe in a suffering God.[10] First, love involves the possibility of suffering. Any loving relationship makes us vulnerable to the possibility of frustration, pain, or suffering. "God is love" (1 John 4:8) is central to our faith, so God must be able to suffer. Second, the central place of Jesus' crucifixion points to divine suffering. The cross reveals God's suffering love. Jesus the Son agonizes over his sense of abandonment by the Father, and the Father grieves over the necessary death of his Son. Third, divine suffering helps us deal with the problem of human suffering. We do not suffer alone, since God suffers alongside of us. Fourth, the contemporary way of understanding the world stresses the interdependence of all of reality. An organic rather than mechanical model of God's involvement in the world prevails in contemporary thought. Fiddes here mentions the contribution of process theology, which is based on the observation that the world is constantly changing—or is constantly in the process of becoming something else. As a result, process theologians contend, God is constantly increasing his knowledge and experience of humanity and his created order. During the incarnation, for example, God experiences what it is like to be human, including what it is like to suffer as a human being suffers. Process theology is one of the major movements in contemporary theology that embraces the notion of divine suffering.[11]

Another modern theologian, Alister McGrath, has also addressed that recent shift away from understanding God as impassible. He suggests three major factors are responsible for the shift.[12] First, McGrath notes the emergence of protest atheism as a form of opposition to the notion of an invulnerable God. Protest atheism is the rejection of belief in God because of the existence of massive innocent suffering. The character Ivan Karamazov in Dostoyevsky's *The Brothers Karamazov* is often counted as an example of protest atheism. Second, scholars rediscovered Martin Luther, especially his theology of the cross, in the early twentieth century. This theology of the cross stresses that God is best understood in light of Jesus' death on the cross rather than abstract theology.[13] Third, the history of dogma movement highlighted the role of Hellenistic philosophy in predisposing early Christian theology to affirming divine impassiblity. Scholars increasingly argued that the Hellenistic conception of divine perfection obscured biblical teaching on God's suffering for and with his people.

The scholarly literature on divine suffering has become vast and the issues are complex. Perhaps one more issue can be raised to illustrate what is at stake in answering the question, "Does God suffer?" The Bible frequently uses feeling language to describe God's relationship to people. Scholars call this feeling language "anthropopathism," which comes from the Greek words for human (*anthropos*) and feeling (*pathos*). The second word is part of our words *empathy* and *sympathy*. In stressing the personal nature of God, the biblical writers used anthropopathic language often. Words such as love, hate, jealousy, and wrath would count as anthropopathisms.

Interpretation of this feeling language about God is crucial to the debate about God's suffering. Those who oppose divine suffering insist that this language is part of God's condescension to the human level: He really did not suffer, but the authors were inspired to use language we might understand. Those who affirm divine suffering argue that this language must be taken more seriously as a clue to God's character. God experiences human-like suffering, but he is still God. Or, in the words of Abraham Heschel's paraphrase of Isa 55:8–9, "For my pathos is not your pathos, neither are your ways My ways, says the Lord."[14]

HOW DOES GOD SUFFER?

To examine all of the arguments for and against divine suffering would require a full book or perhaps a series of books. Since the main focus of our study is what the Bible says about suffering, especially human suffering, I will draw from some recent studies of divine suffering in the Bible. The best single work is Terence Fretheim's *The Suffering of God: An Old Testament Perspective*.[15] Fretheim's work is a fresh, provocative study of divine suffering, although he relies on some classic studies, such as Abraham Heschel's pioneering study of divine pathos. After examining God's relation to the world and some of the divine attributes (e.g., omnipotence and omniscience), Fretheim distinguishes three forms of divine suffering:

God suffers because, God suffers with, and God suffers for. Although I will not follow Fretheim exclusively in the following discussion, his outline is helpful.[16]

God Suffers Because of Us

First, God suffers because of problems in his relationship with humans. An example of a broken relationship between God and humans can be seen in Genesis 6:5–6. God is displeased with the activity of the sons of God and the daughters of men. This text points to divine sorrow rather than divine anger as the expression of God's displeasure. "The Lord was sorry that he had made humankind on the earth, and it grieved him to his heart" (Gen 6:6). Parents often recognize that there is a fine line between being *mad* at and being *sad* for their wayward children. Although God's wrath is a prominent theme in the Bible, texts such as this one highlight another dimension of divine feeling: divine grief.

Fretheim notes texts that recall a time when the Israelites were faithful to God, but unfaithful to their covenant obligations. For instance, Hosea develops the parent-child analogy in his prophecy. God loved his child, Israel, and taught him how to walk, but Israel rejected God. Hosea's prophecy reflects God's broken heart: "My heart recoils within me; my compassion grows warm and tender. I will not execute my fierce anger; I will not again destroy Ephraim; for I am God and no mortal, the Holy One in your midst, and I will not come in wrath" (Hos 11:8b–9). Fretheim notes

How does God suffer?

that the image of God in this text is one of "the long-suffering parent" and "not that of some heavenly General Patton having difficulty tolerating acts of insubordination."[17]

God Suffers with Us

Second, God suffers with us in our suffering. Many times in the Bible God reassures his people that he knows about their sufferings and will help them. For example, at the burning bush God tells Moses that he is aware of the oppression of the Israelites as slaves in

Egypt (Exod 3:7). God often tells suffering people that he will be with them in their pain. Elie Wiesel's conviction that God was with the three people executed by the Nazis reflects this biblical theme. The familiar words of Psalm 23 remind us of God's intimate presence while we suffer (Psa. 23:4).

One of the key attributes of God, his compassion, reinforces our awareness of divine suffering with us.[18] God instructs Israel to be concerned about the poor. "If your neighbor cries out to me, I will listen, for I am compassionate" (Exod 22:27b). God is not apathetic in any Stoic sense; he actively identifies with the suffering of his people.

Another expression of divine suffering with us, according to Fretheim, is divine mourning.[19] Jeremiah, for instance, reports God's grief over Israel's suffering: "Is Ephraim my dear son? Is he the child I delight in? As often as I speak against him, I still remember him. Therefore I am deeply moved for him; I will surely have mercy on him, says the Lord" (Jer 31:20). Although God punishes his people for their sins, he empathizes with their suffering. "The God who in anguish visits judgment upon the people does not thereby sever the relationship. God immediately turns from the role of judge to that of fellow-sufferer."[20]

Although Fretheim highlights the Old Testament view of divine suffering, he sometimes shows the relationship of these texts to the New Testament. That God is with us in our suffering reaches its climax in Jesus, who bears the symbolic name Immanuel, which means "God with us" (Matt 1:23).

God Suffers for Us

Third, God suffers for suffering people. Fretheim warns us that the biblical passages that fall into this category are "the most difficult of the divine suffering materials."[21] God suffering for us ultimately involves his sending his Son as the fulfillment of the Suffering Servant texts in Isaiah. In our earlier discussion of retribution, I mentioned that the vicarious, substitutionary suffering of the Servant of the Lord in Isaiah 52–53 was understood by the early church as the model for Jesus' death. Although the suffering servant texts in Isaiah do not develop a full-fledged doctrine of the atonement, according to Fretheim, they provide important clues that were developed by the church.

> **What is the relationship between the suffering of God and the suffering of Jesus?**

This third type of divine suffering raises an important concern for some who debate the pros and cons of divine suffering. A suffering person can feel some consolation from the fact that God suffers with her. But does God help as well as hurt with us? I could tell someone that I feel their physical pain, but if I could render medical help for their condition that would be even more welcome. One of the reasons many earlier Christians resisted the notion of divine suffering was that a suffering God seemed weak or impotent. They preferred a strong, invincible God who might perform a miracle.

FROM THE CROSS TO THE SUFFERING GOD

I have highlighted Fretheim's valuable study because he distinguishes different dimensions of God's suffering. Some discussions of divine suffering are more philosophical or theological and less rooted in the Bible. For many Christians the key to affirming divine suffering is Jesus' experience on the cross.[22] Evangelical theologians today often stress the relation of Jesus' suffering to God's experience of suffering. For example, D. A. Carson concludes, "The biblical evidence, in both Testaments, pictures God as a being who can suffer. Doubtless God's suffering is not exactly like ours; doubtless metaphors litter the descriptions. . . . Here, then, the cross is climactic. God's plan of redemption cost the Father his son; it cost the Son his life."[23] John R. W. Stott discusses "the pain of God" as part of the conclusion to his fine study of *The Cross of Christ*.[24] "If God's full and final self-revelation was given in Jesus . . . then his feelings and sufferings are an authentic reflection of the feelings and sufferings of God himself."[25]

Christians who affirm the suffering of God because of the suffering of Jesus are usually aware of the complex issues of Christology and Trinity. Christology is the traditional term used by theologians for the study of the "person" of Christ, which includes his divinity, his humanity, and how Jesus is both human and divine. Trinity refers to the relations of God the Father, God the Son, and God the Holy Spirit. Christians throughout the centuries have struggled to find the best way to describe the relation of Jesus' humanity and divinity and the relations of the "persons" of the Trinity.

This is not the place to try to sort out all of these complex christological and trinitarian issues, but they have a bearing on our question, "Does God suffer?" In order to avoid the charge of reviving the ancient heresy of patripassianism, some contemporary advocates of divine suffering have carefully worded the relation of the passion or suffering of Jesus and the suffering of God the Father. For example, Jürgen Moltmann states, "In the passion of the Son, the Father himself suffers the pains of abandonment. In the death of the Son, death comes upon God himself, and the Father suffers the death of his Son in his love for forsaken humanity. Consequently, what happened on the cross must be understood as an event between God and the Son of God."[26] Moltmann has made significant contributions to the doctrines of the Trinity and Christology throughout his career. In the last few decades he has consistently affirmed that God suffers as he has developed his views of the Trinity and Jesus.[27]

BE COMPASSIONATE

This chapter may have been the most difficult one so far for some readers. The issues are tough ones to simplify, and the reader may be ready to ask "So what?" Perhaps you had already decided that God suffers. Perhaps it makes sense to you that a loving God would empathize with human suffering. An all-knowing God would certainly know about our pain, and the feeling language of the biblical portrait of God has never created intellectual problems for you. S. Paul Schilling, commenting on the episode in Elie Wiesel's *Night* that introduced our discussion, notes that divine suffering is "the most profound of all responses to human anguish."[28] Many Christians today agree that divine suffering has a biblical basis. When they suffer, they find it consoling to know that God feels their pain with them.

God's Suffering—Our Action

So, since God does suffer, what is the practical pay off of this belief? The key to my response is Luke 6:36 (NEB): "Be compassionate as your Father is compassionate."[29] Throughout the Bible the behavior of God's people is, ideally, patterned after God's character and behavior. Sometimes called the imitation of God theme, this emphasis is consistent in both testaments. T. B. Maston argues, "The dominant ethical appeal in the Bible is for the people of God to be like Him."[30] For example, God is holy, so his people should be holy (Lev 19:1–2). God identifies himself as compassionate (Exod 22:27b), and Jesus urges us to imitate this aspect of God (Luke 6:36). The Apostle Paul describes God as "the Father of compassion and the God of all comfort" (2 Cor 1:3 NIV). Since God feels our pain and helps us, we should help other suffering people (2 Cor 1:4).

Some people seem to have a stronger sensitivity to the feelings of others. Personality type, education, or other environmental factors may be involved in developing a kind of interpersonal extrasensory perception. Some people are good listeners or seem to have a sixth sense about the pain others are feeling. The Apostle Paul includes compassion as one of the virtues we should put on as followers of Jesus (Col 3:12).

Jesus' compassion should be a concrete model for Christians to follow as they respond to the suffering of those around them. William Barclay notes that the word translated "compassion" in reference to Jesus (*splagchnizesthai*) derives from the word for "the nobler viscera, that is, the heart, the lungs, the liver and the intestines."[31] This Greek word for compassion occurs only in the Synoptic Gospels and is primarily used to describe Jesus' response to people. For example, Jesus is moved with compassion when he sees the people "harassed and helpless, like sheep without a shepherd" (Matt 9:36). Another time Jesus' compassion leads to healings and the feeding of the 5,000 (Matt 14:14–21). A careful study of Jesus' ethical behavior and teaching would further demonstrate the importance of compassion for him.[32]

Christians realize we should be compassionate, as God is compassionate. Wayne Floyd, Jr., identifies three aspects of compassion. "Compassion . . . includes (a) a disposition of solidarity toward the neighbor's sufferings plus (b) the action of entering into the context of that suffering as one's own, with (c) a commitment to overcoming the cause of the suffering itself. Indeed, compassion might best be described as a dynamic process which included both affective and active dimensions."[33]

The Dangers of Compassion

Even if we realize we must identify with suffering people and try to help them, we face at least two dangers in trying to be compassionate toward the suffering people we encounter. First, we might be tempted to say to a suffering person, "I know just how you feel." Too often a person in the midst of suffering hears that comment as a pious, trite platitude rather than a sincere expression of concern. Unless I have experienced the exact same kind of suffering (leukemia, death of a spouse, etc.), I should say "I am trying to understand what you're going through" or "I can barely imagine what you're feeling." Or, perhaps the best way to demonstrate genuine Christian concern would be to simply sit with the suffering person. After all, Job's friends become his enemies when they speak to him. As long as they sit quietly, he has no reason to doubt their understanding (Job 2:11–13).

Second, Christians today may experience what is commonly called compassion fatigue. Some Christians in the helping professions, such as social work or counseling, often experience such emotional drain that they find it hard to continue in that profession. They care deeply, and they find themselves drained of spiritual and emotional resources. The Apostle Paul urges us to "not be weary in doing what is right" (2 Thess 3:13), but even Jesus occasionally withdrew from the crowds that demanded so much of his energy.

Our recognition that God suffers should motivate us to be more compassionate and aware of the suffering around us. We should also take divine suffering as a motivation to help alleviate the suffering we observe. James Cone, a prominent theologian, affirms divine suffering, but insists "Christians are called to suffer with God in the fight against evil in the present age."[34] As we will see in the next chapter, the total elimination of suffering awaits the return of Jesus, but we can work to lessen the amount of suffering in the world today. Our compassion for the suffering should not stop with a warm feeling; compassion should lead to action.

Chapter Four

HOW LONG, O LORD?

Suffering occurs in all shapes and sizes. One of the most difficult types of suffering is long-term, chronic sickness. This kind of suffering is difficult, for both those who die slowly and those who watch them die over days, weeks, months, and sometimes even years. Frank Tupper wrote a magisterial study of providence after his wife, Betty, died of cancer. She was diagnosed with breast cancer in 1981 and she died in 1983. Throughout his book Tupper, then a professor of theology at the Baptist seminary in Louisville, Kentucky, reflects on his wife's pain and his own grief. One day, when he was emotionally exhausted, Tupper said to his wife, "I'll be glad when this is all over." Her angry response was, "When this is all over, I'll be dead."[1]

Earlier we saw that people often respond to suffering by going through stages or phases. "Suffering is a process. It takes time (usually much more than people think), it requires work, and it proceeds through phases."[2] In this chapter, however, our concern will not be so much with either the personal or the corporate process of suffering. Here we will focus on the larger picture of suffering in human history. In the technical jargon of theologians, we will look briefly at the relation of eschatology and suffering. The term "eschatology" means the study of last things. The term "last things" includes many topics, such as heaven, hell, judgment, and the return of Jesus.[3] Theologians often divide the large field of eschatology into three major divisions: personal eschatology, corporate eschatology, and cosmic eschatology.[4] In this

> **Will we ever be free from suffering?**

chapter we will not look at personal eschatology, which includes death and afterlife, since we will have a chapter on these topics later. We will not look in detail at cosmic eschatology, which includes the creation of a new heaven and a new earth, since these relate to animal suffering, the topic in another chapter.

Our primary interest in this chapter, then, will be with corporate or historical theology. All of our discussion of suffering in this book fits within the larger context of a Christian view of time. Most Christians understand that the Bible presents a teleological view of time. The word teleological is based on the Greek work for "aim, goal, or purpose" (telos). Although, as we saw earlier, Christians may debate how closely God directs the course of events, the consensus Christian view is that God is guiding the course of history toward an ultimate consummation.[5] The NEW ENGLISH BIBLE translation of Romans 11:36 captures the essence of the traditional Christian view of God's relationship to time: "Source, Guide, and Goal of all that is—to him be glory for ever! Amen."

The category of corporate or historical theology usually includes topics such as the millennium, the tribulation, and the kingdom of God.[6] In this brief chapter, however, we will focus on the general theme of God's relation to time. We will examine this theme from the standpoint of sufferers who are not sure about the reality of God's providence. Sufferers sometimes wonder whether God is truly guiding history. How much longer will they suffer? Will they ever be free from their pain?

MY GOD, MY GOD, WHY HAVE YOU FORSAKEN ME?

Many sufferers feel that God has abandoned or forgotten them. They do not sense God's providential guidance of history; nothing makes sense to them when they are suffering. A literary example of the despair felt by some believers appears in Peter DeVries' haunting novel, *The Blood of the Lamb*. The central character's name, Don Wanderhope, captures the tension between hope and wandering through the tragedies of life that many people feel today.[7]

Laments

Cries of agony from biblical sufferers are often recorded in a kind of literature scholars identify as laments.[8] The genre of lament appears in several places in the Bible. The book of Lamentations reports the agony of the Jews when their nation was destroyed by the Babylonians. Jeremiah's "confessions" reveal his distress at trying to proclaim God's message to a hostile audience. For example, in one confession Jeremiah accuses God of tricking him, and Jeremiah begs to be allowed to quit preaching (Jer 20:7-9). Jeremiah begins to wonder if he can trust God.[9]

> **Has God abandoned us?**

Defined simply, a lament is "a prayer offered up to God in times of deep trouble."[10] A typical lament includes the following elements: an address to God, a statement of the sufferer's complaint, a confession of trust in God, a petition for God's intervention, a statement of assurance that God will help, and a vow that the sufferer will praise God when he helps the sufferer.[11] Many laments appear in the book of Psalms. Perhaps the most famous individual lament is Psalm 22, since Jesus quotes the first verse as he dies on the cross (Matt 27:46; Mark 15:34).[12] Here the psalmist feels forsaken by God and expresses concern that God does not answer his prayers (Ps 22:1-2). He is sure of God's holiness and that God helped his ancestors, but in the first half of the psalm he experiences ridicule from other people. In the second half of the psalm the author expresses his confidence that God will indeed help him (2:22-24).

One of the most helpful analyses of laments in the Psalms is by Walter Brueggemann. This Old Testament scholar organizes his discussion of the book of Psalms around three types: psalms of orientation, psalms of disorientation, and psalms of new orientation. Psalms of orientation address times of well being, when life is going well. Psalms of disorientation include laments, which reflect the "anguished seasons of hurt, alienation, suffering, and death."[13] Finally, psalms of new orientation address those times when we receive gifts from God, when we feel joy rather than despair.

In American culture we often like to accent the positive rather than the negative. Many scholars have noted the tendency of contemporary Christians to neglect the laments of the Bible. They are "downers" to some Christians, especially those looking for some hope via glib answers or spiritual quick fixes. Daniel Simundson identifies six reasons why Christians avoid the biblical laments.[14] First, they seem too pessimistic, perhaps encouraging an unhealthy preoccupation with personal problems. Second, the laments encourage harsh feelings toward other people. Third, they seem irrelevant to Christians in light of God's continued revelation in Jesus. Fourth, the laments are often harsh and demanding in their attitude toward God. Fifth, people today assume we should be patient when we suffer, and laments demonstrate impatience. Sixth, the lamenter stresses his or her innocence, sounding self-righteous.

Although some Christians are put off by the biblical laments, we can appreciate these laments as honest, candid statements of human pain and suffering. They also reflect the lamenter's conviction that God is just and will make the situation right eventually. Some Christians who suffer today find the laments liberating, since they remind them that God's people can be honest with God. As Simundson notes, the laments provide sufferers "some balance over against the constant pressure to pretend, to smile when they feel like crying, to say thanks to God when they are furious with God, to say they believe when they are full of doubts."[15]

The biblical laments correlate with our earlier study of the stages of suffering. For example, after the initial numbness and shock of a medical diagnosis wears off, the person with cancer may need to ventilate with God. The sense of hopelessness or despair may last for a while, but the suffering person may eventually move on to an experience of new orientation, as described in Brueggemann's interpretive scheme.

THE GOD OF HOPE

The Bible consistently affirms that we should place our ultimate hope in God. Paul even describes God as "the God of hope" (Rom 15:13). Sometimes, however, God's people experience hopelessness or despair. Their suffering is so intense, chronic, or both that they find it difficult to have any hope for the future. Throughout the Bible, especially in texts such as the laments, the sufferer asks the question, "How long, O Lord?" For example, the psalmist writes, "My soul also is struck with terror, while you, O Lord—how long?" (Ps 6:3). The lamenter turns to God in anguish, wondering when the pain will cease, when God will do something to help the situation. The sufferer feels like God has forgotten him or hidden his face from him (Ps 13:1-2).

Sufferers today ask similar questions. Is my suffering hopeless? Will God intervene here and now to help me, or do I have to wait until death for relief from my problems? Questions such as these point to the relation of God, suffering, hope, and the future.

The Bible provides several perspectives on the relationship between suffering and God's role in the future. A key perspective to guide our thinking will be our basic understanding of God's character. As Shirley Guthrie expresses the guideline, "The best insight we have into what God will do is found by looking at what God has done."[16] God will relate to us and our suffering in a consistent manner. We can trust in God now, and we can trust God to help us in the future. That message is stated more clearly in some parts of the Bible than others, but God is always the God of hope who hears our question, "How long, O Lord?"

> **What if we lose hope?**

Hopelessness

The Bible is candid about the experience of hopelessness. God's people sometimes despair. At one point in his life, Jacob cries out "Everything is against me" (Gen 42:36b NIV). Jacob thinks his son Joseph is dead, he knows his son Simeon is a hostage in Egypt, and he now learns he must send his youngest son to Egypt! Life looks very bleak to this patriarch.

Hopelessness is also a major theme in the opening chapters of Ecclesiastes. The "Teacher" has tried to find meaning in life through such avenues as pleasure, building projects, and wisdom, but his conclusion is "Vanity of vanities" (Eccl 1:2) or "Meaningless! Meaningless!" (NIV). His life was so meaningless at one point that he "hated life" (2:17). The early Israelites had no strong belief in life after death to provide an eschatological balance to this despair. Indeed, the Teacher asks if the ultimate destiny of a human is any different than an animal's fate (3:19–21). The Teacher does not despair completely, however, since he recommends finding some satisfaction through food and labor (e.g., 2:24; 3:22). Once described as the most dangerous book in the Bible, Ecclesiastes is open to many interpretations.[17] A consensus view is that Ecclesiastes does not offer much hope for suffering people. Physical death seems to be the end of human experience.[18]

Patience

Sometimes biblical authors tell us to be patient when we suffer. In the Old Testament, especially, we are told that suffering will not last forever. For example, the psalms that deal with the prosperity of the wicked often stress that the wicked person's prosperity will be temporary (Ps 37:8–9, 35–38). God's justice will prevail eventually, and he will not forsake his people (37:27–28). The frame of reference in these kinds of texts is usually human history. The Old Testament writers mention Sheol occasionally, a shadowy underworld where dead people reside, but they rarely offer an otherworldly eschatological hope.

The response "Be patient" also appears outside of the Psalms. For instance, God tells Habakkuk to wait for his response to the prophet's concerns about the Babylonian invasion. Habakkuk appeals to God's moral character, and God responds by giving the prophet a vision. "If it seems to tarry, wait for it; it will surely come, it will not delay" (Hab 2:3b). Habakkuk learns that "the righteous live by their faith" (2:4), but he never receives a complete theological answer to his questions. He is assured of God's guidance of history, and his faith in God is restored (3:17-19).

Many Christians are also familiar with James's instruction to be patient in the face of suffering (James 5:7). Although the KING JAMES VERSION of the book of James refers to the "patience of Job" (5:11), Job eventually grows very angry and impatient in the middle of that book. Other translations refer to Job's "perseverance" (NIV) or "endurance" (NRSV).

Prophetic Hope

A stronger, clearer affirmation of hope in God appears in some Old Testament prophecy. The Hebrew prophets often interpreted international events in light of God's will for his people. They frequently followed the doctrine of retribution, suggesting that their nation's defeats were due to divine punishment, not merely the military superiority of their enemies. For example, Isaiah reports God calling the Assyrian empire "the rod of my anger" (Isa 10:5). Amos has a series of visions in which God announces his plans to destroy the northern kingdom for its sinfulness. God compares his relation to the unfaithful Hebrews to Hosea's relation to his adulterous wife, Gomer.

Despite the frequent emphasis on divine judgment in the Hebrew prophets, they also note God's plans for the future of his people. Jeremiah, for example, records God's promise of a new covenant (Jer 31:31-34). Generally, the prophets deal more with the future of the nation Israel than with individual hope, such as death and afterlife. Ezekiel, for instance, receives a vision about the reviving of a valley of dry bones. The skeletons, representing the defeated Israelite nation, will become a living army again when God's breath, or Spirit, moves over them (Ezek 37:1-14).

Daniel Simundson makes a helpful distinction between two emphases in the prophet's hope. "Sometimes the prophets appear to be still hoping that *this* world will be renewed. At other times, their hope is for a completely *new* world."[19] The prophets are convinced that God is active in history. Eventually, God will change the Israelites' situation and remove their suffering.

Apocalyptic Hope

Another biblical hope emerges in the apocalyptic literature. The word *apocalyptic* derives from a Greek word for "unveiling" or "revealing." This type of literature puzzles many Christians, but it offers a distinctive message of hope to suffering people. Although Daniel and Revelation are the two clearest examples of apocalyptic literature in the Bible, some sections of other books are usually classified by scholars as apocalyptic (e.g., Isa 24–27).

Apocalyptic books typically deal with the future and are often full of symbolism. Sometimes the books reflect a situation of persecution or oppression of God's people. The problem of evil or suffering, therefore, is central to the books. For example, John sees some martyrs who are perplexed by the apparent triumph of evil over good. "Sovereign Lord, holy and true, how long will it be before you judge and avenge our blood on the inhabitants of the earth?" (Rev 6:10). These martyrs are "told to rest a little longer" (Rev 6:11). The theme of waiting has a different context in apocalyptic literature than in the Old Testament laments.

One of the major characteristics of apocalyptic thought is temporal dualism, the belief that God has divided time into two major periods, the present and the future. In the present God's people will suffer, but God will dramatically intervene in the future to change history and remove the suffering. This temporal dualism reassures the suffering people that God will eventually help them. The waiting is only temporary, although God's time table is not the same as human calendars (e.g., 2 Pet 3:8–9). When history is consummated, all evil and suffering will disappear. God will "wipe every tear from their eyes. Death will be no more; mourning and crying and pain will be no more, for the first things have passed away" (Rev 21:4).

Sometimes apocalyptic literature looks like a reaffirmation of the doctrine of retribution. The good will eventually be rewarded, and the wicked will be punished. Good will eventually triumph over evil. Temporal dualism, if pushed too far, could create problems for some sufferers. Being patient is difficult for many sufferers. They might feel that God should help them now, not later. Delaying relief from their present suffering may seem like a confirmation that their lives are unimportant to God.

Apocalyptic theology is, however, an essential element in the overall biblical view of suffering. Apocalyptic literature reminds us that ultimately God is Lord of time and space. Richard Bauckham notes that a central question in the book of Revelation is "who is Lord over the world?"[20] Although suffering occurs in this life for all of us, God will eventually eliminate all of life's prob-

> **What do we do in the meantime?**

lems. As Simundson wisely noted, "Apocalyptic seems most appropriate as a message for those at the end of their rope, in hopeless situations, with no place else to turn, and with this world no longer offering any solutions."[21]

IN THE MEANTIME

Our ultimate source of hope is God, and God will eventually eliminate all suffering. But, what do we do in the meantime? We could prooftext and highlight the passages that suggest we merely wait for the end, either death or the end of time, when our suffering will cease. The Bible, however, does not commend total passivity in the face of suffering. As someone once said, waiting is not the same as loitering. What can we do about our suffering and the suffering of others while we wait?

Already, but Not Yet

One of the most helpful concepts about the future to emerge in recent biblical scholarship is the balance between the "already" and the "not yet" of God's activity.[22] This jargon is often used in discussions of Jesus' teaching about the kingdom of God. Sometimes Jesus proclaims a kingdom that is already present among those who follow him (e.g., Luke 11:20). At other times Jesus announces a coming, future kingdom (e.g., Matt 6:10, "Your kingdom come"). Although Bible scholars have presented a wide variety of interpretations, a consensus view is that Jesus inaugurated the kingdom during his earthly ministry, but the kingdom will be completed at the consummation of history. Oscar Cullmann popularized this view with his analogy from World War II. Jesus' death and resurrection are the pivotal events in human history, just as D-Day was the turning point in that war. More fighting went on in Europe after June 6, 1944, but the tide had turned. V-Day, when the peace treaty was formally signed, parallels the return of Jesus and the consummation of history.[23]

According to this view of the kingdom, Christians are living between D-Day and V-Day. God did not promise that all suffering would disappear when we became Jesus' followers. The total elimination of suffering is eschatological, at the end of time.[24] Salvation, for instance, includes deliverance from our slavery to sin (Rom 6:17–18), but God never promised a pain-free, trouble-free life here and now. In this life and in time as we know it, pain and suffering will remain. Our hope is still in God, but we will face suffering along life's journey. The Apostle Paul knew through personal experience that a strong relation to God did not guarantee a pain-free life. Whatever the thorn in the flesh might have been, it troubled Paul a lot, and he prayed for relief from it. God did not remove the thorn, but Paul learned that God's gracious presence would be adequate for him to cope with the thorn (2 Cor 12:1–10).

While We Wait

What do we do while we wait? Sometimes the biblical authors recommend patience (James 5:7–11). But the Apostle Paul tells the Christians at Thessalonica, who had a severe eschatological itch, to attend to their everyday duties. Paul is especially concerned about Christians who have apparently quit their jobs and are passively waiting for Jesus' return (2 Thess 3:6–12).

The Bible encourages active waiting, not passive waiting or quietism.[25] Stanley Grenz highlights two aspects of a Christian's life in light of the end. First, our actions are "effective." Christians can participate in God's kingdom. They do not build the kingdom on their own, of course, but they are commissioned to follow a kingdom agenda. Second, our actions are "penultimate." Our actions are significant, but they are not ultimate. "God, and not our feeble actions, is the final hope of the world."[26]

Dealing with our suffering as we live between D-Day and V-Day also means that we must avoid false hopes and expectations about life. I like to listen to Garrison Keillor, a radio humorist who tells stories about his fictional hometown, Lake Wobegon, Minnesota.[27] At the end of each monologue, he describes the town as the place "where all the women are strong, all the men are good looking, and all the children are above average." I usually smile at that concluding comment because the story Keillor has just told obviously contradicts that utopian description. The people in Lake Wobegon, as in any home town, are ordinary people facing ordinary suffering, such as racism, cancer, poverty, and depression. Life is often difficult, but for Christians, our relation to the God of hope is always a source of hope.

PART TWO

SUFFERING FROM WOMB TO TOMB

Chapter Five
INFERTILITY

This first chapter of Part Two begins our survey of various types of suffering in the human life cycle. Some of us will escape some of these concrete examples of suffering, although aging and death will confront most people. In the biblical narrative Enoch and Elijah escape physical death, and those who die untimely deaths will miss the aging process. One impression a reader might get from the review of human suffering in Part Two is that life is always hard. Indeed, Job's friend, Eliphaz, states that "human beings are born to trouble, just as sparks fly upward" (Job 5:7). Sallie McFague notes that "Life is a mess and a misery."[1] Indeed, life is often hard. A major purpose of Part Two is to draw wisdom from the Bible for facing the typical troubles and struggles of life from womb to tomb.

The title for Part Two could be, Out of the Depths. "Out of the depths I cry to you, O Lord!" said the psalmist (Ps 130:1). A typical lament, this psalm continues to express confidence in God's goodness (130:7-8). The types of suffering we will study in Part Two often cause believers to feel that they are in "the depths"; like the psalmist, they plead for God's help.

Do we suffer differently as we age?

Although suffering may be prevalent among humans, we may not have a negative view of life. Life is punctuated with problems, but life, for a Christian, also has happiness, joy, and a keen awareness of the presence of God. I hope that Part Two will help Christians gain a more realistic view of life as we survey God's response to our suffering.

Part Two is loosely organized chronologically, suiting what I earlier called a "womb to tomb" approach. The first type of suffering we will explore is infertility. Problems such as illness, poverty, and racial discrimination are not localized in any one stage of human life, so the sequence of those chapters is not strictly chronological. Later in Part Two, however, we will look at aging and death, events typical of the end of life. As in Part One, my primary concern here will be to seek biblical insights for responding to these life problems and to encourage Christians as they seek to help suffering people.

THE BIBLE AND BABIES

The desire to have a child can be very strong. The story of Rachel, Leah, and Jacob illustrates the Hebrew view that having children is desirable. After Leah bears four children for Jacob, her infertile sister Rachel laments to Jacob, "Give me children, or I shall die!" (Gen 30:1). Jacob assumes that God plays a role in the conception of a child, and he will not take the blame for Rachel not having children: "Am I in the place of God, who has withheld from you the fruit of the womb?" (Gen 30:2). Eventually Rachel bears two children, Joseph and Benjamin, but she dies giving birth to Benjamin (Gen 35:16-20).

Infertility and conception are frequently mentioned in the Bible, especially in the Old Testament. The ancients did not have our contemporary, scientific understanding of biological processes, but they offered a faith perspective on how God was involved in them.

In general, the Bible is pro-children. Children are seen as a gift from God, and most families portrayed in the Bible have several children. The psalmist notes, "Sons are indeed a heritage from the Lord, the fruit of the womb a reward. Like arrows in the hand of a warrior are the sons of one's youth. Happy is the man who has his quiver full of them" (Ps 127:3-5). The fact that "sons" are especially desired reflects the patriarchal ethos of Hebrew soci-

Does God cause infertility?

ety. In our discussion of sexism in chapter ten we will return to the issue of patriarchy. Here my main concern is that children were seen as a gift from God. At the beginning, God had told Adam and Eve to "Be fruitful and multiply" (Gen 1:28).

Many passages in the Old Testament depict God as the direct cause of conception or barrenness. When the first child, Cain, is conceived, Eve gives God rather than Adam the credit! "I have produced a man with the help of the Lord" (Gen 4:1). When Abimelech takes Sarah from Abraham, God punishes Abimelech's family by closing the wombs; when Abimelech repents, God enables the women to conceive again (Gen 20:17–18). Rachel conceives Joseph after God "opened her womb" (Gen 30:22). Ruth and Boaz conceive Obed with the help of God (Ruth 4:13). Although a woman's barrenness is sometimes mentioned without reference to divine intervention (Gen 11:30; 25:21; Judg 13:2), the impression some Christians have is that infertility or conception always involve divine hindrance or help.

Infertility serves as another case study in the different ways Christians view God's power and providence. On the one hand, those who lean toward what I earlier called monergism will insist that all conceptions and all infertility are the will of God. No conceptions are accidents; God is actively involved, according to this view. On the other hand, those who advocate a self-limiting God, who builds some flexibility into the universe, will note that some conceptions are not the will of God. For instance, God does not will or intend incest or rape, but sometimes a child is conceived in these ways.

The key issue could be phrased as a pair of questions, "Is every conception the direct action of God? Is God the direct cause of infertility?" Although I would grant that God might be directly involved in some cases, especially the ones mentioned in the Bible, I am reluctant to argue that God is the direct cause of all conceptions or all barrenness. I fear those who hold to a monergistic view of God's action have universalized or absolutized biblical texts about specific situations so that they apply to all situations. Just as I do not believe God causes all tornadoes, even though he stirs up the storm that threatened the ship Jonah was on, I do not believe God caused my friend's infertility.

People who experience infertility often raise the same kind of questions about the justice of God that survivors of tornadoes or victims of cancer pose. Lynda Stephenson, an infertile married woman, devoted a chapter in her book *Give Us a Child: Coping with the Personal Crisis of Infertility* to the spiritual crisis she and her husband went through. She reviews many of the same issues we surveyed in Part One, wondering why God caused or allowed her infertility.[2]

HOPE FOR THE INFERTILE

Infertility Is God's Will

How should a Christian couple respond to infertility? Depending on your view of God's relationship to your condition, you have a wide range of options. On the one hand, if a couple believes that infertility is God's will, then they have fewer choices.

Childfree

First, an infertile couple could decide to stay childless or childfree.[3] Some Christians extend Paul's argument about the value of remaining single to remaining childfree. Paul argues that a single person will have more time to serve God than a married person (1 Cor 7:32-35). If a couple is married but infertile, then they can devote more time and energy to Christian causes.[4] I know some couples who have chosen to be childfree, and they have led productive, happy lives. Sometimes they are embarrassed by questions from curious friends about why they have chosen to remain childless, but they generally have not let infertility hinder their moving on with their lives. They might agree with the view of Gilbert Meilaender:

> Those who desire children, but, it turns out, can have none are understandably saddened. Nevertheless, we must learn to pursue our projects in faithfulness to God's creative will. The couple who cannot have children may—and should—find other ways in

which their union may, as a union, turn outward and be fruitful. God blesses in many different ways, and the task he does not lay upon us may be replaced by other tasks less open to those who have children and equally significant for the care and preservation of the creation.[5]

Adoption

A second option for those who believe their infertility is God's will is to adopt children. These couples suggest that God, for some unknown reason, does not want them to bear children but will allow them to raise children as adoptive parents. Children put up for adoption need a loving, Christian home, and these infertile couples have a valid ministry through being the adoptive parents of children conceived by others.

Infertility Is Not God's Will

On the other hand, if a couple believes that their infertility is not necessarily the will of God, they have a wide range of options. Of course, they can consider the first two options discussed above: remaining childfree or adoption. Advances in medical technology, however, have opened up several more options. Although the technology is constantly changing, some of the traditional methods are artificial insemination (of semen from the husband or a donor), *in vitro* fertilization, or surrogacy.[6] I will not elaborate on the medical or scientific data on these methods but focus on biblical perspectives and principles for dealing with infertility.

> **How should Christians respond to infertility?**

Surrogacy

Some people believe something like surrogate mothering was practiced in the Bible. When Sarai could not conceive a child with Abram, she offered her servant Hagar to Abram (Gen 16:1–4). Although no sophisticated technology was used, a child was conceived that Sarai hoped would count as the child God had promised. God responded that Abram and Sarai would eventually have their own child, Isaac. Probably the most famous case of a surrogacy in the United States was the case of "Baby M" born to Mary Beth Whitehead in 1986. For a fee Mrs. Whitehead agreed to be artificially inseminated with sperm from William Stern, and to give up the child she carried for Stern and his wife. When Mrs. Whitehead changed her mind, refusing to give up Baby M, a long legal negotiation resulted in the court deciding that Baby M would live with the Sterns. Mrs. Whitehead would have visitation rights.[7]

In vitro fertilization

To simplify our discussion, I will focus on one of the older versions of technologically assisted conception, in vitro fertilization.[8] The Latin phrase in vitro literally means "in glass," and children conceived this way are often called "test tube babies." Fertilization or conception occurs outside of the woman's womb, usually in a petri dish, not a test tube, and the developing embryo is later placed in the mother's uterus. Louise Brown, the first child conceived in this manner, was born in 1978, and several thousand more children have been conceived through in vitro fertilization since then. Although this technique has become widely accepted, even among Christians, we need to explore several issues related to the Christian theology and ethics of in vitro fertilization. For the sake of simplicity, I will assume that the eggs and sperm used in in vitro fertilization come from the husband and wife, although in some cases donors are used.

Questions to Be Asked

Why have children at all?

This fundamental question underlies a wide range of contemporary issues.[9] Because God instructed Adam and Eve to "Be fruitful and multiply," many Christians believe that having children is expected. Some Christians, however, interpret that instruction as specifically for the first couple, not all couples. Some Christians insist that the "Be fruitful" statement is a blessing rather than a command.

"God gave this *blessing* to the human race as a whole. He does not direct it to everyone."[10]

In the ancient world, and in some cultures today, people had several practical reasons to have several children. For example, children can be laborers, they can support their parents in their old age, and they can carry on the family name.[11] Some of these reasons seem less significant today. For example, many couples prepare financially for their senior years and do not depend on their children for financial support. Stanley Hauerwas notes that many couples have difficulty explaining why they feel the need for children.

> They say it is fun (obviously these never had children), that it is a manifestation of their love (but then what do you do with your children if the love fades), or it is to please the grandparents or to prevent the couple from being lonely (again less than good reasons, since then the child is being used for some purpose other than him or herself), or that children are our hope for the future (and then they always disappoint us).[12]

Hauerwas's comment will startle some Christians. Many Christians would respond to the question, Why have children at all?, by pointing to biblical teaching on the purposes of sexual intercourse. One purpose of sex is to conceive children. A fertile couple might use contraceptives at times, but they are often open to the possibility of a conception as a natural consequence of the way God designed sex. A husband and wife would welcome children as an expression of their love for each other.

Is technology legitimate?

Second, what is the Christian view of technology? This question, like the first one, is a large, complex question, and Christians have held a wide range of opinions about the use of technology in solving life's problems in general. Daniel McGee has proposed a simple, twofold typology: Our view could be pro-technology or anti-technology.[13] Another scholar suggests that three views of technology are possible: technology as an antimoral, amoral, or moral enterprise.[14]

In relation to infertility in particular, Christians have disagreed about the use of technological assistance such as *in vitro* fertilization. Some Christians insist that methods such as *in vitro* fertilization are not "natural," that humans are "playing God." The Roman Catholic church, for instance, has generally held this perspective.[15]

This resistance to *in vitro* fertilization fits into a longer history of Christian rejection of medical science and technology. For example, some Christians opposed the use of inoculations for smallpox in the 1700s. Some Christians also rejected the use of anesthesia in surgery or in childbirth.[16]

Many Christians, however, are more open to the use of technology and medicine, including *in vitro* fertilization. They might argue, for example, that developing technology is a valid expression of God's command to have "dominion" over the created order (Gen 1:26, 28). God encourages humans, they continue, to be co-creators with him. Also, the creation of technological solutions to life's problems is a responsible form of Christian stewardship of our God-given talents: "From this perspective, numerous opportunities available in modern medicine are interpreted as invitations from God to advance. Here, God is seen as working through human effort to reduce suffering and to heal."[17]

Christians who affirm the use of technology such as *in vitro* fertilization usually avoid a total endorsement of all forms of technology. They realize the need for a theological assessment of technology; the fact that we can do something technologically does not mean we necessarily should do it. The Apostle Paul urges us to "test everything; hold fast to what is good, abstain from every form of evil" (1 Thess 5:21-22).

Christians who are open to the possibility of technologically assisted conception still need to evaluate the pros and cons of those techniques. Without attempting a full-scale study of *in vitro* fertilization, a few of the commonly mentioned theological and ethical concerns can be mentioned.

For example, assuming the genetic material comes from the husband and wife and no third party is involved, some Christians would be concerned about the use of masturbation by the husband to provide the sperm used.[18] Contemporary discussions of masturbation reveal a wide range of opinions. One conservative Christian author, for example, identifies four viewpoints among Christians today, ranging from "Masturbation is a gift of God" to "It is certainly wrong."[19]

Another potential problem for *in vitro* fertilization is the inefficiency of the process. *In vitro* fertilization generally creates several embryos, but only about 25 per cent are implanted in the woman's uterus. The woman who conceives with this method may produce a large number of children; ironically, couples who have agonized over infertility for years may now have many children to rear. A related inefficiency issue is the disposal of the unnecessary embryos created by this process. For those who believe that human life begins at conception, disposing of these embryos is actually the killing of innocent children.[20]

Another significant ethical issue is the expense of *in vitro* fertilization. This procedure costs several thousand dollars, and the success rate is fairly low (about 20 per cent).[21] Should an infertile couple spend that much money when they have other options such as adoption and remaining childfree? Money is almost always a major issue in life's dilemmas. Christians are expected by God to be wise stewards of all of their resources. Could the thousands of dollars needed for *in vitro* fertilization be used better for some other worthy cause? Raising these kinds of questions may be offensive to some infertile couples. They already agonize over their inability to have a child, and they may resent someone questioning their motives in pursuing technological assistance. Still, how we use our money is an important aspect of Christian discipleship and decision making.

Some critics of *in vitro* fertilization suggest that a key issue is community. Stanley Hauerwas phrases the issue bluntly:

> Put starkly, for the Christian the question of the use or non-use of *in vitro* fertilization will be determined primarily by whether such a procedure is appropriate to our understanding of what kind of community we should be and in particular what kind of attitudes about parenting we should foster.[22]

Hauerwas argues that Christians should see children as gifts from God. A childless couple should prefer adoption as the best response to their situation. For Hauerwas, the most basic Christian community is the kingdom of God, not the family.

> Therefore, it was not incumbent on every Christian to marry or have children, since, after all, the community was primarily to grow through the conversion of those outside of it. Put simply, Christians broke the assumption that marriage was a natural or moral necessity and thus made it a vocation. . . . They had to think about why they were having children, because their own beliefs now convinced them they were not obliged.[23]

Techniques such as *in vitro* fertilization, however, might reinforce the notion that the biological family, and not the kingdom of God, is the fundamental social institution for Christians.

Hauerwas's elevation of the Christian community over the biological family does have some merit. In light of the criticism of the traditional Christian view in contemporary culture of the family as a man and a woman married and, typically, bearing children, however, Christians need to examine their beliefs about marriage, sexuality, procreation, and children in light of the Bible's teachings. An infertile couple's decision needs to be informed by the Bible.

CHILDREN AND THE CHILD

Many years ago a friend told me about an unusual conversation she had with a college student. The student told her that the only reason she would go to heaven after death was because she had borne children on earth. He used 1 Tim 2:15 to defend his position: "Yet she will be saved through childbearing, provided they continue in faith and love and holiness, with modesty." The student assumed, wrongly I think, that having children was essential to female salvation. Other translators and interpreters have suggested that the verse could mean women will be saved because of the birth of the Child, meaning Jesus, or that women will be brought safely through the trauma of childbirth. A recent commentator, reviewing several options, noted, "No serious interpreter accepts the first alternative that Paul promised women salvation by their having children."[24]

Although this obscure, debated text is a proverbial can of worms, the college student's erroneous interpretation raises the fundamental issue we have tackled in this chapter: how important are children to a Christian couple living a happy, productive life? Having a child will not give a woman spiritual salvation, and neither are all women protected from physical harm in childbirth. But will childbearing remove the agony felt by an infertile couple? Having children has provided satisfaction and meaning for many Christian couples, but should Christians have the attitude that life is somehow incomplete without children? Gilbert Meilaender suggests, "Without in any way undervaluing the presence of children, we should also be free of the idolatrous desire to have them at any cost—as our project rather than God's gift."[25] God blesses our lives

| **How important is having children?** |

in many ways. The inability to have children is tragic for the infertile couple and their concerned family and friends. There are no easy answers.

Without wanting to sound trite, I hope that an infertile couple realizes that a strong relationship to God is ultimately more important than having children. The prophet Isaiah reports God's blessings on faithful eunuchs: "To the eunuchs who keep my sabbaths, who choose the things that please me and hold fast my covenant, I will give, in my house and within my walls, a monument and a name better than sons and daughters; I will give them an everlasting name that shall not be cut off" (Isa 56:4–5). Being infertile is not, obviously, the same as being a eunuch except in the sense of being unable to have children. God's promise of blessing to eunuchs does have relevance for those who struggle with infertility today.

Jesus notes that our relation to God is more important than biological or family relations. When a woman calls the womb that carried him blessed, Jesus replies, "Blessed rather are those who hear the word of God and obey it!" (Luke 11:27–28).

Being infertile presents believers with a major spiritual crisis. Being angry at God is a natural response. Lewis Smedes recounts an agonizing personal tale in *Forgive and Forget*. He and his wife, Doris, thought they could not conceive a child. Eventually she became pregnant, but she went into premature labor in her seventh month. At first the doctors thought the child would be deformed, but a healthy baby was born. Tragically, the child soon died. At one stage in the grieving process, Smedes wrote, "I felt as if I were the butt of a cruel divine joke. Would I end up hating God?"[26] Although Smedes and others who suffer horribly are tempted to hate God, God continues to love us.

While I do not believe God causes infertility directly, he has created a world in which infertility can occur. Christians can responsibly use technological advances to cope with their situation, but their ultimate consolation must be in God, not technology.

_ꕔ_ **Chapter Six**

ILLNESS AND DISABILITY

Sickness can occur at any time in the human life cycle. This chapter and the next few chapters are not arranged in a strict chronological order, since they are not tied to specific events in the womb to tomb sequence of Part Two.[1] For example, a relative suffered a major stroke many years ago when she was a young adult. Although she recovered well, she still has some partial paralysis.

> **If death is inevitable, why do we suffer long, painful illnesses?**

Continuing bouts of depression about her medical condition have contributed to marital difficulties and problems with employment.

Some illnesses are temporary nuisances, such as colds or the flu, but some are life-threatening. Some sicknesses are chronic, debilitating conditions. Some people cannot recall a time when they did not feel bad. For these sick people and their care givers, the topic of this chapter addresses the form of suffering most real and meaningful to them.

Although I will use words such as illness, sickness, and disease interchangeably, many scholars make clear distinctions. For instance, Edwin Hui calls sickness the state of unhealth, while disease refers to the biological dimension of sickness. He limits illness to the subjective dimension of sickness.[2] Such distinctions are useful, but in ordinary conversation I notice many people use these words as synonyms.

The best-selling book _Tuesdays with Morrie_ captured the attention of many because of the candid observations of Morrie, who was dying of Amyotrophic Lateral Sclerosis (ALS), often called Lou

Gehrig's disease.[3] The agony of someone with a serious disease far transcends our experience with colds, allergies, and the flu. Serious illness prompts us to reflect on our relation to God and the Christian view of life in general.

One of the most famous contemporary accounts of a religious person struggling with evil and suffering is Harold Kushner's *When Bad Things Happen to Good People*. A Jewish rabbi, Kushner began to think more seriously about God's relation to evil when his son was diagnosed with progeria, or rapid aging. Kushner asked, "How could this be happening to my family? If God existed, if He was minimally fair, let alone loving and forgiving, how could He do this to me?"[4]

Other gripping accounts by Christians deal with their struggles with the diagnosis of a child or spouse with a severe illness or disability. John Goldingay, an Old Testament scholar, wrote a series of essays after his wife was diagnosed with Multiple Sclerosis.[5] Frances Young, a theologian, composed a narrative essay about her son's severe handicap. Arthur was born brain-damaged, a condition known as microcephalia.[6] German theologian Jürgen Moltmann has written briefly about his older, severely disabled brother.[7] Some insightful accounts have been written by survivors of cancer.[8]

One extremely frightening illness is Alzheimer's disease. Elizabeth T. Hall offers many helpful suggestions about how to care for a person with Alzheimer's disease as she reports on her relationship with her mother. Hall's perspective is unusual because she also suffers from a debilitating medical condition.[9] David Keck identifies Alzheimer's disease as the "Theological Disease." Keck chose this intriguing nickname because the ravaging impact of this disease provoked theological reflections on issues such as the image of God, memory, and salvation. His reflections on the theological dimensions of this terrible condition were prompted by his mother's situation.[10] Robertson McQuilkin wrote a moving account of his taking care of his wife as her Alzheimer's disease developed.[11]

In this chapter I will explore biblical perspectives on physical illness. Realizing that the Bible does not make a hard distinction between the spiritual and physical dimensions of life, I will still highlight conditions that are primarily physical. What today we call mental illness will not be addressed in depth. Depression, for example, is a complex experience and can be addressed by medication and counseling.[12] Serious personality disorders can be studied in light of the riches of the Bible, Christian theology, and contemporary psychology.[13] Illnesses typically associated with older people and the topics of death and dying will be mentioned in later chapters. This chapter will include some treatment of physical handicaps or disabilities, since the Bible often includes blindness and lameness in it discussions of sickness. The suffering of the mentally challenged or retarded presents a special case for a theology of suffering. Christian ethicist Stanley Hauerwas has devoted significant attention to this topic.[14]

SIN, SICKNESS, AND SUFFERING

The Bible has a lot to say about sickness and health.[15] Conditions such as leprosy, blindness, lameness, and demon possession are frequently mentioned. Since the amount of biblical material on sickness can be overwhelming, I will start with two stories that are representative of the themes we need to explore.

Biblical Examples of Illness

First, 2 Kings 5 recounts the familiar story of Naaman's leprosy. Scholars generally agree that the disease labeled "leprosy" is not the same as the modern leprosy, or Hansen's disease.[16] Leprosy in biblical times referred to a serious skin condition, and lepers were typically treated as social outcasts. Naaman's case may not have been too severe, since he continued to serve as a leader in the Syrian army.

The biblical storyteller does not indicate the source of Naaman's leprosy. As we will soon see, sin and sickness are often linked in the Bible. Many texts suggest that the doctrine of retribution applies to illness. Sin leads to suffering, perhaps as a form of divine punishment. In the case of Naaman, however, no hint of the doctrine of retribution appears.

When Naaman visits the king of Israel with a letter from the king of Syria requesting a cure, the Israelite king responds, "Am I God, to kill and to make alive, that this man sends word to me to cure a man of leprosy?" (2 Kgs 5:7). The king's comments reflect the typical Israelite view that God is ultimately in charge of human health and sickness.

After Naaman has been healed by following the prophet Elisha's instructions, Elisha's servant Gehazi becomes greedy. When Gehazi requests a reward from Naaman for the healing, Elisha is upset and announces that Gehazi will be afflicted with the leprosy that had departed Naaman (2 Kgs 5:27).

The second story I will use as a case study is Jesus' healing of a paralyzed man. Before he heals the man, Jesus says, "Take heart, son; your sins are forgiven" (Matt 9:2). In this situation Jesus echoes the traditional Israelite view that sin and sickness are linked as cause and effect. The religious leaders accuse Jesus of blasphemy for claiming the divine prerogative of forgiving sins, but Jesus continues to heal the paralytic.

Key Biblical Themes

An exhaustive study of sickness and health in the Bible is beyond the scope of this book, but these two stories and a few others point us to some key biblical themes.

God as the source of sickness

First, the Bible generally presents God as the ultimate source of sickness and disability. As we saw in the chapter on tornadoes, Christians disagree on the details of interpretation of divine sovereignty, but they agree that God is ultimately lord of all of life. For instance, when Moses protests that he is not eloquent enough to speak for God, God responds, "Who gives speech to mortals? Who makes them mute or deaf, or seeing or blind? Is it not I, the Lord?" (Exod 4:11). Some Christians interpret this verse to mean that God is the direct cause of all sickness and disabilities. Others insist that this passage means that God can use whatever ability Moses has. "He who has made everyone certainly has the power to effectively use anyone."[17] A similar text is Deuteronomy 32:39, where God is the one who heals and wounds. God can be the ultimate source of the human condition without being the direct cause. He created a world in which sickness happens, but he does not directly cause every sickness.

Sickness as connected to sin

Second, the Bible often explains sickness as the result of sin. The doctrine of retribution was the focus of an earlier chapter, and sickness is a classic illustration of the widespread acceptance of this view. For example, when Miriam criticizes Moses, she is punished by God with leprosy, resulting in her temporary expulsion from the camp (Num 12:9-15).

Despite the many texts that support the linkage of sin and sickness, punishment for sin is not the only biblical explanation for illness. Jesus, for example, rejects the retributive view of sickness in the case of the man born blind (John 9:3). In some passages no explanation of the medical condition or its cause is offered by the biblical writer.

Another source of sickness is Satan or demons. Job's suffering, including his sores, are not the result of Job's sin but of Satan's activity, permitted by God (Job 2:7-8). The role of demons is especially highlighted in the New Testament. Satan and the demons are rarely mentioned in the Old Testament, but the gospel writers in particular mention conditions caused by demonic powers.[18] Perhaps the most famous example of Jesus exorcizing demons is the story of the man with "an unclean spirit" living among the tombs (Mark 5:1-3). Jesus' deliverance of the demonic Legion transforms him into a healthy man. Although some Christians distinguish exorcisms from healings of disease, some link illness and demon possession (e.g., Matt 4:24).

God as the source of healing

Third, God is the ultimate source of health and healing. If the Hebrews are faithful to God, they will experience long life and good health. After reminding the Hebrews that he has sent the plagues on the Egyptians, God announces "I am the Lord who heals you" (Exod 15:26b). Later God states, "I kill and I make alive; I wound and I heal" (Deut 32:39). As we will see shortly, this emphasis has been the source of some controversy among Christians today. If God is the direct source of health and disease, should Christians seek medical help? Or, should they trust in divine intervention alone?

God's people are to help the sick

Fourth, God's people are encouraged to help the sick. Although lepers were considered outcasts in Hebrew law (Lev 13–14), the law also expresses concern for the sick. The Hebrew servant girl who tells Naaman's wife that help for her husband's leprosy is available in Israel reflects a typical compassion for those suffering sickness. One manifestation of holiness is avoiding ridicule of the deaf or putting a hindrance in the path of the blind (Lev 19:14). Whether or not the deafness or blindness is the result of sin is not mentioned, only that a holy person will not afflict them with more pain.

> **How should we respond to sickness?**

MEDICINE, MIRACLES, AND FAITH

The numerous biblical examples of sickness and health can be overwhelming, but many Christians today focus on a few key issues that relate to their situations. How should a believer respond to sickness? Should she pray for a miracle? Should she pray that God's will be done? Should he seek medical help?

Biblical Suspicions of Medical Care

God is ultimately the source of healing, but does the Bible allow the use of medical science today? Some Christians have found a few passages that seem suspicious of medical care. For example, King Asa had a foot disease, "yet even in his disease he did not seek the Lord, but sought help from physicians" (2 Chr 16:12). To some Christians, this text clearly points to an either/or choice between divine help and futile medical care. The passage might, however, mean Asa sinned by not trusting God; his reliance on doctors was not wrong in itself. Asa had in fact relied on God previously (2 Chr 14:3–4). The word translated "physicians" might here refer to pagan medicine men rather than medical physicians.[19] The ancient near east did not have medical doctors in our modern sense. Religion and medicine were so intertwined that many doctors were identified with pagan religion.[20]

Two passages in the New Testament are often used to discourage medical care. The woman who bled for many years "had endured much under many physicians, and had spent all that she had; and she was no better but rather grew worse" (Mark 5:26). Likewise, James 5:14–15 is sometimes cited in these discussions. The Christian response to sickness, it is argued, is to pray and anoint the sick person with oil, not to summon a physician.

Although some Christian groups take these selected texts to build a case against medical care today, the majority Christian view has been that medical care is an appropriate part of a believer's response to illness. Is the majority wrong? How does the Bible support medical care?

Biblical Support of Medical Care

Scholars who have studied Hebrew and early Christian texts, comparing them with writings from the surrounding cultures in the ancient world, have generally concluded that the Israelites and early Christians knew little of medical science: "In general a sick person [in Israel] had virtually no *aids* at his disposal worth mentioning, no physicians in the real sense, and no knowledge of medicine." So, the debate between medicine and faith in God would not have been the same kind of issue for people in the ancient world as it is today. Today Christians may debate whether to use traditional medicine, holistic medicine, or rely on faith in God alone. In the ancient near east the issue was often whether to put one's faith in God or to use medicine practiced by pagans.

As medical science and practice improved, the Israelites gained a healthy appreciation for what medical care could do. Even though the doctors of that day were not as qualified as contemporary medical specialists, they knew their insights ultimately came from God. Sirach, a book in the Old Testament Apocrypha, praises physicians and medicine, insisting that they are gifts from God. "Honor physicians for their services, for the Lord created them; for their gift of healing comes from the Most High. . . . The Lord created medicines out of the earth, and the sensible will not despise them" (Sir 38:1–2a, 4). This writer also encourages the sick to pray for God's healing (Sir 38:9).

The early church advocated a healing mission. Luke was "the beloved physician" (Col 4:14), and Jesus' healing ministry inspired the eventual establishment of hospitals.[22]

A Christian's attitude towards medical care today will partially reflect her general perspective on technology, mentioned in the chapter on infertility. Those who reject techniques such as artificial insemination or *in vitro* fertilization may typically be reluctant to use other forms of medical care. Those who are more pro-technology will see no major problem with medical care.

A simple example might focus the issues. I have worn eyeglasses since I was a child. Without my glasses I would be unable to function very well in my career or life in general. According to Exodus 4:11, interpreted literally, my poor eyesight is an act of God, and wearing my glasses is sinful! As someone who is generally pro-technology, I would argue that God gives humans the right and privilege to solve some of life's problems technologically and medically. God gives humans the privilege and responsibility of having "dominion" over the created world (Gen 1:28). That responsibility includes the development of human culture in general and the development of medical science and technology in particular. As I mentioned in the last chapter, we need to make a theological assessment of new technologies, but, in general, medical care is acceptable to me.

The Effect of Prayer

Most Christians accept both medical care and prayer for healing as valid responses to sickness. When they pray, however, mature

Christians realize that God may not heal all sickness.[23] David prays and fasts for his son, but the son dies (2 Sam 12:15-18). The Apostle Paul prays for removal of the thorn in his flesh, but the affliction remains (2 Cor 12:1-10).

Recent scientific studies have revealed that prayer has a therapeutic effect. Even when God does not provide miraculous healing, prayer has some medical benefits.[24] Medical experts and theologians still debate whether the therapeutic effect of prayer is psychological in origin or due to divine intervention.[25]

The numerous healings recorded in the Bible and a belief in God's control of health and sickness have encouraged Christians across the centuries to pray for healings. The topics of miracles, faith healings, and the so-called health and wealth gospel are complex, but perhaps a few comments will stimulate the reader's thinking. The health and wealth gospel, also known as the prosperity gospel, has brought these issues before the public in a prominent way in recent years. Advocates of this viewpoint insist that miraculous healings are available now, and people with strong faith in God can be cured of medical problems and can avoid financial problems. Some even insist that Christians should refuse medical care, relying completely on God for healing.

Medical Miracles

A fundamental issue in this discussion is the nature of a miracle. C. S. Lewis begins his book-length study of miracles with a simple working definition: a miracle is "an interference with Nature by supernatural power."[26] Lewis's explanation of this definition depends upon his particular worldview. In some views of reality, the unusual or miraculous is ruled out completely. Miracles are not possible, a naturalist would insist, so whatever looks like a miracle can be explained some other way.[27] Supernaturalists understand miracles as events that are not governed by natural law. Weighing all the pros and cons of the naturalist versus supernaturalist worldviews is a complex theological issue, but mainstream Christianity has generally allowed for the possibility of miracles.

Although much of American society is heavily secularized, there has been a resurgence of interest in miracles, heaven, and angels in the popular media in recent decades. For example, *Time* magazine's cover story for April 10, 1995, was "Can We Still Believe in Miracles?" In their poll, 69 percent of Americans believe that miracles are possible.[28] A national poll in the fall of 2003 reported that 82 percent of Americans believe in miracles.[29] Epitomizing this popular interest is Dan Wakefield's *Expect a Miracle*.[30]

Assuming that miracles are possible, then, Christians still debate whether they are possible today. In particular, Christians debate whether or not spiritual gifts such as healing are still available. The Apostle Paul mentions "gifts of healing" as well as "the working of miracles" in his catalogue of spiritual gifts (1 Cor 12:9-10). The early Christians were empowered to perform miracles similar to those in Jesus' ministry (e.g., Acts 3:1-10). Should Christians expect to do miracles, including healings of disease, today?

Can people perform miracles?

The major Christian views on the possibility of divine healing today can be classified into three categories.[31] First, some Christians are cessationists, meaning that they believe miracles ceased after the first century. Cessationists are often from the Reformed (Presbyterian) tradition or are dispensationalists. They argue that miracles, healings, and speaking in tongues were essential to confirm that God was working through Jesus and the early Christians. Now that Christianity is established and the biblical canon is available, miracles are not needed.

Second, Pentecostals and charismatics insist that all of the spiritual gifts are still available. Early in this century Pentecostalism was usually identified with specific denominations, such as Assemblies of God, but by mid-century this view of spiritual gifts had become trans-denominational and began to be called the "charismatic movement." In the 1980s a new stage of this trajectory appeared. This movement, called the "third wave," has been popularized through the works of John Wimber and the Vineyard churches.[32]

Third, a large group of Christians fit into a mediating category, the "open, but cautious" group.[33] They believe that God can still heal today, but they are cautious about the excesses of some "faith healers" in the second category. I would fit most comfortably in this third camp. I have never directly seen a miracle occur, but my theology allows for that possibility. I have read several reports of miraculous healings, and I have no doubt that God still heals.

If a Christian fits within the second or third category, they believe prayer for miracles is still legitimate for Christians. A significant difference between the two groups might be the level of expectation of a miracle. A charismatic Christian, or someone from the health and wealth gospel, has a higher degree of expectation that God will heal them. Growing up in the 1950s, I recall seeing Oral Roberts's healing services on television. The movie *Leap of Faith* satirized the excesses of this view.

A Christian in the open but cautious category would sincerely pray for a miracle, but she would more quickly acknowledge that God sometimes says "No" to these requests. The theological dilemma that many Christians in this third camp feel is expressed poignantly in C. S. Lewis's essay, "Petitionary Prayer: A Problem without an Answer."[34] Lewis says that the Bible teaches us two patterns of petitionary prayer. On one hand, we are told to pray "Thy will be done," but, on the other hand, we are encouraged to pray for miracles and healings. Praying for miracles seems supported by the times Jesus says a miracle is due to the healed person's faith response to him (e.g., Matt 9:22). Lewis said he had found no answer to his dilemma, but he offered an observation. Faith

> does not mean any state of psychological certitude such as might be—I think it sometimes is—manufactured from within by the natural action of a strong will upon an obedient imagination. The faith that moves mountains is a gift from Him who created mountains.[35]

WHOLENESS AND WELLNESS

A chronically sick person may become so accustomed to his condition that he takes it for granted. No, he's not happy about being ill, but he sees no realistic chance for significant change. When Jesus encounters a man who has been paralyzed for 38 years, he asks "Do you want to be made well?" (John 5:6). The question may sound strange, because we assume everyone wants to be well. Jesus' question is a wake-up call; he is saying, "Your condition is not normal."

Daniel Simundson begins a splendid essay on "Health and Healing in the Bible" by noting that "Health and wholeness is the 'normal' state."[36] The world in which

| **What is wellness?** |

we live, punctuated by sickness and disabilities is not the way it is supposed to be. "The present interlude in which there is sickness is the aberration, the abnormality, not what is either normal or permanent."[37]

Eschatological Healing

The total elimination of sickness, pain, and suffering is eschatological (Rev 21:4–5); it will not happen until Jesus returns. Until then, most of us will be sick at times, or we will try to minister to sick people. Most Christians will seek medical help for our illnesses and divine assistance as well. Even Oral Roberts, who popularized faith healing in the 1950s, later built a hospital in Tulsa, Oklahoma. Many Christians could find themselves in synch with Oral Roberts on this issue, that prayer and medicine are compatible ways to address illness.

The Comprehensive Wellness of the Bible

One final observation is necessary, however, to avoid what may be a misleading impression from this discussion of illness. The Bible does not totally separate the physical and spiritual dimensions of life. Medical practitioners have long acknowledged the interaction of mind and body. The popularity of alternative or holistic medicine today signals a fresh awareness of the interdependence of all aspects of human nature. The biblical perspective is that the total person is affected by an illness.[38]

A recent, exhaustive study of the biblical terms for healing has stressed the comprehensive nature of God's action. When God "heals" us (e.g., Exod 15:26), he is more than "Israel's 'Great Physician,' in twentieth century, Western terms. Rather, he was the Restorer, the One who made them whole."[39]

Two examples must suffice to support the holistic emphasis of the Bible on the well-being of the total person. First, Paul tells Timothy "Physical exercise has some value, but spiritual exercise is valuable in every way, because it promises life both for the present and for the future" (1 Tim 4:8; Good News Bible). Paul expresses a preference for spiritual well-being, but physical well-being is important as well. John supports this notion when he tells Gaius, "I pray that all may go well with you and that you may be in health; I know it is well with your soul" (3 John 2).

Simundson notes that "Healing is more than attaining physical health" in the Bible.[40] If we do not have complete wholeness in this life, then God will give that to us in the next life. "If God's intention for us is wholeness, *shalom*, health, we need a life beyond this one in order for this to be accomplished."[41]

Christian Responses to Sickness

How does a Christian respond to a chronic illness or a life-threatening condition? T. B. Maston, long-time seminary ethics professor, wrote an inspirational book about his experiences with suffering. His son had been injured in child birth, and he was confined to a wheel chair throughout his life. Maston himself had a critical case of pneumonia and almost died, but he felt God had enabled the medical team to save his life. He also tells the story of a medical doctor friend who experienced a miraculous healing after a car wreck. Although he had experienced and heard about miraculous healings, his son was never cured. He concluded faith in God and medical care were compatible: "Prayer and the physician belong together. Both have a place in the relief of suffering in general and in the healing of the sick in particular."[42] Maston further concluded that God's greatest miracles may not be the healing of physical problems but the inner peace God offers.

 **Chapter Seven**

BETRAYAL OF TRUST

Which hurts more, a broken leg or a broken heart? A broken leg can be very painful, and wearing a cast and using crutches is an inconvenience for several weeks. For many people, however, a broken heart is even more painful. The phrase "broken heart" will remind many readers of problems with romantic relationships, such as unrequited love, being jilted by a lover, or the death of a spouse. The phrase could also apply to any significant interpersonal relationship that turns sour. We are often disappointed with other people, and that frustration can be an intense form of suffering.

In this chapter we will focus on the emotional or psychological suffering we experience from failed or fractured relationships. The title of the chapter is borrowed from a recent book on sexual misconduct among the clergy, but the phrase "betrayal of trust," much like "broken heart," is fitting for many forms of mental anguish that result from relationships that fail to meet our expectations.[1] Rather than highlighting problems such as the abuse of power by pastors or other betrayals of trust in the workplace, I will look primarily at two other arenas of life in this chapter. First, we will study some biblical examples of friendships gone awry. Second, we will explore betrayals of trust within the family. Although the subject of the last chapter, illness and disability, has often been studied in works on the biblical view of suffering, there has been considerably less attention to the subject of broken relationships as a form of human suffering. The major exception is books on forgiveness.[2]

> **What do you do with a broken heart?**

FAILED FRIENDSHIPS

Although the Bible tells of several friends, the topic of friendship is often neglected in biblical scholarship. For example, an excellent six-volume Bible dictionary does not have a single article on friends or friendships.[3] Friendship has been a consistent theme in world literature, but Christian theologians have not explored this subject as well as they should.[4]

Typically we think of friendship as the close relations between humans. One Bible dictionary defines *friendship* as "a close trusting relationship between two people."[5] Perhaps the best-known example of human friendship in the Bible is David's relation to Jonathan, son of King Saul. David and Jonathan seal their close relationship with a covenant (1 Sam 18:1–3), and David deeply grieves after Jonathan's death (2 Sam 1:25–26).

One of the most unusual descriptions of friendship in the Old Testament is that of God as friend (e.g., 2 Chr 20:7; Isa 41:8).[6] The New Testament continues this emphasis, mentioning again that Abraham is "the friend of God" (Jas 2:23). Moreover, Jesus describes his followers as his friends (John 15:14).

One of the Greek words for love, *philia*, describes the admiration that makes up friendship. This term has been the focus of some significant studies. C. S. Lewis devoted a book to all four of the Greek words for love. Lewis makes some strong claims for the distinctive character of *philia*. For instance, friendship is "the least *natural* of loves" since it is not based on any biological need.[7] Friendship love differs from romantic love: "Lovers are normally face to face, absorbed in each other; Friends are side by side, absorbed in some common interest."[8]

Although a close friendship can be a very satisfying, enriching experience, it can also be the source of agony. Conventional wisdom might say that ideally "A friend loves at all times" (Prov 17:17), however, wise persons also know that "Some friends play at friendship, but a true friend sticks closer than one's nearest kin" (Prov 18:24).

Biblical Betrayals

Proof that friendships can sometimes become the source of emotional and social anguish can be found in the Book of Job. Job's friends are a disappointment to him when they try to explain his suffering. They come to offer comfort as he is suffering, but their dogmatic application of the doctrine of retribution frustrates him. Job knows that he has not committed the kinds of sins that would merit so much suffering, and he grows increasingly frustrated with their unwanted advice. For example, he compares them to "worthless physicians" (Job 13:4), and he has no use for their so-called wisdom: "Your maxims are proverbs of ashes, and your defenses are defenses of clay" (Job 13:12). Job's experience is similar to that of many suffering people today. Their friends have a hard time understanding their feelings, and any advice seems trite.

In Psalm 55 David complains bitterly that he has been betrayed by a close friend. David says he can bear the opposition of an enemy, "But it is you, my equal, my companion, my familiar friend" (Ps 55:13) that he cannot abide. Although David does not identify his false friend, some Bible students suggest it could be Ahithophel, who deserts David to join Absalom's rebellion against the king (2 Sam 15:12). David reports a similar experience of betrayal by a friend in Psalm 41:9, saying his "bosom friend" has turned against him.

The prophet Jeremiah is betrayed by some of his friends. In one of his "confessions" he mentions that some of his friends are "watching for me to stumble" (Jer 20:10). Jeremiah's message about the Babylonian threat is so unpopular that his so-called friends hope for him to fail.

Several New Testament stories illustrate flawed or failed friendships. John the Baptist may have felt betrayed by or at least disappointed with Jesus. John the Baptist announces Jesus as the Messiah, but Jesus does not match the typical messianic expectations of that day. John sends his own disciples to ask Jesus if he is really the Messiah (Matt 11:2). Jesus tells John's disciples that he is fulfilling his agenda by doing miracles and preaching the good news.

The Apostle Paul is apparently disappointed when John Mark deserts the team on the first missionary journey (Acts 13:13). When Barnabas wants to take John Mark on the second trip, Paul refuses, resulting in a serious division between the companions. Later, however, Paul seems to reconcile with John Mark, since he writes favorably of him (Col 4:10). In 2 Timothy, Paul compares the faithfulness of Onesiphorus to the infidelity of two others (2 Tim 1:15-18). He also mentions that at one point everyone deserts him except God (2 Tim 4:16-18).

Probably the most famous cluster of stories about betrayal by close friends occurs in the life of Jesus. Judas's betrayal of Jesus has puzzled readers. Perhaps Judas was a frustrated Zealot, hoping that a confrontation with the authorities would force Jesus to fight Roman occupation as many expected a messiah would. Further, Scripture mentions the role of Satan in prompting the betrayal (John 13:2). Jesus is also troubled by the inability of Peter, James, and John to watch and pray in the garden of Gethsemane. Jesus may have been especially disappointed in Simon Peter's denials. Jesus' long conversation with Peter after the resurrection is often interpreted as a reconciliation process (John 21:15-23). Peter uses the word for friendship love to express his affection for Jesus, but he had not been a trustworthy friend earlier.

These biblical stories of stresses within friendship may remind us of times we have felt betrayed by a friend or a co-worker. The severity of our suffering over failed friendships will typically depend on the depth of that friendship. I have several close friends and many more acquaintances. If I were wronged by an acquaintance, I would be troubled, but if a close friend betrayed a confidence or was disloyal I would be deeply grieved.

Mending Broken Friendships

Jesus' relationship with those who were fickle toward him is instructive for us. Although Judas committed suicide before there was any chance for reconciliation, Jesus carefully restores his relationship with Simon Peter and the other disciples. Jesus not only teaches about forgiveness (Luke 23:34), he practices that forgiveness.

How should a Christian respond to betrayal by a friend? The ideal response, epitomized by Jesus, is to forgive the other person. Despite the popularity of the old saying, "Forgive and forget," forgiveness does not require developing amnesia. Forgiveness means not holding a grudge or brooding over the damage to a relationship. If the person who betrayed you is repentant, the relationship may be restored and even become stronger than it was before the betrayal. If the other person is unrepentant, you can forgive them without there being a mutual reconciliation. Paul encouraged us to do what we can to bring about peace in our relationships: "If it is possible, so far as it depends on you, live peaceably with all" (Rom 12:18). Forgiveness is often a process rather than a one-time patching-up of a broken relationship, but we can begin the process by being willing to forgive others.

FAMILY FEUDS

The betrayal of trust among friends and colleagues creates mental anguish for many of us. The pain is different than physical pain, but the hurt sometimes lasts longer. In his fictional correspondence with Malcolm, C. S. Lewis notes a sudden discovery: "I had really forgiven someone I have been trying to forgive for over thirty years."[9]

Despite the severity of suffering when friends betray us, many of us experience betrayal of loyalty most often in our families. Some of our deepest life commitments are made within this arena of life, yet family members often hurt each other. We will not look primarily at the issues of verbal and physical abuse in this section, but we will highlight biblical stories of painful disruptions of family relationships. Although I will try to classify these situations (e.g., sibling rivalry), in most of the stories several members of the family are involved.

The Bible occasionally offers us didactic, or teaching, passages about the ideal family. For example, Proverbs 31:10–31 is often taken to be a description of the ideal Hebrew wife and mother. Ephesians 5:21-6:9 is frequently interpreted as the ideal pattern for a Christian home. More often than depicting the ideal, however, the Bible describes real families experiencing the joys and tragedies of real life. Most of these stories are in the Old Testament, although we have a few glimpses of family life in the New Testament as well.

Sibling Rivalry

A common source of family strife is sibling rivalry. For instance, the rivalry of Jacob and Esau, the twin sons of Isaac and Rebekah, begins even in the womb (Gen 25:22-23). As an adult, Jacob realizes that his older brother will benefit greatly from being the first born. Jacob convinces the hungry Esau to trade him the treasured birthright of the first born for some food. With the help of his mother, Jacob also tricks the elderly Isaac into giving him the blessing which rightly belongs to his older brother, Esau. When Esau discovers that Jacob had twice lived up to his name, which can be translated "supplanter," he promises to kill Jacob (Gen 27:36-41). Esau's anger prompts Jacob to flee to another country. Only after several years does Jacob return and reconcile with Esau.

Sibling rivalry surfaces again in the story of jealousy among Jacob's sons. Jacob plays favorites with Joseph, the son of Rachel. The other sons are naturally jealous, and they sell Joseph as a slave. Eventually Joseph rises to power in Egypt, but when given the chance, he does not punish his brothers for their earlier cruelty. When he first identifies himself to his brothers, who had come to Egypt to find food for the family, he assures them that God has providentially guided the course of events in his life and he has no animosity toward them (Gen 45:5-8). When their father Jacob dies, the brothers worry that Joseph might now exact revenge on them, but he again reassures them he will not retaliate. "Do not be afraid! Am I in the place of God? Even though you intended to do harm to me, God intended it for good, in order to preserve a numerous people, as he is doing today" (Gen 50:19-20).

Joseph's forgiving spirit may be difficult for some of us to emulate. When we are mistreated by our brothers and sisters, we may feel more wronged than when a colleague or friend betrays us.

The disbelief of Jesus' brothers provides another example of tension between siblings. Although Jesus was born of the virgin Mary, many Protestant scholars believe that the brothers and sisters mentioned in the gospels were born to Mary and Joseph later (Mark 6:3). Jesus' brothers do not accept Jesus as the promised Messiah during his earthly life (Mark 3:21, 31; John 7:3-5), although his brother James does become a leader in the early church after encountering the risen Jesus (1 Cor 15:7; Acts 15:13-21). According to many evangelical scholars, two biblical books were written by half-brothers of Jesus, James and Jude.

Wayward Children

Another source of suffering in family life is wayward children. Proverbs 22:6 suggests that good parenting will typically result in good children: "Train children in the right way, and when old, they will not stray." Unfortunately, too many Christians today take this verse as a divine guarantee rather than a probability. This assumption adds to parents' frustration when their children depart from their guidance. Hebrew wisdom literature, especially Proverbs, most often offers generalizations or probabilities rather than no-exception promises. Ezekiel uses the analogy of a good father with a bad son to illustrate personal responsibility (Ezek 18:5-13), acknowledging that this proverb does not fit every situation. The analogy unexpectedly suggests that the bad son could have a good son (18:14).

Perhaps the most notable biblical story of a rebellious son is the account of Absalom's political revolution against his father. Disappointed that David has not punished Amnon for the rape of his half-sister, Tamar, Absalom eventually conspires to take over the kingdom (2 Sam 15:1-6). Although David regains his throne after Absalom is killed in battle, he grieves so deeply over his son's death that Joab warns him that his grief is demoralizing his troops (2 Sam 18:33-19:8). David is passionate about many of his relationships, and even though Absalom betrays him he still loves him deeply.

The prophet Hosea gives another illustration of wayward children. Although Hosea often compares God's relationship to Israel to that of a husband and wife, in Hosea 11 he compares God to a parent agonizing over the disobedient child, Israel. God teaches Israel how to walk, but Israel walks in the wrong direction, sinning against God. God practices a tough love, allowing the northern kingdom to be defeated by Assyria, but he does not completely abandon Israel (Hosea 11:8b–9). God's enduring love for his wayward people sets a high standard for Christians today dealing with rebellious children.

Parental Problems

While children sometimes disappoint their parents, the Bible also notes times when parents cause suffering for the children. Some of the most gruesome tales in the Old Testament, labeled "texts of terror" by Phyllis Trible, describe these situations. For example, the Israelite judge, Jephthah, in the heat of battle against the Ammonites, makes a desperate, rash promise to God (Judg 11:1–11). If God will give him victory, he will sacrifice whatever first comes out to meet him when he returns home (Judg 11:30–31). After he wins the battle and returns home, the first living being to come out from his house is his daughter, his only child. Although human sacrifice is often condemned throughout the Old Testament, Jephthah keeps his vow sacrificing his daughter (Gen 22; Deut 18:10, Jer 32:35; Ezek 20:31).[10]

Lot does not sacrifice his daughters in the same way, but he does offer them to the men of Sodom for sexual pleasure. When two angels arrive in Sodom, Lot practices typical Hebrew hospitality. Then, when the men of Sodom want to attack the two visitors, Lot offers his two daughters as substitutes (Gen 19:7–8). Lot and his daughters later flee the destruction of Sodom, and then the daughters commit incest with the drunken Lot in order to guarantee that they will have children (19:31–38). There are no heroes or heroines in this story, and it illustrates an extreme kind of betrayal in a family.

The stories of the Hebrew patriarchs are full of illustrations of family problems. One more example will illustrate how a father-in-law fails to follow through on a moral obligation to his daughter-in-law.

Judah, one of Jacob's sons, had three sons of his own. The first son, Er, had married Tamar but then died. According to a custom scholars call "levirate marriage" (see Deut 25:5-10), the widow should be married to a male kinsman of her dead husband in order to produce a child that will carry on the name of the dead man. Judah follows this custom, and Tamar marries Onan, Er's brother. Onan, however, refuses to complete sexual intercourse with Tamar, and therefore prevents her from bearing a son in the name of her first husband. God kills Onan for his refusal to follow biblical law (Gen 38:8-10). Fearful about allowing his third son to marry Tamar, Judah lets Tamar remain destitute. According to an old saying, desperate times call for desperate measures, and Tamar decides to trick her father-in-law. Disguising herself as a prostitute, she has sex with Judah and becomes pregnant. When her pregnancy becomes public knowledge, Judah is ready to have Tamar executed. Tamar, however, reveals that her accuser is the father of her child. Judah then admits, "She is more in the right than I, since I did not give her to my son Shelah" (Gen 38:26). We might use the traditional phrase the lesser of two evils to compare the actions of Tamar and Judah, since they each betrayed the other. One gospel writer, however, later makes mention of Tamar's place in the family tree of Jesus (Matt 1:3)!

Marital Strife

The husband-wife relationship is another common source of suffering in the family. Miscommunication between the two genders has been the subject of investigation by psychologists and family experts for years. John Gray's *Men Are from Mars, Women Are from Venus* was a best-seller for several years, partly because he addresses problems with communication in a popular, readable manner.[11] My concern here will be to highlight a few examples of betrayal between husbands and wives.

Abraham is famous as the first patriarch, but he betrays his wife Sarah at least twice. On two occasions Abraham tells political leaders under whose control he is living, that Sarah is his sister. According to one of the stories, Abraham is technically only telling a half-lie (if there is such a thing), for Abraham and Sarah had the same father

(Gen 20:12). Abraham tells the Pharaoh and Abimelech that she is his sister in order to avoid being killed (Gen 12:10-20; 20:1-18). If he identifies himself as Sarah's husband the Pharaoh and Abimelech might eliminate him to get Sarah. Although ethicists often discuss the possible legitimacy of lying to save a life, Sarah may have felt betrayed by her husband's deception.

Another form of betrayal of trust between husband and wife occurs when a spouse cooperates with the other spouse's enemies. Samson's wife betrays him by revealing the secret of his strength to his enemies. As a result, Samson is captured by his enemies, made a slave, and has his eyes gouged out (Judg 15:18-22). He almost certainly felt betrayed by his wife's collaboration with his opponents. He eventually commits suicide in order to escape a terrible life and to kill his tormentors.

The story of Abigail and Nabal is complicated, but Nabal may also have felt betrayed when Abigail helped his enemy, David. While David is a fugitive from King Saul, he asks for supplies for his men from the prosperous Nabal. When Nabal refuses to help David, Abigail takes supplies to David and pleads with him not to attack Nabal (1 Sam 25:23-31). Because of Abigail's intercession, David does not attack Nabal, but Nabal dies after Abigail reveals what she has done. The most interesting twist to this story is that David then "wooed Abigail, to make her his wife" (1 Sam 25:39).

Adultery

Perhaps the most common form of marital betrayal both in the Bible and today is adultery.[12] The most famous biblical story of adultery is probably David's affair with Bathsheba. Although the biblical writer does not disclose Bathsheba's motives or make clear if she was forced into the affair, she and David are both unfaithful to their marriage commitments. David causes the death of Uriah, Bathsheba's husband, and she later marries David. David's poetic confession of his sin is sincere, but he fails to acknowledge that he has wronged Uriah. To God, David says, "Against you, you alone have I sinned, and done what is evil in your sight" (Ps 51:4). Although the major consequence of human sin is always a broken relationship with God, sin also has consequences for ourselves and our relations with other people.

Anyone who has been close to an adulterous situation can testify to the long-term impact of that sin on marriage. Contemporary Christian ethicists often note, however, that other forms of infidelity are also possible. Lewis Smedes, for instance, warns of the dangers of "sexual friendships."[13] A sexual friendship is when a married person allows a person of the opposite sex—other than their spouse—to become a very close confidant. Although male-female friendships do not inevitably become sexual, they may threaten a marriage because of the level of emotional intimacy created. Richard Foster examines the category of "emotional adultery."[14] A husband or wife might, for example, commit emotional adultery when he or she devotes so much time and energy to a career or other activity that the marriage relationship is neglected.

Adultery always strains a marriage relationship, and sometimes the adultery leads to divorce. Although some divorces are described as amicable, many divorces produce severe emotional, financial, and psychological suffering for the divorced people, their friends, and their other relatives, especially their children.

Divorce

Biblical teaching on divorce includes several key texts. For example, Old Testament law describes the process for a husband divorcing his wife because he finds something "objectionable about her" (Deut 24:1). Later the Jewish teachers Shammai and Hillel debated the meaning of this "objectionable" basis for divorce. When the Pharisees ask Jesus his view of the Deuteronomy text, he directs them back to God's ideal for marriage: "they are no longer two, but one flesh. Therefore what God has joined together, let no one separate" (Matt 19:6). In the famous "exception clause," as it is called by Bible scholars, Jesus notes that "unchastity" is a basis for divorce (Matt 19:9; 5:32). The Apostle Paul hints that a Christian might divorce a non-Christian spouse who abandons the relationship (1 Cor 7:15), a provision sometimes called the Pauline Privilege by scholars.

Christian discussions of the legitimate biblical grounds for divorce, the ways to prevent divorce, and the best responses when divorce occurs cover a wide range of views.[15] One useful typology presents four major Christian views.[16] First, some Christians believe divorce is never permissible. Second, some others believe divorce is allowed but not remarriage. Third, some allow divorce for adultery or desertion and then affirm the possibility of remarriage. Fourth, some Christians accept the possibility of divorce and remarriage for reasons beyond adultery and desertion. For example, Craig Keener wants Christians to consider situations such as physical and psychological abuse as possible grounds for divorce.[17]

When people suffer in a marriage, especially over a long period of time, they wonder what God wants them to do. Stay in the marriage? Seek counseling? Seek a divorce? Different denominations and biblical scholars have disagreed over the best response to this kind of suffering. Ideally, a couple will seek to preserve the marriage, but the physical and emotional suffering may become so severe that one spouse must seek release from the relationship. A legal separation may be one way to buy some time to see if the relationship can be salvaged, but in some cases a divorce may be the only way to protect the suffering spouse from irreparable emotional or physical harm. I believe that biblical principles such as justice, love, compassion, and forgiveness need to guide the marriage partners in their decision making and the church in its response to any divorce.

CAN GOD BE TRUSTED?

Our review of broken relationships might have one unfortunate result: the reader might decide that nobody can be trusted! I do not want to paint such a bleak picture of interpersonal relationships. Although everyone is a sinner, relationships with friends, children, spouses, and coworkers often add meaning and depth to life. Whenever we make an emotional investment in a relationship, however, we open ourselves to the risk of emotional and psychological suffering.

Years ago the singing duo Simon and Garfunkel sang about being a rock and an island. Rocks and islands, the song said, feel no pain. By emotionally isolating ourselves, we might escape some of the suffering described in some biblical stories, but our lives would be stale, monochrome, and flat.

Broken human relationships cause some to ask, "Can God be trusted?"[18] People who suffer physical or emotional pain often raise questions about the goodness of God. The trustworthiness of God is fundamental to our entire study. Philip Yancey builds his powerful book *Disappointment with God* around conversations with a Christian who becomes disillusioned with God. Yancey focuses on three questions rarely articulated by Christians, lest they seem impolite or even heretical. The questions are: Is God unfair? Is God silent? Is God hidden?[19]

Throughout our study we have dealt and will continue to deal with these sorts of questions because they are central to any study of the biblical view of suffering. Many people in the Bible, especially in the laments, voice concerns like these. Our earlier explorations into the doctrine of retribution, the laments, and the "confessions" of Jeremiah revealed how often a suffering person might express anger or disappointment with God.[20]

> **Can God be trusted?**

Without sounding trite, I want to reemphasize that the Bible affirms the goodness of God. Someone in the midst of suffering may doubt the goodness of God, but the overwhelming message of Scripture is that God can be trusted. Questions such as "Where is the God of justice? Can I trust God? Why is God silent?" are natural expressions of our pain and frustration whenever we suffer. In the process of suffering, however, we may come to realize that God is just, fair, and loving.

Two illustrations reinforce what I have said in earlier chapters about God's love and concern for us. First, the author of Lamentations offers graphic testimony to the pain he and other Jews feel during the exile. Although he acknowledges that the Babylonian captivity is deserved suffering, or God's punishment for the nation's sin, he still agonizes, comparing desolate Jerusalem to a lonely widow (Lam 1:1–2). In the midst of his suffering, however, he recalls God's goodness: "The steadfast love of the Lord never ceases, his mercies never come to an end; they are new every morning; great is your faithfulness" (3:22-23).

Second, the Apostle Paul affirms that "God is faithful" (1 Cor 1:9; 10:13). Although Paul experienced many different kinds of suffering, he clings to his conviction that God is trustworthy. The author of Lamentations struggles with questions about God's goodness after a national tragedy; Paul wrestles with personal difficulties such as imprisonment and the thorn in the flesh. Both biblical authors deal realistically and deeply with their suffering and emerge to affirm the goodness of God.

 **Chapter Eight**

VIOLENCE

Now the earth was corrupt in God's sight, and the earth was filled with violence" (Gen 6:11). Although these words originally referred to the situation before the flood in Noah's day, they are equally true today. We live in a society saturated with violence.

Have you read the newspaper or watched television news lately? How many stories dealt with violence? My daily newspaper usually has several stories about murder, rape, armed robbery, and child abuse. Television shows, motion pictures, and other media often include violent scenes, and many Americans pay money to watch such displays of blood, gore, and humiliation at the theater or on video.

In recent years the threat of terrorism has become a new illustration of the prevalence of violence in our world. The images of airplanes flying into the World Trade Center and the Pentagon on

| **Where, in our violent world, is God?** | September 11, 2001, will be etched in the memories of Americans for a long time. In recent years Christian scholars have begun to reflect on this particular violent event, but violence has a long history.[1] |

Violence is one of the most common forms of suffering in our time. Although social scientists and other scholars continue to debate whether humans are naturally prone to violence or whether violent behavior is a learned response, violence has been around at least since Cain killed his brother Abel.[2] The nature-nurture debate about the origin of violence may never be resolved, but the prevalence of violence today constitutes a major cause of much of our suffering.[3]

When we are the victims of violence, we often wonder where God is and why he does not stop attacks on us. The basic issue of our study—Is God just?—relates to violence as much as sickness, infertility, or broken relationships. The Hebrew prophet Habakkuk expresses this concern at the beginning of his dialogue with God. "O Lord, how long shall I cry for help, and you will not listen? Or cry to you 'Violence!' and you will not save?" (Hab 1:2). Habakkuk complains to God that everywhere he looks he sees violence and justice perverted (1:3-4). Habakkuk's concern was provoked by the imminent invasion of his country, Judah, by the Babylonians. To the prophet the bad guys were about to defeat the good guys.

Habakkuk's quandary about war anticipates one of the issues we will discuss in this chapter. Violence occurs in diverse ways, including physical violence like murder, abuse, robbery, martyrdom, and persecution. One dictionary defines violence as "the use of physical or psychological force so as to injure or coerce someone either physically or psychologically or both to damage something."[4] Other Christian ethicists describe violence as "any physical act intended to injure, damage, or destroy a person or thing. Force need not be violence, but all violence involves force."[5] Although these definitions are comprehensive and helpful, I will bracket out two types of violence from our discussion. First, I will not treat verbal or emotional attacks, such as slander, psychological manipulation, or bullying. Second, I will not discuss physical abuse associated with persecution, martyrdom, or torture.[6] Although these are serious concerns, I will limit this discussion to three representative examples of violence which are highlighted in the Bible: murder, rape, and war.[7] The insights we gain from this study should be relevant to the other types of violence.

IT ALL BEGAN WITH CAIN

Great literature often stimulates our ethical and theological reflection. Oscar Hijuelos's novel *Mr. Ives' Christmas* is a gripping story about how a Christian man responds to his son's murder. Across the years Mr. Ives struggles with the question whether his son's murder was God's will.[8] Reading this novel can generate serious thinking about God, violence, and suffering, even if the reader has no direct experience of violent crime.

Murders often make the headlines in the news media. Some murders are crimes of passion and others are premeditated. Our legal system differentiates several kinds of murder, with manslaughter being less serious than premeditated murder. According to Hebrew law, a man who accidentally kills another person, can flee to a city of refuge to escape execution (Deut 19:4–10).

The Motivations of Murder

Murder cases such as the trials of Scott Peterson, Robert Blake, or notorious serial killers often grab the headlines for months and occasionally claim the title "trial of the century." The first murder in human history did not result in a court case, but Cain was judged by God for killing Abel. What prompted Cain's violent act? The book of Genesis does not disclose Cain's motivation; it simply reports that Cain was angry because God preferred Abel's offering (Gen 4:4–5). John later comments, "And why did he murder him? Because his own deeds were evil and his brother's righteous" (1 John 3:12). Cain lures Abel out into the field and kills him. When God confronts Cain, the murderer asks the

> **Am I my brother's keeper?**

now famous question, "Am I my brother's keeper?" (Gen 4:9). Surprisingly, God does not execute Cain but, rather, gives him a protective mark so that other humans will not harm him. Cain's punishment is to be a wanderer.

The Bible records many more murders after this first fratricide. Usually we learn more about the motivation behind the murder than we do in the account of the first murder. Depending on the motivation for the killing, we might not even want to call the killing a murder. Moses, for example, kills an Egyptian who is beating a fellow Hebrew (Exod 2:11–15). Like Cain, Moses becomes a fugitive, but God does not condemn him for his killing, and Moses later guides the Hebrews out of Egyptian bondage.

Although some murders might be for humanitarian reasons—what we might today call justifiable homicide—most murders are for more selfish reasons. For instance, David arranges for the death of Uriah, the husband of Bathsheba, after their adultery leads to her pregnancy. David first tries to get Uriah to sleep with Bathsheba, hoping to hide the fact that she is pregnant from her adultery with David. When Uriah refuses to go home to his wife, David has Uriah placed in a dangerous position in the next battle, where he is killed. When the prophet Nathan confronts David about his sin, Nathan accuses David of murdering Uriah, even though David's hand never literally strikes the blow (2 Sam 12:9). God does not kill David, but David's family suffers the consequences of his adultery and Uriah's murder.

Ahab, another Israelite king, is partially responsible for the death of Naboth. In this case again the king does not kill a man directly, but he sets in motion a chain of events that lead to the death of an innocent man. When Naboth refuses to sell his vineyard to the king, queen Jezebel helps her husband by having false charges brought against Naboth. Naboth is convicted and executed, allowing Ahab to claim the vineyard. God sends the prophet Elijah to accuse Ahab of murder (1 Kings 21:19). Ahab's greed, like David's concern to cover up his adultery, leads indirectly to the murder of an innocent man.

King Herod kills John the Baptist at the request of the daughter of Herodias. John the Baptist had criticized Herod's illegal marriage, and Herod had imprisoned him. When Herodias's daughter dances at Herod's birthday party, pleasing the king, he offers her a reward. After conferring with her mother, the young woman requests the death of John the Baptist (Matt 14:1–12). Although Herod is reluctant to kill John, his rash promise to his step-daughter leads to a murder.

Can Some Murders Be Condoned?

Some biblical killings are not condemned. Scholars have debated whether to translate the sixth commandment "Thou shalt not kill" (Exod 20:13 KJV) or "You shall not murder." Clearly some killing, such as war or capital punishment, is justified in Hebrew law. Murder, however, is always wrong. Killing such as assassination is allowed because it fits into a war context. Ehud is famous as the left-handed judge. Rather than lead the Hebrew army into battle against its oppressor, he gains a private audience with the king of Moab and kills him. This political assassination liberates the Hebrews from Moabite threat for eighty years (Judg 3:12–30).

The old saying "All's fair in love and war" might apply to the killing of Sisera by Jael (Judg 4:12–22). Sisera, the commander of the enemy army, runs away from battle and seeks refuge in the tent of the Hebrew woman, Jael. While he rests, she drives a tent peg through his temple. Her action saves the Hebrews just as effectively as if a soldier had killed him in battle.

Although some killings, such as these wartime assassinations, might not technically count as murders, they remind us that any kind of killing is a violent act. When Jesus interprets the Hebrew law, he retains the prohibition on murder, but he adds prohibitions on verbal abuse, slander, and character assassination (Matt 5:21–22). A murder deprives a person of his or her life, but verbal attacks can ruin a person's reputation and livelihood. As Dallas Willard notes, "Violence is the sure overflow of anger and contempt in the heart."[9]

The Suffering Murder Causes

How can we measure the amount of suffering caused by a murder? Our contemporary legal process allows for the family of a murder victim to testify about the severity of their loss in the penalty stage. Although all humans are created in the image of God, and thereby equally valuable, the death of a young mother, for example, has different consequences for her husband and young children than the death of an elderly person. A jury might try to assess the dead person's potential earning power over a lifetime, but measuring the potential contribution of an artist, author, or world leader is almost beyond the reach of our imagination.

Christians can undoubtedly agree that murder is a terrible sin, a violent act that erases a human life and creates long-term suffering for the victim's family. Where Christians have long disagreed is about the proper legal response to murder. [10] Some believers and Christian ethicists insist that the death penalty is warranted by Scripture, while others urge forgiveness and lesser legal penalties. Some, for example, prefer the legal option of life in prison without parole. Advocates of the death penalty often note issues such as the support of the Old Testament, the principle of justice, the possible deterrence of others considering serious crimes, and the sanctity of human life. Critics of capital punishment often stress issues such as the danger of economic and racial bias and the risk of executing an innocent person. Whether the execution will lessen the suffering of the murder victim's family is a key issue in the discussion.

Have you ever wanted to kill someone? Most Christians would probably answer "No," but many have experienced strong anger, even rage, at another person. John, commenting on Cain's murder of Abel, contrasts the attitudes of hatred and love. "All who hate a brother or sister are murderers" (1 John 3:15). Strong words, indeed. Like Jesus' teaching about the commandment not to kill (Matt 5:21–26), John's teaching goes beyond the physical act of killing someone. John knows that one of the primary motivations behind murder is hatred.

RAPE

Violence by men against women has a long history. Physical and mental abuse by a boyfriend or husband is a major problem in society today.[11] In this section, however, I will focus on one specific act of violence toward women, rape.

Rape is one of the most horrible violent acts a human can experience. Although some rapes may be random acts of violence, many rapes are acquaintance rapes and even rapes within a marriage.[12] Rape is not primarily an action motivated by sexual desire but rather by the need for control. Rape victims, usually but not always women, generally feel a range of emotions. They may wonder what they could have done to protect themselves or prevent the attack. They might think they were somehow at fault. They often feel abused, humiliated, and damaged. Occasionally pregnancy or sexually transmitted diseases result from the attack. The victims of rape often cope with emotional scars for years after the attack. In this discussion I will bracket out the case of statutory rape, which may involve so-called consensual sex between a minor and an adult.

Rape in the Bible

As in the case of murder, Hebrew law acknowledges that rape can occur in a variety of circumstances. If the attack occurs in the city and the woman, engaged to another man, does not cry out for help, she and the man are both considered guilty. If the attack occurs in the open country and she cries out, only the man is guilty because no one was near to help the woman (Deut 22:23-27). The relevance of Old Testament law for Christians today is a controversial issue, but it is important to note that the Old Testament law codes recognize that a woman's attempt to seek help is a factor in her situation.

Two stories in the Old Testament illustrate the horrible nature of rape.[13] In the first story, Amnon rapes his half-sister Tamar (2 Sam 13:1-39).[14] Amnon thinks he is in love with Tamar, although his behavior looks more like an obsession than true love. He pretends to be sick and asks his father, David, to send Tamar to prepare food for him in his bedroom. When he is alone with her, Amnon attacks her. Tamar resists, even reminding him that they could be married (13:13). Earlier Abraham had been married to his half-sister (Gen 20:12), but Hebrew law later condemns such marriages (Lev 18:9). Perhaps Tamar uses this argument to try to outwit her attacker. After he rapes Tamar, Amnon then kicks her out. He now hates her as much as he thought he had loved her (2 Sam 13:15). The New Revised Standard Version of this verse suggests that he had actually feels "lust" for her rather than love for her.

Amnon's rape of Tamar is tragic enough, but the rest of the story illustrates the deep problems in David's family. Tamar's brother, Absalom, is outraged at the attack, but David does not punish Amnon. Perhaps surprising to modern readers, Absalom tells his sister to remain quiet about the attack (13:20). It is possible that Absalom thinks such silence will protect his sister from further consequences after the rape (see Deut 22:23-27). David is angry about the attack, but his lack of punishment further infuriates Absalom. Later, Absalom instructs his followers to kill Amnon, and Absalom flees Jerusalem. When Absalom is allowed to return home, he begins the conspiracy that results in David temporarily losing the throne.

Although the biblical author does not focus on Tamar's feelings, he notes that she grieves over the event and lives with Absalom as a "desolate woman" (13:20). As a rape victim, she realistically had little chance of being married or fulfilling the traditional roles of wife and mother in a patriarchal society.

In the second biblical story, a woman is attacked by several men. Any rape is horrific, but a gang rape can only illustrate human depravity at its worst. The story begins with a Levite going to Bethlehem to win back his concubine. She had returned home, but he wooed her and she rejoined him on his journey (Judg 19:2-3).[15] They later stop at the town of Gibeah, where an older man welcomes them into his home for the night. During the night some of the men of Gibeah demand that the Levite be brought out so that "we may have intercourse with him" (19:22). The elderly host knows their intention is immoral, and he offers his own virgin daughter and the guest's concubine for their pleasure. The Levite pushes his concubine outside of the house, and the townsmen rape her repeatedly during the night. The woman finally falls at the doorstep, and the Levite discovers her dead the next morning.

Outraged at what had happened to his concubine, he cuts her body into twelve pieces and sends them to the Hebrew tribes as a battle cry. The Hebrews decided to punish the tribe of Benjamin for this atrocity, and a civil war ensues. After the Benjaminites are defeated, the Hebrews have compassion on them and want to provide wives for them. Since no Hebrews want their daughters to marry Benjaminites, the Hebrews attack a town that had not helped in the earlier battle and give the virgin prisoners of war to the Benjaminites (Judg 21:8-15). Needing more brides, the Hebrews capture the women of Shiloh during a festival dance (21:20-23). This episode reflects a patriarchal view of women. The men of Benjamin need wives, and during the chaotic and lawless period of the judges' kidnapping and perhaps further rape of the victims was the order of the day. This story, perhaps more than any other, makes clear just what is meant when the author of Judges depicts that period in Israelite history as a time when "all the people did what was right in their own eyes" (Judg 21:25).

Even though other stories might illustrate rape, such as Solomon's public intercourse with David's concubines (2 Sam 16:20–22), the reader is surely already convinced of the suffering caused by rape. Have you or someone you know ever been raped? How did you and fellow Christians respond? Did some suggest, "She must have done something to mislead him?" Or, did family and friends surround the victim with love and compassion? Rape victims need professional medical and psychological care to help them move on beyond the attack. A concerned Christian should urge a rape victim to find the appropriate medical, psychological, and legal resources she needs. A loving Christian community can help the victim understand that God still loves her.

WAR AND PEACE

John Macquarrie once noted, "Peace is in Biblical teaching, both eschatological and primordial."[16] In other words, history began with an age of peace, and it will end in peace, but in between there have been numerous wars. Although the news media and politicians used to talk about the "cold war" in the mid-twentieth century, in this section we will look briefly at the violence of actual armed conflict. Some readers may be veterans of military service, including combat, but others know about war only from the stories of veterans or the media. The 1998 movie *Saving Private Ryan*, according to the testimony of some D-Day survivors, gave a realistic depiction of the battles that helped stop Hitler in World War II. The bloody scenes in the first part of that movie should have deglamorized war for anyone.

The Bible is decidedly pro-peace in its overall message, but it is equally candid about wars in the ancient world. The Hebrew prophets looked forward to a time when all war weapons would be changed into farm implements (Isa 2:2–4; Mic 4:1–3). Indeed, the future Messiah is called the "Prince of Peace" (Isa 9:6). The Hebrew word for peace, *shalom,* means more than the absence of war; it suggests completeness, harmony, and reconciliation.[17] The corresponding Greek word, *eirene,* has the same rich meaning in the New Testament.

Christian Views of War

Holy war

Despite the pro-peace attitude of Scripture, however, Christians have often disagreed on the best Christian response to the reality of war. Many analysts describe three major views of war in Christian history.[18] First, the holy war or crusade view is based on the Hebrew's conquest of Canaan. The theory of holy war is sketched out in Deuteronomy 20, and the practice of holy war is recorded in Joshua and Judges 1. Many Christians

> **Holy war or just war?**

have expressed concern about the slaughtering of innocent people in the conquest, and ethicists have proposed several theories about the morality or immorality of holy war.[19] For example, some scholars note that the inhabitants of Canaan had the opportunity to learn about Yahweh in the patriarchal period and therefore had a chance to convert to the worship of Yahweh. If they were not driven out by the Hebrews, their pagan religions would be a constant temptation to the Hebrews (e.g., Deut 7:1–5). Still, no major Christian group endorses holy war today in the literal sense of a war ordained by God. Some Christians have adapted holy war language for spiritual warfare (Eph 6:10–17).

Pacifism

The second view of war is pacifism, or the total rejection of Christian participation in combat. The historic peace churches, such as the Amish, Quakers, and Mennonites, refuse to support any war. They may resist evil nonviolently, but they will not take up arms. They usually seek conscientious objector status with the Selective Service system, meaning they ask the government if they can serve in nonviolent ways in the event of a draft. With the advent of nuclear weapons, a related position known as nuclear pacifism has been promoted. These pacifists reject any war using nuclear weapons since these weapons cannot distinguish between combatants and noncombatants. Pacifists in general look to Jesus' teaching on non-resistance to evil as literal rules for today (Matt 5:38–42). Turning the other cheek is not compatible, they argue, with shooting an enemy on the battlefield.

Just war

The third view, the most popular in Christian history, is the just war theory. According to this perspective, war is sometimes necessary. When negotiations and diplomacy have failed, a country must use force to stop an aggressor or for some other "just" cause. Among the several criteria for just war usually mentioned is the ability to distinguish between armed forces and innocent civilians. The introduction of nuclear weapons and guerrilla warfare has made it increasingly difficult for this criterion to be honored. The most popular saying in American history about war is probably General Sherman's, "War is hell." Hawkeye Pierce, a character on the television series *M*A*S*H* which depicted the Korean War of the 1950s, countered Sherman by saying that war is not hell, since in hell there are no innocent bystanders. Another major issue in recent years has been the question of whether or not a just war can be a preemptive war; can a nation launch an attack in anticipation of an attack by an aggressor?

Suffering Caused by War

The violence of war produces many kinds of suffering. People are killed or maimed. Buildings, homes, and farm land are devastated. Many people flee the conflict, becoming refugees. Veterans often try to cope with the trauma of war for years, and that slow healing process sometimes disrupts family life.

Is the suffering of war avoidable? The easy answer is that wars, like other forms of suffering, will continue until the end of time. Some Christians, however, insist that the level of conflict can be reduced through means such as better diplomacy, education, and prayer. The famous Ecclesiastes passage about times and seasons might be used to suggest there will always be wars: "a time to love, and a time to hate; a time for war, and a time for peace" (Eccl 3:8). One interpretation of this whole text is that it presents what typically occurs in human life, not what is fated to happen.

Dr. Seuss, the author of books for children, addresses the topic of war in *The Butter Battle Book*. Two countries, the Yooks and the Zooks, are ready to fight over which side of bread should be buttered. They have their own version of the arms race, until in the final scene a representative of each group holds a small bomb in his hand. When a child asks if either one will drop his bomb, the grandfather says "We'll see. We will see . . ." Dr. Seuss leaves the conclusion of the story open-ended, implying that humans today have some control over when, if ever, wars occur.[20]

THE POLITICS OF SUFFERING

The three topics of this chapter, murder, rape, and war, require a multifaceted Christian response. Many Christians respond to the suffering of others on a personal level by words of encouragement and the ministry of presence. Sometimes suffering people need more than our presence; they need medical help and professional psychological assistance. Rape victims, for example, may need long-term counseling. Military veterans may also need medical and psychological care. Christians can collectively respond to these kinds of suffering with financial support for institutions such as Christian counseling centers.

Christians can also respond to violence in the political arena. Christian political activity can be a complicated and sensitive subject, especially since different denominations hold varying views on overall strategy. Some Christian groups, for example, discourage any organized political activity, since they only support "spiritual" solutions to life's problems. Evangelism, not lobbying, they insist is the right way to improve the world. At the other extreme are Christians who want to create a theocracy in our country. Problems such as violence would disappear or be lessened considerably if our government were based on Christian principles, they argue. Perhaps the majority view today is that Christians should work with political and religious groups on common objectives such as reducing the crime rate and the chances of international conflict.

How should Christians respond to violence?

In the next several chapters we will explore other forms of suffering that call for both personal and political responses. Realistically, we will never eliminate all forms of suffering in this world, but we can reduce suffering as much possible without playing God. Some of our political responses will be remedial, attempting to undo the suffering caused by violence. Other political efforts will be preventative, trying to reduce the chance of violence occurring in the first place.[21]

Many Christians follow the approach epitomized in the Serenity Prayer. American theologian Reinhold Niebuhr penned the prayer for a worship service, and it is still used by various support groups. "God, give us grace to accept with serenity the things that cannot be changed, courage to change the things that should be changed, and the wisdom to distinguish the one from the other."[22] Once Christians discern what things can be changed, they should work diligently to alleviate suffering as much as possible.

Chapter Nine
POVERTY AND HUNGER

Imagine that one Sunday morning two visitors come to your church for the worship service. One is dressed in expensive clothing, and you would guess she is a banker or lawyer. The other person wears ragged clothes, suggesting she is poor, probably on welfare, or so you and other members might presume. How would you and the other members of your church react to these two visitors? Unfortunately, in some congregations the wealthy person would be welcomed with open arms, but the poor person might be ignored.

Years ago I read that a pastor disguised himself as a poor person and waited outside his church on a Sunday morning. Some of his church members welcomed him, but others deliberately avoided him. Later he preached on James 2:1–13. James warned his readers against "acts of favoritism" (2:1) by telling a story similar to mine. He then criticized some early Christians for breaking the "royal law," which he identified by quoting from the Old Testament: "You shall love your neighbor as yourself" (Jas 2:8; Lev 19:18).

> **What are we to do for "the least of these"?**

This chapter will highlight several interrelated forms of suffering. Poverty, hunger, homelessness, and other forms of physical deprivation are chronic, pervasive forms of suffering. Unlike a broken arm or a tornado, these types of suffering may, at times, be more subtle. Poor people may have grown so used to their condition that they fail to see how bad their situation is. Some Latin American liberation theologians, for example, propose conscientization or consciousness raising as an essential step in educating and liberating the poor.[1] They often classify poverty as a form of institutionalized violence.[2]

YOU ALWAYS HAVE THE POOR WITH YOU

Poverty is a perennial problem. When Mary anoints Jesus' feet, Judas Iscariot objects to her extravagance, insisting that the expensive ointment could have been sold and the money used to help the poor. Jesus' famous response is "You always have the poor with you, but you do not always have me" (John 12:8). Instead of being wasteful, Mary's anointing points to Jesus' death and burial a few days later.

Some Christians have taken Jesus' comment to be a dismissal of any attempts to eliminate poverty. "We'll never get rid of poverty," they argue, "since Jesus said so!" Many scholars, however, note that Jesus' comment is a paraphrase or quotation of Deuteronomy 15:11. Although poverty will never be totally eradicated in human history, Hebrew law encourages a continuing concern for the poor. "Since there will never cease to be some in need on the earth, I therefore command you, 'Open your hand to the poor and needy neighbor in the land'" (Deut 15:11).

> **Will we ever get rid of poverty?**

Defining Poverty

Concern for the poor and needy is a consistent theme in the Bible, but some Christians today differ on what kind of poverty truly needs our attention. Defining poverty is notoriously difficult. Richard Foster reminds his readers that if they can afford to buy his book they are wealthy by global standards. He too should be counted as wealthy since he has the time to write that book.[3] The same would be true of you and me; we are wealthy by third world standards.

Some Christians distinguish two types of poor people, the deserving and the undeserving. Those who are poor because of punishment for sin, these Christians argue, do not deserve our help. The undeserving poor, however, need Christian compassion and ministry; they are poor because of circumstances beyond their control. Other Christians hold the opposing view: "Nowhere in the Bible is a distinction made between our responsibility to the deserving poor and our responsibility to the undeserving poor."[4]

Although these two categories are traditional, a larger frame of reference or typology on poverty is needed. D. A. Carson helpfully distinguishes six types of poverty.[5] First, the unfortunate poor are those made poor by circumstances such as illness, drought, or some other factors beyond their control. The poverty of Ruth and Naomi, caused by a drought and the deaths of their husbands, illustrates this first category. Second, the oppressed poor include people made poor by the immoral actions of others, the oppressors. Hebrew prophets such as Amos often note this cause of poverty (Amos 2:5-7). James identifies the oppressors of the poor as rich people who withhold their workers' wages (5:1-6). Third, the lazy poor deserve their poverty. This would be the economic equivalent of the doctrine of retribution, which we studied earlier. Proverbs often mentions this kind of poverty, especially in contrast to the classic illustration of the hard working ant (Prov 6:6-11). Fourth, Carson discusses those who are poor because of someone else's actions. Someone else sins, but the poor person is affected by the sinner's punishment. Fifth, some people voluntarily choose poverty. The Jerusalem church of early Christians, for instance, shared its goods, so many of its members would be technically poor after being generous. Sixth, Carson notes Jesus' beatitude for the poor in spirit. People who acknowledge their spiritual poverty may or may not be economically poor.

Carson's list of types of poverty clarifies some of the causes of suffering. Someone who holds to the divine monergism view we studied earlier would stress that ultimately God is the cause of wealth and poverty. "The rich and the poor have this in common: the Lord is the maker of them all" (Prov 22:2). Monergism would discount most discussion of stewardship, oppression, and work ethic; God is the supreme, solitary architect of economic status. The beautiful hymn "All Things Bright and Beautiful" includes a verse, not often printed today, which reflects this view:

> The rich man in his castle,
> The poor man at his gate,
> God made them high and lowly,
> And ordered their estate.[6]

Along with those who highlight God's role as the cause of poverty, there are those who hold to more political and social origins of poverty. Ronald Sider discusses the debate between liberals and conservatives about the causes of poverty. Liberals tend to highlight the role of structural causes; conservatives accent the role played by bad moral decisions.[7]

In this chapter we will focus primarily on the so-called undeserving poor. All poverty is painful, but we will look primarily at biblical teaching on responses to poverty caused by others' sins, natural disaster, and oppression.

A BROTHER OR SISTER IN NEED

The Poor in the Old Testament

The Bible consistently teaches the obligation of God's people to help the poor. Although our primary concern will be with New Testament teaching, a few examples from the Old Testament will lay our foundation. Hebrew law frequently addresses the needs of the poor. For example, if the poor are able to work but have no land to cultivate, they are allowed to glean in other people's fields. The land owner should not reap the field to its border or strip his vineyards; a little should be left for the poor to gather (Lev 19:9–10). Hebrew laws about tithing often mention that part of the tithe will be used to help the needy. For example, part of the third year tithe is shared with "the resident aliens, the orphans, and the widows" (Deut 14:29). These three groups, the resident aliens, orphans, and widows, were often dependent on extended family or the Hebrew community for their economic well being. The Hebrews were expected to be compassionate to them.

The Poor in the New Testament

The New Testament builds on the humanitarian foundation laid in the Old Testament. Here I will focus primarily on a few key texts to illustrate the variety of New Testament teaching. Rather than highlighting the causes of poverty, we will look at Christian responses to the poor.

The Jerusalem church

The church at Jerusalem offers a famous response to the needy. After the Day of Pentecost, that congregation experiences rapid growth in membership. About 120 heard Peter preach before Pentecost (Acts 1:15), but soon the group numbered about 5,000 (Acts 4:4). This prosperity apparently brought problems, however, and the church included several poor people.

The so-called Jerusalem experiment involved the voluntary sharing of possessions to help the needy. People "would sell their possessions and goods

> **What does the Bible say about how to treat the poor?**

and distribute the proceeds to all, as any had need" (Acts 2:45). No one claimed their right to their private property, and many sold land and houses (Acts 4:34). The role model in this story was Barnabas, the son of encouragement (Acts 4:36-37). Not everyone had this spirit of giving, however, as evidenced by the story of Ananias and Sapphira. They lied to Simon Peter about their generosity and dropped dead (Acts 5:1-11).

Across the centuries, some Christian groups have taken the voluntary sharing of the Jerusalem church as the ideal for all Christians. As far as we know, no other first-century church copied this model, so other Christians are reluctant to elevate the Jerusalem practice to the level of ideal or norm for today. Since the Jerusalem church eventually needed economic help from other churches, some Christians argue that this sharing was a failed experiment, and therefore not a model for later churches. Perhaps the Jerusalem church was so effective in its witnessing that it outgrew its resources.

Paul as fundraiser

A second New Testament example of a response to poverty is Paul's fund raising on his third missionary journey. Luke mentions this project only once in his record of Paul's travels (Acts 24:17), but Paul frequently mentions his collection for the Jerusalem church in his letters to Corinth. Paul's relationship with the Corinthian church is convoluted, with scholars proposing that he wrote four or five letters to that church. In 1 Corinthians he proposes a systematic collection for the needy in Jerusalem (16:1-4).

After their relationship breaks down and is restored, he reminds them of their obligation (2 Cor 8-9). Paul uses several arguments in his attempt to persuade the Corinthians that they should help the Jerusalem church. For instance, he notes that their stewardship will be an appropriate expression of their gratitude to God for his gift (9:15). Christ "became poor, so that by his poverty you might become rich" (8:9). Paul probably has in mind Jesus' humiliation when he became human (Phil 2:6-8) rather than Jesus' financial status. Gratitude for God's generosity is crucial to Paul's case.

Paul also uses more pragmatic arguments with his Corinthian audience. For example, he proposes a friendly rivalry between the Corinthian Christians and the Macedonian churches. Those believers in Macedonia had given generously, and the Corinthians would not want to be outdone (2 Cor 8:1-7; 9:1-5).

The goal of Paul's financial campaign is "a fair balance" among the churches (8:14). The Jerusalem church is in need, and the church at Corinth is prosperous. If the Corinthian church ever found itself in need, other churches should share with them. Rather than there being "haves" and "have nots" among the churches, the ideal is equality.

The importance of work

The third text that will illustrate the New Testament response to hunger and poverty is 2 Thessalonians 3. Paul's two letters to the church at Thessalonica highlight eschatology, or the doctrine of last things. In particular, some of these Christians are concerned about the apparent delay in Jesus' return. Some Christians had died already, and the others worried that these dead Christians might miss out on Jesus' return. Paul assures them that their dead Christian friends will not fall through any eschatological cracks (1 Thess 4:13-18).

Paul's first letter does not erase all of their eschatological fervor, and some remain so sure that Jesus will return momentarily that they quit their jobs. Paul writes that the church has no obligation to support those "living in idleness" (2 Thess 3:6). Helping the poor is good, but when the need is created by disobeying Paul's insistence on working up until Jesus' return the church has no obligation to help those poor people. Paul's famous line is: "Anyone unwilling to work should not eat" (3:10). One commentator paraphrases Paul: "No loaf to the loafer!"[8]

Paul's advice to the Thessalonian Christians does not conflict with his concern for the needy at Jerusalem. The poverty at Jerusalem may have been caused by the large influx of new members into the church, straining the resources of those Christians. The believers at Thessalonica, however, had created a need for help by rejecting Paul's teaching. People who mooched off the church because they misinterpreted the date of Jesus' return could support themselves easily by returning to their jobs.

John summarizes the overall biblical perspective on the proper response to suffering due to poverty: "How does God's love abide in anyone who has the world's goods and sees a brother or sister in need and yet refuses to help?" (1 John 3:17). Genuine Christian love motivates us to help the poor out of our abundance.

GOD OR MAMMON?

Poverty is a problem that will not go away. Government social programs and church humanitarian activity can lessen the amount of poverty in the world, but the problem will continue to trouble the poor and those who try to help them.

The larger context for a discussion of the suffering caused by poverty is the Christian view of topics such as money, stewardship, and vocation. While a full analysis of these important subjects would occupy a large book or a series of books, a few comments are necessary for our discussion of poverty as a form of suffering.[9]

A Christian's overall view of money is crucial to his view of poverty. I often ask my college students to fill in the blank in this sentence: "Money is _____." I usually get a variety of good answers, but my favorite is the earthy saying "Money is like manure. If you pile it up in one place, it stinks a lot. If you spread it around, it does a lot of good."

The Bible and Money

The Bible presents what Richard Foster calls the "dark side of money" and the "light side of money."[10] Or, as another writer puts it, money can be seen as a blessing from God or as "highly dangerous."[11] Money in itself is not good or bad, but it can become very seductive to the naive. The Bible often warns against the sins of greed and covetousness. The last of the Ten Commandments prohibits coveting another person's possessions or family members (Exod 20:17).[12] Paul compares covetousness to idolatry (Col 3:5), and some people still worship the "almighty dollar." When a man asks Jesus to force his brother to share his inheritance, Jesus warns him to watch out for covetousness, or greed (Luke 12:15).

> **Can we serve more than one master?**

Perhaps Jesus' most definitive statement on money is "You cannot serve God and mammon" (Matt 6:24 RSV). "Mammon" refers to money or possessions. Jesus insists that a person can have only one primary allegiance in her life. Ideally, our ultimate loyalty is to God. Other legitimate concerns, such as money, family, and politics, must have a secondary role in our value system. Several years ago, however, an opinion poll asked Americans if they thought Jesus was right about God and mammon. As the income levels of the respondents went up, they started to disagree with Jesus![13]

The Bible often notes that the greed of some people produces poverty for others. Amos, for example, criticizes the rich for trampling the poor into the dust (Amos 2:7). James criticizes the wealthy for withholding the wages of their employees (Jas 5:4). Christians who misuse their power or position to oppress others should repent. John the Baptist, for example, tells the tax collectors to collect no more than the law requires (Luke 3:12). After Zaccheus becomes a follower of Jesus, he repays the money he had taken immorally from the tax payers (Luke 19:8).

One of the New Testament teachings that most challenges contemporary culture is the instruction to be content with what we have. John the Baptist tells the soldiers who question him about how to live rightly to "be satisfied with your wages" (Luke 3:14). These soldiers might be tempted to use the power of their position to gouge civilians. Paul states that he has learned to be content (Phil 4:11–13). Paul did not, however, adopt a Stoic stance of apathy toward life's deprivations. Rather than self-sufficiency, he learned the lesson of God-sufficiency. His basic needs were met by God.[14]

John the Baptist and Paul did not necessarily mean that every poor person should be satisfied with their poverty. Their concern probably was with both the abuse of power by soldiers and other officials and greed as a temptation for immature Christians. Still, our consumer culture encourages us to want more and to buy more. Several contemporary Christians have identified consumerism as a challenge to the Christian view of money.[15] Consumerism tempts us to think of ourselves primarily as consumers. Consumption is not bad in itself, but excessive consumption is bad for others because, contrary to popular sentiment, there are a limited number of resources on our planet.[16] Moreover, people are increasingly addicted to easy credit until they have bought themselves into bankruptcy.

One of Jesus' most memorable stories involves a poor man, Lazarus, and a rich man, traditionally called Dives (Luke 16:19–31). Although the main point of the story may not be poverty, Jesus does note while on earth that the rich man lived well while the poor man lay at his gate. In one of Jesus' typical reversal of fortune twists, after death the poor man goes to Abraham's bosom, and Dives ends up in Hades. If Dives had worked more diligently to care for the poor person he could see every day, would he have been in heaven as well?

Money and Modern Christians

Christians today have developed a wide range of perspectives on money.[17] Perhaps two examples will suffice to represent the current diversity. First, the simple-living movement encourages a modest lifestyle for Christians. Richard Foster's *Freedom of Simplicity* has been widely influential, especially in evangelical circles.[18] Ron Sider's *Rich Christians in an Age of Hunger* has made popular notions such as the graduated tithe. A Christian family, he suggests, should adopt a modest lifestyle, tithing their remaining income and then giving larger and larger percentages as a "graduated tithe" as their income increases.[19] Sallie McFague and other ecological theologians urge Christians to adopt a frugal lifestyle that will help preserve the health of our planet.[20]

The health and wealth gospel, however, promotes financial success as a proper byproduct of the Christian life. A favorite proof text for this group is Mark 10:29-30. People who dedicate themselves to Jesus will receive "a hundredfold now in this age."

Some of the discussion between groups such as the simple-lifestyle group and those who espouse the prosperity gospel focuses intensively on personal and family finance. Another facet to the problem of poverty as suffering, however, is its global dimension. Although there are many poor people in our country, poverty is a major concern in other countries as well. Assuming, for example, that farmers produce enough food to feed the world, the debate among Christians and others is about the distribution of that food.

If there is not enough food and other resources to go around, the debate involves the allocation of scarce resources. A popular analogy used in this discussion among ethicists is labeled "lifeboat ethics." The movie *Titanic* illustrates this concept. If there are more people on the cruise ship than the lifeboats can handle, then who gets a seat in the life boat and who winds up in the water? Christians who stress the distinction between the deserving poor and the un-deserving poor argue that nations with a poor track record on family planning, agricultural technology, and other methods for helping themselves do not deserve humanitarian aid. Other Christians insist the right to survival is basic, and we should help all poor people, de-serving and undeserving.[21]

Since poverty is a perennial concern, how should Christians respond? John insists that a humanitarian response to the needy is a necessary expression of *agape*, or unconditional, selfless, love (1 John 3:17). James argues that responding to the needs of the hungry is one expression of genuine faith (James 2:14–17).

One of the most cited biblical texts on this subject is Jesus' par-able describing the separation and judgment of the sheep and the goats (Matt 25:31–46). A spontaneous, concerned response to the needy characterized the "sheep," who were called to the right hand of God. Those who had ignored the needy were the "goats," who were sent away from God. Some Christians have debated the appli-cation of this text to humanitarian actions in general. They insist that the aid is to fellow Christians, not the world population in general. Many mainstream Christians, however, see the parable as Jesus' call to offer assistance to all of the needy.

Several years ago a comic strip dealt with the relationship be-tween God and humanity, as well as questions about poverty. In one picture a character states, "sometimes I'd like to ask God why he al-lows poverty, famine, and injustice when he could do something about it." A friend asks, "What's stopping you?" The first speaker re-plies, "I'm afraid God might ask me the same question." Certainly God expects his people to struggle against poverty and hunger. An-other episode in that same comic strip pictures one character say-ing, "I wonder if God can really hear me. Hey, God! What should I do with my life?" God replies, "Feed the hungry, right injustice, work for peace!" Startled, the first person responds: "Just testing!" God's reply is "Same here."

Christians may debate public policy about domestic welfare, federal budgets for humanitarian aid for foreign countries, and the details of biblical interpretation. The overwhelming evidence of the Bible is, however, that Christians have an obligation to relieve the problems of poverty and homelessness as much as possible. Many Christians, for instance, are actively involved in humanitarian projects such as Habitat for Humanity. Others provide assistance to the poor and needy of their communities through local church programs.

Chapter Ten

DISCRIMINATION

To some people the problem of suffering primarily involves types of suffering that are visible and traumatic: sickness, natural disaster, and violence. As we saw in the chapter on poverty, however, suffering can sometimes be more subtle and invisible. Discrimination is another form of suffering that is easily overlooked, unless you are its victim. Discrimination can be like pollution in the air we breathe. We are so used to polluted air that we get used to it; only when we catch a breath of fresh, clean air do we realize the extent to which invisible forces can affect us. Discrimination is not limited to any one stage of human life. A child in school might suffer discrimination on the playground because of a physical limitation. An employee might be passed over for a promotion or a raise due to ethnic or gender prejudice. An older person might be neglected because of her age.

Jesus' ministry is like a breath of fresh air in the first century. He welcomes all types of people and confronts several forms of economic, social, and gender discrimination. His conversation with the Samaritan woman in John 4 illustrates his challenge to two common forms of discrimination, sexism and racism. Traveling from Judea to Galilee, Jesus

> **How does Jesus address discrimination?**

decides to pass through Samaria (John 4:3-4). Most Jews wanted to avoid the Samaritans, a mixed race that was partly Jewish. The Samaritans were descendants of the tribes in the old northern kingdom, but their ancestors had married foreigners. The Jews of Judea considered the Samaritans half-breeds. When Jesus asks the

Samaritan woman at the well for a drink of water, she is startled that a Jew will have contact with a Samaritan (John 4:9). Jesus' openness to all kinds of people is exemplified in his willingness to minister to this Samaritan. When the people from her town acknowledge Jesus, they proclaim him "the Savior of the world" (John 4:42).

While Jesus talks to this woman, his disciples are shopping in town. When they return, they are surprised that Jesus is talking to a woman in public. A good Jewish man avoided public association with a woman (John 4:27). Some Pharisees were nicknamed the bruised and bleeding Pharisees because they shut their eyes when they saw a woman and then ran into walls.[1] Again, Jesus is willing to break some social customs to demonstrate his openness to all kinds of people and to minister to them.

Discrimination takes many shapes and forms. For example, ableism is generally defined as prejudice or discrimination against people with physical or mental limitations. In 1990 the Americans with Disabilities Act was passed to address this kind of discrimination. Homophobia is an irrational fear or extreme prejudice against homosexuals. Several major Christian denominations have struggled to deal with their perspectives on homosexuality in light of the Bible in recent years.[2] Ageism is discrimination against people based on their age. Since ageism is often directed at older people, we will look at it in chapter eleven.

Although there are many forms of discrimination, this chapter will focus on the two types represented in John 4, racism and sexism. The victims of discrimination suffer in many ways, including verbal abuse, violence, and ostracism. The biblical witness is overwhelmingly negative about discrimination.

YOU HAVE TO BE TAUGHT HOW TO HATE

Scholars use several terms to analyze discrimination. Normally, "prejudice" refers to a biased attitude while "discrimination" refers to actions based on prejudice. Attitudes and actions are obviously interrelated, and sometimes a person might learn to treat others in a discriminatory way and then develop the belief system to justify the actions.

Discrimination can be directed in many ways. Dr. Seuss, the author of popular books for children, illustrated a generic kind of discrimination similar to racism, in his delightful story of the Sneetches. Although all Sneetches are basically the same, some have stars on their bellies and some do not. Jealousy and rivalry develops, but eventually they learn that their similarity outweighs the presence or absence of a star.[3]

Discrimination expresses itself in a wide range of actions. Verbal comments, such as crude jokes or stereotypes, are common. Avoidance of other kinds of people, including segregation of races, was part of public policy for much of this country's history. Physical threats, violence, and hate crimes seem to be common today, despite federal civil rights legislation. Extreme forms of discrimination include genocide, or the attempt to eliminate an entire ethnic group, and ethnic cleansing.

Scholars have offered several theories about the origin of prejudice and discrimination. A consensus view is that prejudice is learned, not innate. A song from the Broadway musical *South Pacific* suggests that children have to be taught how to hate. In this musical a female nurse from Arkansas is attracted to a civilian in the south Pacific during World War II. Her feelings become confused when she learns that he had been married to a local woman, and therefore, in the mind of the nurse part of an interracial marriage. Her racial prejudice becomes a stumbling block in their relationship.

Some scholars suggest that prejudice and discrimination are rooted in xenophobia. This term derives from the Greek words *phobia*, or "irrational fear," and *xenos*, meaning "strange" or "alien." An underlying fear of anything or anyone different from us may surface in the form of racial bias or sexual discrimination.

SEXISM

Gender discrimination can be directed against men or women, but I will focus on bias against women. Although women have more opportunities in American society today than a century ago, many women still struggle against gender bias, especially in the work place and in the church.

Women in the Bible

In order to introduce the subject of sexism to my college students I sometimes give a quiz about women in the Bible. Although most of my students are biblically literate, they often have difficulty with some of my questions. Here is a sample:

1. The first people to see the risen Jesus.

2. The female judge.

3. The sister of Moses and a prophetess.

4. A female deacon.

5. The first surrogate mother and mother of Ishmael.

6. The two women who have Old Testament books named after them.

7. The elderly widow who acknowledged the baby Jesus in the temple.[4]

The Bible includes a tremendous amount of material on women. In the last few decades scholars have produced a veritable flood of articles and books on the biblical view of women.[5] This literature represents a wide range of viewpoints, moving from a defense of biblical patriarchalism to more radical forms of feminism.[6]

Even if we limit the scope of the discussion to evangelical authors, diversity of opinion remains. Two major schools of thought are currently prominent in evangelical life. One view, often called traditionalist or hierarchalist, insists that women and men are equal in status in the eyes of God, but God assigned them distinct and complementary roles. The other view, often labeled egalitarian, stresses the equality of men and women even more and is more open to women in leadership positions in church and society.[7]

Women in the Church

Gender discrimination against women is sometimes called patriarchalism or patriarchy. A patriarchal view of society often leads to limitations on opportunities for women. Feminists, both Christian and non-Christian, have argued for a broader role for women in church and society. Theoretically we could look at sexism in the home, church, and society. In order to keep the discussion more manageable, however, I will focus our attention briefly on two arenas: church and the workplace.

The role and status of women in the church has been a hot topic in many denominations in the last few years. *Time* magazine's cover story for November 23, 1992, was "God and Women: A Second Reformation Sweeps Christianity."[8] Some denominations allow women ministers and deacons, others do not. Many in the Roman Catholic Church, for example, reject the notion of female priests, although women do fulfill lay leadership roles and there are those who support the ordination

> **Are there women deacons in the New Testament?**

of women. My denomination, Southern Baptists, generally frowns on women in leadership positions, but discussion continues among some Baptists.[9] For instance, in 2000 the Southern Baptist Convention messengers approved this statement: "While both men and women are gifted for service in the church, the office of pastor is limited to men as qualified by Scripture."[10] Some Southern Baptist churches have, however, ordained women as deacons, church staff members, and senior pastors. Some of these churches have been criticized by fellow Baptists.

For more conservative denominations, the discussion often revolves around key biblical texts.[11] Those who oppose women in

leadership positions usually cite Paul's "husband of one wife" quali-
fication for bishops and deacons (1 Tim 3:2, 12 RSV). While they are
much debated in their interpretation, Paul's instructions to women
to be silent in the church (1 Cor 14:34–35) and not to have authority over men (1 Tim 2:11–12) are crucial to the prohibition on
women ministers and deacons.

Those who are more open to women in leadership positions
often note the actual roles women played in Hebrew and early
church life. Women, for example, were prophetesses (e.g., Exod
15:20; Judg 4:4; 2 Kings 22:14). Phoebe may have been a deacon
(Rom 16:1), and Priscilla, along with her husband, taught Apollos
(Acts 18:26).

Beyond the texts that deal directly with leadership positions,
other relevant Bible passages include the creation of women in the
image of God. The Bible does not teach that women are inferior to
men; even those who argue for different roles for men and women
agree on the equal status of both genders.

Women who feel called to the ministry often encounter resistance, even in denominations that officially ordain women. Patriarchal cultural and social attitudes still hinder the full acceptance of
women in leadership positions. A bishop might, for example, ap-
point a female minister to smaller, less prominent church. Women
in ministry encounter the same kind of glass ceiling (or stained glass
ceiling) women have seen in the workplace for years.

Women in Society

As a result of sexism, women encounter suffering in several
ways. This is especially true in the workplace. Discrimination in hiring, promotions, and dismissals are chronic in some careers. An extreme form of gender bias is sexual harassment. Most workplaces,
even those that have avoided sexual harassment problems, have a
formal policy in order for their staff to be aware of the issue.

Despite continued discrimination against women, the status
quo stance of patriarchalism in the family, church, and society continues to undergo careful scrutiny by men and women who want to
affirm biblical teachings without discriminating against women.

RACIAL DISCRIMINATION

Discrimination based on ethnic category or race is another frequent source of suffering today. Racism is also called ethnocentrism, or the belief that one ethnic group is inherently superior to other ethnic groups. Although people in minority groups have more legal opportunities today, the frequent reference to hate crimes in the media reminds us that racial discrimination, hatred, and violence have not disappeared. Blacks, Hispanics, Native Americans, and Jews are often targets of racial stereotypes.

Discrimination against Native Americans

Discrimination against Native Americans has a long history in America. In the 1830s several thousand Indians were moved to reservations along what became known as the Trail of Tears.[12] In response to the United States government's attempts at the genocide of Indians in the nineteenth century, contemporary Indians have begun to develop a Native American liberation theology.[13] Personal and systemic examples of discrimination against Native Americans continue today.

> **What color is God?**

Anti-Semitism

Anti-Semitism has haunted Christianity throughout its history. Discrimination against Jews has resulted in many atrocities, but the Holocaust in Germany during World War II is the most obvious example. Although there were many political and economic factors in Hitler's policies, his attempt to practice genocide against the Jews is a graphic example of the suffering endured by Jews. Jewish and Christian authors continue to discuss the theological implications of the Holocaust. How could a good, loving God allow his chosen people to be slaughtered? The views of these writers cover a wide range. For example, Richard Rubenstein developed a Jewish version of the death of God theology.[14] Jewish scholar William Scott

Green avoids this extreme view and calls for Jews and Christians to continue to study the justice of God in light of the Holocaust.[15] Christian scholars have begun to focus on the attitude of Christians towards Jews during the war.[16] Some Christians tried to help Jews escape Hitler's assaults in the 1930s and 1940s, but too many Christians failed to help.[17]

Any discussion of ethnic discrimination needs to take into account Jesus' ethnic identity. One of the common themes in recent treatments of the historical Jesus is his Jewishness.[18] Christians who have suffered discrimination often want to enlist Jesus' life and ministry to support their pleas for justice. James Cone, a leading black theologian writes: "For too long Christ has been pictured as a blue-eyed honky. Black theologians are right: we need to dehonkify him and thus make him relevant to the black condition."[19] An earlier black leader, Marcus Garvey, argued that Jesus was not white or black; Jesus represented all races.[20]

Discrimination against African Americans

Although discrimination against Jews and Indians is a major issue today, in this section I will focus on discrimination against blacks. This form of racism has been at the center of a major public policy debate since the Civil War. Growing up in Arkansas in the 1940s through the early 1960s, this form of racism was the one I observed most often.

The opening lines of Ralph Ellison's *Invisible Man* remind us how blacks have been ignored in our culture:

> I am an invisible man. No, I am not a spook like those who haunted Edgar Allan Poe; nor am I one of your Hollywood-movie ectoplasms. I am a man of substance, of flesh and bone, fiber and liquids—and I might even be said to possess a mind. I am invisible, understand, simply because people refuse to see me.[21]

The civil rights movement of the 1950s and 1960s brought about needed change, but racial discrimination still abounds.

Christianity and racism

Some blacks have criticized Christianity for being a white person's religion. In light of the pervasive suffering among black people, William Jones raises the provocative question *Is God a White Racist?*[22] James Cone and other black theologians have responded to Jones' challenge, affirming that God is concerned about the plight of black people, just as he identified with the Hebrew slaves in Egypt.[23]

Racism can appear in at least two forms: personal racism and institutional racism. Personal racism is the use of racial slurs or violence in personal behavior. Institutional racism is "the intentional or inadvertent practice of institutional behavior which yields negative effects on a group based on the concept of race."[24] Some contemporary Christians may still be guilty of personal bias based on race. Moreover, some Christian institutions still struggle with institutional racism. Others, without resorting to quotas in hiring and promotions, try to be more aware of how race issues affect decision making.

Some earlier Christians argued for the separation or segregation of the races using selected proof texts such as the so-called curse on Ham (Gen 9:22-27).[25] Although slavery has not always been based on ethnic bias, some of these texts were used for centuries to justify the enslavement of blacks.[26] Later opposition to open housing laws was sometimes based on Acts 17:26, where Paul mentions the "boundaries of the places where they would live." The fear of interracial marriage, or miscegenation, was another concern for people who opposed the mingling of ethnic groups.[27]

Biblical arguments against racism

The vast majority of Christians eventually realized that texts such as Galatians 3:28 expressed a biblical principle that should eliminate racial bias as well as gender discrimination. Paul writes, "There is no longer Jew or Greek, there is no longer slave or free, there is no longer male and female; for all of you are one in Christ Jesus." Many Bible commentators note that Paul may be consciously responding to a common prayer said by Jewish men, thanking God that they were not foreigners, slaves, or women.[28] In Christ, Paul argues, traditional ethnic, economic, and gender distinctions are not important. All people are created in the image of God, and all people can become disciples of Christ. As a child I learned the chorus, "Jesus loves the little children, All the children of the world. Red and yellow, black and white, They are precious in his sight—Jesus loves the little children of the world."[29] Growing up in Arkansas in the 1940s and 1950s, I saw the conflict between the faith my church sang about and the segregation practiced in our society. Years later I saw a comic strip in which a child asked her mother, "Is God white, black, brown, yellow, or red?" The mother wisely answered "Yes." God transcends ethnic boundaries, and his people should imitate his love for all people.

Jesus' ministry illustrates his openness to other races. He speaks openly to the Samaritan woman at the well, and he casts a Samaritan as the hero in the parable of the good Samaritan. He instructs his disciples to take the gospel to all nations (Matt 28:18-20; Acts 1:8).

Other parts of Scripture present foreigners or non-Jews as good people. The Moabite woman, Ruth joins the Hebrew community and moves to Bethlehem with her mother-in-law, Naomi. Ruth, along with the Canaanite, Rahab, are part of Jesus' family tree (Matt 1:5). The Bible reports several interracial marriages without condemnation. For example, Abraham (Gen 16:3), Joseph (Gen 41:45), and Moses (Exod 2:21, Num 12:1) married non-Hebrew wives.[30]

One of the most remarkable stories about racial relations in the Bible is the story of Peter and Cornelius. Cornelius was a Gentile, a Roman soldier, and a God-fearer. He prayed to God every day, but he had not converted to Judaism. In a vision, God tells him to send for a certain man named Peter. Before Cornelius's men arrive to fetch him, Peter falls into a trance and has a vision of a sheet being lowered from heaven with animals standing on it. When a heavenly voice tells him to kill the animals and eat them, Peter protests that the animals are unclean. The voices replies, "What God has made clean, you must not call profane" (Acts 10:15). While on the surface Peter's vision is about the repeal of kosher food laws, the vision also prepares him to encounter Cornelius. When Cornelius and his associates accept Jesus, Peter concludes, "I truly understand that God shows no partiality, but in every nation anyone who fears him and does what is right is acceptable to him" (Acts 10:34-35).

Although Luke's emphasis in this story might be the conversion of Cornelius, the reader can also see a second conversion here. Peter is converted away from his traditional bias against Gentiles. Even though Peter's primary ministry is to the Jews, just as Paul's is focused on Gentiles (Gal 2:7), Peter's encounter with Cornelius liberates him from his inherited bias against Gentiles.

Recent approaches to the problem

Christians today agree that racial discrimination is sinful. One lingering debate is about how racial equality can best be manifest in local church life. On the one hand, some Christians argue that every congregation in a multiethnic context should strive for multiethnicity in its membership. Sid Smith, for instance, argues against paternalism and ministry by proxy as ministry strategies because they assume the superiority of the mother church. Paternalism refers to when one church assumes the role of the "parent" and forces the minority group to be the "child" in the relationship. Ministry by proxy involves one ethnic group trying to help another group without any personal or direct involvement; assistance is offered long distance rather than by working side by side with the minority group. Smith advocates fraternalism as the best expression of multiethnic ministry, because ethnic groups treat each other as equals.[31]

On the other hand, the Church Growth Movement has promoted the homogeneous unit principle, or the collecting together of people with similar backgrounds and concerns, as central to church growth. Although leaders in this movement are not racist, their emphasis on the homogeneous unit could lead to a church that is *de facto* segregated.[32] Churches continue to be interested in membership growth, but one temptation to be avoided is consciously attracting people of one ethnic group. The old saying "Birds of a feather flock together" may be a sociological truth, but Christians need to avoid encouraging monoethnic churches that are segregated in practice, even if not in theory.

LOVE, THE LAW, AND LYNCHING

How should Christians lessen the amount of suffering caused by sexual and racial discrimination? As in addressing any complex problem, the solution will need to be multifaceted. Education, worship, legislation, and social reform are all possibilities.

Biblical Principles

Many Christians appeal to biblical principles such as the image of God, love, justice, and forgiveness in making their decisions about ethnic relations. Certainly any form of prejudice or discrimination reflects a misunderstanding of the image of God. All people are created in the image of God. Differences such as gender, skin color, economic status, or social class should not be the basis for a Christian response to anyone. James's critique of economic discrimination in the story of the rich and poor visitors to his church (Jas 2:1-13) is relevant to other forms of discrimination as well.

> **How can Christians respond to discrimination?**

Public Policy

Although Christians generally agree on these biblical principles, they sometimes differ on their public policy implications. Christians in the 1960s debated the pros and cons of the civil rights movement. Some who disliked segregation still could not accept Martin Luther King Jr.'s strategy of nonviolent resistance. The practice of civil disobedience in particular was debated by whites and blacks. King's "Letter from Birmingham Jail" is a classic defense of Christian political action in general and civil disobedience in particular.[33] For example, King insists that the church should be a thermostat, not a thermometer in its relation to society. A thermostat is a change agent, while a thermometer reflects the status quo.[34]

Christians continue to debate the merits of public policies such as affirmative action. Some favor affirmative action, but others call such policies reverse discrimination. These public policies try to address discrimination in arenas such as the workplace and public schools.

The civil rights movement and other social justice campaigns highlight the tension between law and love in Christian ethics. Ideally, education, worship, and other church programs would convince prejudiced people to stop their discrimination. Realistically, Christians sometimes have to work for legislation that will protect the rights of minorities. Martin Luther King Jr., often dealt with the old issue of legislating morality.

> It is not a question of either education or of legislation. Both legislation and education are required. Now, people will say, "You can't legislate morals." Well, that may be true. Even though morality may not be legislated, behavior can be regulated. And this is very important. We need religion and education to change attitudes and to change the hearts of men. We need legislation and federal action to control behavior. It may be true that the law can't make a man love me, but it can keep him from lynching me, and I think that's pretty important also.[35]

Christians should try to alleviate the suffering caused by racial and sexual discrimination through education and legislation. In an ideal community, distinctions such as gender and ethnic category should not be barriers in communication and cooperation.

Chapter Eleven

AGING

The popular movie *Driving Miss Daisy* illustrates some of the difficulties of growing old. Miss Daisy is an elderly Jewish woman who wants to maintain her independence as long as possible. Her driving skills have deteriorated, however, and her son hires a chauffeur to drive her. Miss Daisy resists for a while, and the plot develops around her relationship to her son and her new chauffeur.

Older people often experience the role reversal Miss Daisy resisted. An older person becomes increasingly dependent on those who once depended on them: the parent begins to be taken care of by his children. Experts in ethics sometimes talk about the danger of paternalism in any relationship when one person assumes the role of "parent," thereby claiming authority to do what is best for the "child." Some older people suffer when their grown children restrict their autonomy sooner than they wish.

> **How do we suffer differently as we grow old?**

In this chapter we will focus on the suffering of elderly people. We are moving along the life spectrum I earlier called womb to tomb. We may suffer poverty, illness, discrimination, or acts of violence at any age, but aging presents its own challenges and its own forms of suffering.

Recent Studies on Aging

Aging has been a popular subject for social scientists such as psychologists and sociologists to study in recent years. The graying of

America is obvious to most social analysts, since many members of the post-war baby boom, including myself, have turned fifty and started planning for retirement. For example, Gail Sheehy, drawing on much prior research, popularized the idea of transition points in the adult life span in her 1970s bestseller, *Passages*.[1] Many universities now have programs in gerontology and geriatrics. Christian theologians, ethicists, and counselors have also focused attention on this important stage in the life cycle.[2] Students of aging have begun to divide old age into separate stages. For example, old people might be young old (65–74), old (75–85), and very old (85 and older).[3] Until recently elderly women had been neglected in studies of aging.[4]

Although each older person is unique, some concerns are typical of many older people. For example, retirement can be a traumatic experience or a positive event, both for the person leaving a career behind and for that person's spouse.[5] Also, although people often become grandparents in their forties or fifties, interaction with the grandchildren presents new challenges to aging adults. Death also becomes a concern for many older people, as its inevitability may seem more real than it once did. Elderly people who want to plan for their dying often consider signing a Living Will.

The Spiritual Life of Older People

The spiritual life of older people has also been a concern of many groups. Social scientists have studied how elderly people handle spiritual issues.[6] In his classic study of religious development, Lewis Sherrill identifies simplification as the major concern of people from age fifty on into their senior years.[7] Sherrill defines "simplification of life" as "distinguishing the more important from the less important, getting rid of the less important or relegating it to the margin; and elevating the more important to the focus of feeling, thought, and action."[8] Churches have addressed the needs of the aging population in a number of ways, including counseling and assisted living centers.[9] Several years ago the theologian William A. Hendricks wrote a popular overview of Christian beliefs in light of the experiences of aging.[10]

Biblical Perspectives on Aging

In this chapter my major concern is to review some of the biblical perspectives on aging, demonstrating their relevance for our situation today. The Bible offers some basic schemes for the seasons of human living. Jeremiah 51:22, for instance, suggests four stages: childhood, youth, young married couples, and the elderly. Jeremiah 6:11 refers to five stages: small child, youth, adults, elderly, and "the very aged."[11] We will look at death and dying in the next chapter, although apprehension about impending death is one way older people suffer.

The Bible says a lot about the elderly, but it offers no systematic statement on their plight.[12] After a short introduction, then, we will look at several biblical stories about elderly people to see what they experienced. With the graying of our society, attention to this distinctive form of suffering is crucial to Christian reflection and ministry.

DAYS OF TROUBLE

Perhaps the closest the Bible comes to an overview of the situation of aging is Ecclesiastes 11:7–12:8. Qoheleth, the Teacher, urges the reader to rejoice in his youth, since old age will soon come (Eccl 11:8). The reader should also remember his creator while he is young "before the days of trouble come, and the years draw near when you will say, 'I have no pleasure in them'" (12:1). Quoting from Ecclesiastes is always dangerous, since the author often sounds negative or cynical until the more orthodox conclusion to the book (12:13–14). His description of old age as the "days of trouble" may seem too severe to some readers, but Qoheleth's description of aging stresses the losses experienced by many older people (12:2–7). Job echoes Qoheleth's pessimistic assessment when he speaks of his own life: "My days are swifter than a weaver's shuttle, and come to their end without hope" (Job 7:6).

What Is "Old"?

Two preliminary questions need to be addressed before we look at some biblical examples of aging. First, what is "old"? I often wise crack that to me an older person is someone about thirty years older than me. Age, in other words, is relative. To a teenager, a forty-year-old parent might appear to be ancient. To a person in her seventies, one hundred might be old. Certainly some people feel older than other people do at any age. A tired, frustrated fifty-year-old woman might have less vitality than some people in their eighties.

The Bible does not define old age exactly, but some passages offer clues about who counted as old when various biblical books were written. Psalm 90:10 suggests that seventy years might be a typical life span, but we might reach eighty "if we are strong." Earlier God had announced that because of the prevalence of human sin, the human life span would be 120 years (Gen 6:3). In the book of Genesis, however, extraordinary ages are mentioned. The

> **What is distinctive about the suffering of the elderly?**

oldest person mentioned in the Bible, Methuselah, lived to be 969 years old (Gen 5:27). Some other prominent people in the Old Testament lived past 100.

One unusual text from the law codes divides life into phases or stages. The law code deals with fees that could be paid to be liberated from religious vows. The fee for a boy from age five to twenty was twenty shekels, but the fee for an adult male from twenty to sixty was fifty shekels. After sixty years of age, a man was required to pay only fifteen shekels (Lev 27:1–7). Although the Bible generally has a high regard for the elderly, this text suggests that an older person, past sixty, owed less money in this context.

Although the Bible does not specify a certain year when one becomes old, it does recognize the aging process. As we will see in our survey of biblical seniors, some are strong and vital into their senior years while others suffer physical decline.

The Suffering of Older People

The second question is: What suffering is distinctive or characteristic for older people? Older people encounter many of the forms of suffering we have already studied. They experience infertility, illness, natural disasters, betrayal, and many other types of adversity. One of the most common forms of older suffering is apprehension about one's own death and the death of a spouse. We will look at death and dying in a later chapter, but this concern appears in some of the biblical profiles in the next section of this chapter. I must be clear, however, that being older is not necessarily in itself a form of suffering. Older people may suffer in some different ways than younger people, but they do not necessarily suffer just because they are ninety rather than nineteen.

Older people often face a form of discrimination called ageism. Ageism is discrimination based on age.[13] Younger people could be the victims of such bias, but older people are very familiar with this pattern as well. Forced retirement from work plagued older people for years. Several years ago, for example, a person might be forced to retire at age sixty-five in many businesses, yet a person of the same age could serve as President of the United States.

Ageism is based on familiar stereotypes about the aging process. Although older people do occasionally experience the loss of some intellectual and physical capacities, they can still perform many tasks well. Their accumulated wisdom and maturity often counterbalance their loss of physical dexterity. Movies such as *Grumpy Old Men* perpetuate some of these stereotypes, such as the image of an older male as a dirty old man. Recent movies such as *Space Cowboys,* however, reaffirm that older men can still make significant achievements, such as being astronauts.

PROFILES IN AGING

Although Methuselah was the oldest person in human history, the Bible does not describe his aging experience in any detail (Gen

5:25-27). Both testaments, however, offer profiles or portraits of people in their senior years. Reviewing some of these stories will help us understand the kinds of suffering older people experience and how Christians today can minister to suffering seniors.

Old People in the Old Testament

Abraham and Sarah

The book of Genesis records the long lives and troubles of the patriarchs and matriarchs of Hebrew history. Abraham and Sarah, for instance, struggle with her infertility for many years. Although God had promised Abraham that he would be the father of a great nation, he was still childless as a senior citizen. When God announces that he will finally become a father, Abraham laughs. How could he at one hundred and Sarah at ninety become parents? (Gen 17:17). Sarah laughs later when God repeats that promise (Gen 18:12-15). We looked at infertility as a common contemporary form of suffering earlier. The conception of Isaac is miraculous, considering Sarah's advanced years. Most older couples who have always wanted but been unable to have children, however, carry the burden of childlessness into their later years. When their friends and relatives revel in stories about their children and grandchildren, these childless seniors often suffer silently.

The story of Isaac and Rebekah highlights another dimension of senior suffering. When Isaac is old, his eyesight fails him (Gen 27:10). Both parents play favorites with their twin sons, Jacob and Esau, and Rebekah helps her favorite, Jacob, to deceive the blind Isaac into giving him the blessing reserved for the firstborn, Esau. When Esau discovers he has been tricked he threatens to kill Jacob. Jacob flees and Rebekah apparently dies before Jacob is able to return twenty years later.[14] Isaac's loss of sight is typical of the physical losses experienced by some older people. Several members of my extended family, for example, have been afflicted with macular degeneration.

Moses

Moses lives to be 120 but he does not suffer the same kind of physical decline. Because he had sinned while leading the Hebrews, God does not allow him to enter the promised land. But because his "eye was unimpaired, and his vigor had not abated" (Deut 34:7), he is able to see the entire promised land from the lookout on Mount Nebo before he dies. Amazingly to some in our youth-oriented culture, Moses began his work as liberator when he was eighty years old. Even at this age Moses encounters God at the burning bush and reluctantly agrees to leave the land to which he fled forty years earlier after killing an Egyptian who was beating a Hebrew (Acts 7:23). At an age when some people are slowing down, Moses is able to return to Egypt, confront the Pharaoh, liberate the Hebrew slaves, and lead them across the wilderness for another forty years.

Caleb

Caleb has a similar story of active service for God later in life. One of Caleb's last major appearances in the biblical narrative is his conversation with Joshua as the conquest of Canaan draws to a close (Josh 14:6–15). With the conquest about over, Caleb requests permission to capture the area promised to him by Moses as a reward for his spying out the land forty-five years earlier and bringing Moses back an honest report of the Hebrews' chances of capturing the land. Caleb had helped the rest of the other Hebrews in their battles, and now he is ready to take his land. He is eighty-five, but he announces "I am still as strong today as I was on the day that Moses sent me; my strength now is as my strength was then, for war, and for going and coming" (Josh 14:11).

Although Caleb's continuing physical strength is amazing, even more important is his complete loyalty to God throughout his life (Josh 14:8, 14). Many seniors recognize the difference between loyalty and longevity. They may have worked at a career faithfully for many years, but some co-workers may have simply marked time. Service awards for length of service on the job do not always measure the depth of commitment to the task.

Samuel

Another common experience of older people is the desire to say goodbye in a meaningful way. Samuel gives a farewell address as he steps aside to allow Saul to lead the Hebrews. Acknowledging that he is "old and gray," Samuel addresses the nation rather than his immediate family (1 Sam 12:2). He wants to know if the Hebrews have any criticisms of his leadership. He does not claim sinless perfection, but he wants his record to be clean as he leaves office. Many seniors today try to tie up any loose ends before they leave a career or move to a new phase of life.

Barzillai

One of the best depictions of both the negative and the positive sides of aging is the story of Barzillai (2 Sam 19:31-40). Barzillai helped David while he was a fugitive. After Absalom temporarily takes over Jerusalem, David flees. Later Absalom is killed and David returns home. He invites Barzillai to join him. Barzillai notes that he is eighty years old and had lost some of his physical capacities (2 Sam 19:35). He does not want to join David and be "an added burden" on him (19:35). On the positive side, however, Barzillai demonstrates a tactful autonomy. He politely refuses the king's offer, saying he would rather return home to die among his family (19:37). Frank Stagg notes that his "speech reflects a poised person, far from decrepit or decadent. He does not talk like a defeated old man. He is master of the situation, offering service without reward and giving his king freedom to go on without him."[15] Although not all older people are as wealthy and independent as Barzillai, he exemplifies the desire for autonomy felt by many senior citizens.

David

David's own experience with aging is more traumatic than Barzillai's balanced appraisal. As David's family plots about who will be his successor, David grows old and cold (1 Kings 1:1). His servants brought a young woman to warm him up, but "the king did not know her sexually" (1 Kings 1:4). David is apparently impotent, and

the nation knows that a new king will likely take over soon. It is possible that if the king could not pass a "virility test" he might be dis-
qualified from leadership.[16]

Other Old Testament elders

Several other Old Testament texts mention the experiences of
older people. Elisha, for instance, is ridiculed for being bald by
some youngsters (2 Kings 2:23-24). Although the Hebrews generally showed respect for the elderly, this juvenile behavior led to the
boys being attacked by bears. Mordecai is probably over one hundred years old when he gives advice to Esther about entering the
Persian king's beauty contest and about saving her people from destruction. Although aging is not a major topic in the Hebrew prophets, Zechariah anticipates a day when old men and women can
again sit quietly in the streets of Jerusalem (Zech 8:3). Joel looks forward to the day when God's Spirit will be poured out on all people,
and "your old men shall dream dreams" (Joel 2:28). Even though
Job suffers much, he lives to be 140 years old and dies "old and full
of days" (Job 42:16-17).

Old People in the New Testament

Elizabeth and Zechariah

The New Testament also reports the stories of several older
people although, since the New Testament is shorter than the Old
Testament, there are comparatively fewer stories about older people.
For instance, Elizabeth and Zechariah are both older when they appear in Luke's account of the background to Jesus' birth. Like Abraham and Sarah before them, Elizabeth is barren and they are both
old (Luke 1:7), but the angel Gabriel announces to Zechariah that
they will be the parents of John the Baptist.

Anna

After Jesus is born to Mary, she and Joseph take the infant to
Jerusalem. Anna, an elderly prophetess who lives in the temple
area, recognizes Jesus as the fulfillment of her hope for "the redemp-

tion of Jerusalem" (Luke 2:38). Her spiritual insight may illustrate the maturity typical of many older people who have learned well the lessons of life.

Nicodemus

Nicodemus is apparently an older man when he visits Jesus at night. When Jesus tells him he needs to be "born from above" (John 3:3), Nicodemus wonders how an older person can enter his mother's womb again (3:4). Although John does not report the conclusion to this conversation, Nicodemus seems to support the old saying that it is hard to teach an old dog new tricks. Eventually, however, Nicodemus identifies himself with Jesus, assisting Joseph of Arimathea in burying Jesus (John 7:50–52; 19:39).

Apostles

Three of the apostles have vivid experiences with aging. The Apostle Paul apparently describes himself as "an old man" in his letter to Philemon (Philemon 9 NRSV), but the Greek word in question can also be rendered "ambassador" (RSV). Scholars have long debated the chronology of Paul's life, but quite likely he is in his sixties when he writes his prison letters, including Philemon. F. F. Bruce, for example, suggests Paul was born in the first decade of the first century.[17] According to early Christian tradition, Paul was executed during Nero's persecutions of the Christians in the 60s.[18] Although Paul suffers a lot during his ministry, much of that adversity is due to the rigors of travel and persecution, not primarily the aging process.

Simon Peter's experience with aging is hinted at in his conversation with the risen Jesus. After Jesus asks him three times if Peter loves him, a reconciliation and forgiveness for Peter's triple denial seems to have occurred. Jesus then predicts that "when you grow old, you will stretch out your hands, and someone else will fasten a belt around you and take you where you do not wish to go" (John 21:18). We could see this as a general prediction of the physical decline associated with aging. The gospel writer, however, further comments that Jesus is specifically referring to the way in which Peter will die. According to early Christian tradition, Peter was crucified upside down at the orders of Nero.[19] In the meantime, Jesus instructs Peter to follow him.

Although Peter may have been more chastened and less impulsive after this conversation with Jesus, he immediately asks Jesus about the fate of the beloved disciple (John 21:20–22). Jesus replies politely that John's future is none of Peter's business. "If it is my will that he remain until I come, what is that to you? Follow me!" (John 21:22). John reports that some misunderstood Jesus' remark and assumed that John would not die before Jesus' return. According to more traditional scholars, the beloved disciple was John, the brother of James. Conservative scholars argue that he wrote the gospel, the three Johannine letters, and Revelation. Assuming this is true, John probably lived until near the end of the first century. Revelation may have been written during the reign of emperor Domitian, who persecuted Christians around A.D. 95 Although aging is not a major issue in these later books, the author of 2 John and 3 John identifies himself as "the elder" (2 John 1; 3 John 1). The word *elder* here could refer to an older person or to a church office usually held by older people.

The New Testament, like the Old Testament, generally encourages respect for older people. In his letter to Titus, for instance, Paul tells a younger minister to encourage the older men to "be temperate, serious, prudent, sound in faith, in love, and in endurance" (Titus 2:2). Older women are to "be reverent in behavior, not to be slanderers or slaves to drink; they are to teach what is good" (Titus 2:3).

AGING WELL

Our brief review of biblical profiles of aging people may have confirmed our understanding of the aging process or it may have surprised us. Seniors suffer some of the same problems that afflict young people, but they sometimes suffer physical and mental decline as well.

So, how should Christians respond to the suffering of aging people? Christian responses may differ for younger and older people. A few brief observations will have to suffice regarding this complex topic.

What Younger Christians Can Do

Younger Christians need to be aware of the danger of stereo-types. Ageism, in particular discrimination against older people, is an easy trap to fall into. Our popular culture, such as movies, televi-sion, and advertising, is often directed at a younger audience. Some younger Christians will need consciously to strive to overcome the stereotypical portrayal of older people in popular culture. A recent movie, *Deep Impact*, deals with the government's response to the threat of asteroids hitting the planet. Selected younger people are hidden in caves, along with some political and intellectual leaders, so they can survive the disaster and rebuild society. The implied message is that older people had outlived their usefulness unless they were scientists or the President!

Younger adults need to work in their churches and in the arena of public policy to insure older adults are not ignored or mistreated. Medical care, for example, needs to be insured for all age groups. Public policy issues, such as Social Security and Medicare, are often complex, but Christians need to speak up for the elderly in these de-bates. Churches can also provide for senior adults through their programs. Local churches often host senior adult days in morning worship or have se-

> **How should Christians respond to the suffering of aging people?**

nior adult choirs. Churches can employ staff members that plan ac-tivities for senior adults. Larger Christian organizations provide assisted living facilities at a modest price for senior citizens in their denomination and community.

What Older Christians Can Do

Older Christians have some options as well. First, they need to be realistic about what they can and cannot do. Reading the biblical stories of Moses and Caleb might mislead some of the elderly to think they can do as much at ninety as at thirty years of age. "A more balanced approach, however, takes into account the many heroes in the Bible who suffered infirmities common to aging."[20]

Second, aging Christians need to stay as active as possible as long as possible. We do not need to attempt to be Supermen or Superwomen, but passivity needs to be avoided. William Tuck notes the achievements of many senior citizens. For example, Golda Meir became Israel's prime minister at age seventy-one. Grandma Moses began her painting career at seventy. John Wesley preached until he was in his late eighties.[21] Although most of us will not be internationally famous, we can continue to enjoy life into our golden years. Resignation and depression about the aging process can be counterbalanced by finding as many interesting pursuits as possible.

Third, older adults need to look to the future with confidence in God's presence. Aging sometimes creates so many problems that cynicism is attractive. Nostalgia for the good old days is natural, but regular criticism of the present can sometimes blind an older person to opportunities for service now. William Hendricks begins his insightful book *A Theology for Aging* by noting, "We, the aging, have the best of both worlds. We have retrospect and hope."[22] The prophet Isaiah stresses God's presence throughout the human life cycle. God says his people "have been borne by me from your birth, carried from the womb; even to your old age I am he, even when you turn gray I will carry you. I have made, and I will bear; I will carry and will save" (Isa 46:3-4).

Despite the many negative aspects of aging, including physical and mental decline, a Christian can strive for a faithful response to this final stage of life. One writer notes, "The aging process, being biologically determined, is part of God's providence and is to be accepted with grace."[23]

Former President Jimmy Carter even wrote a delightful book on the virtues of aging.[24] Although he notes the many challenges he and his wife face in the aging process, his strong Christian faith helps him discuss aging in a confident way that should characterize all Christians. Although a former president of the United States probably has financial resources the typical Christian may not have,

Mr. Carter's advice is sound. The aging process can test our faith in the justice of God, but a hopeful faith can sustain us as we face the challenges of aging. Just a few weeks before he died, C. S. Lewis wrote to a friend: "Yes, autumn is really the best of the seasons; and I'm not sure that old age isn't the best part of life. But of course, like autumn, it doesn't *last*."[25] Since aging is typically the prelude to death, the next chapter will focus on death and grief.

✳️ Chapter Twelve

DEATH AND GRIEF

The scene has become all too familiar. After a series of tests your physician tells you that your illness is terminal. You have a short time to live, so you need to get your affairs in order. How do you respond? How do you face your own mortality? What do you do with the time you have left?

Most of us will not know exactly when we will die. A few years ago a close friend was diagnosed with terminal cancer. He and I both identified with C. S. Lewis's poem that compares life to a train ride. We never know exactly when we will get off the train and enter heaven.[1] My friend died within a year of the cancer diagnosis.

If we transport ourselves to the eighth century B.C. this scene would involve the prophet Isaiah and the king of Judah, Hezekiah. Hezekiah had been one of the better kings in the Southern Kingdom, but when he grows sick the prophet Isaiah tells him he will die: "Set your house in order, for you shall die; you shall not recover" (Isa 38:1). Since the prognosis came from a trustworthy prophet, Hezekiah did not seek a second human opinion. Instead, he prayed to God and "wept bitterly" (38:3). Hezekiah later writes a vivid portrayal of his despair at his possible early death (38:9–20). God responds to Hezekiah's prayer by telling Isaiah to tell the king that he will have another fifteen years of life. God assures the king of the authenticity of this message by having the sun's shadow on the sun dial move backwards.

> **How do we face our mortality?**

People respond to death, their own and that of others, in various ways. In this chapter we will look at both kinds of death and dying. Although some Christians distinguish three kinds of death, spiritual death, eternal death, and physical death, our concern in this chapter is primarily with physical death. First, we will focus on how a Christian responds to his or her own death. Second, we will look at the ways believers respond to the death of loved ones. Ideally, our responses will be based on our confidence in "the God of hope" (Rom 15:13) who raised Jesus from the dead and will raise us in the future.

THE TIME OF MY DEPARTURE

Let's go back to Hezekiah's situation for a moment. How would you respond if you knew you had a few months to live? Some of us, like Hezekiah, would hope for more time. We might feel we must finish some projects at work or that we had some relationships to mend. We might spend our time traveling, visiting old friends, or taking care of unfinished business. With the introduction of living wills many Americans have given serious thought to the circumstances surrounding their deaths.

> **How should Christians think about death?**

They have stated preferences about the kind of health care they do or do not want to be given to them, especially if they are unconscious or the medical situation is hopeless.[2]

Several years ago Mitch Albom wrote a best-selling book recording his conversations with a former college teacher who was dying of ALS, or Lou Gehrig's disease. *Tuesdays with Morrie* gave us a case study in how one mature person dealt with his impending death.[3] His former student's reflections captured the attention of many readers because of Morrie's insights into life and the honest way he handled his own dying.

Arthur Ashe's *Days of Grace* reports his life story, focusing on his fight with AIDS, a disease he contracted through infected blood given him during an operation. Knowing he would die before his daughter grew up, he ended his book with a letter to her, expressing his confidence in God and his hope in life after death.[4]

Biblical Teachings about Death and the Afterlife

How you respond to your own death depends partly on how you understand the Bible and its teachings about death and life after death. The Christian view of death can be analyzed or outlined a number of ways. For example, death might be considered a friend or a foe. Hezekiah's response illustrates well the negative view that death is our enemy.

Death is destruction

Another way to sketch out the biblical view of death is to use a threefold typology: death is destruction, death is departure, and death is dead.[5] First, death is destruction. Death destroys the body, but even more importantly for some is death's destruction of relationships. Arthur Ashe's letter to his daughter, for instance, reflects his concern over a disruption of the parent-child relationship. In the next section of this chapter we will glance at some of the relationships that are destroyed, at least temporarily, when someone dies.

Death is departure

Second, death is departure. Many religions and philosophies have stressed that death is the doorway to another life, the afterlife or life after death as we often term it. The Apostle Paul exemplifies this more positive understanding of death in his last letter. In jail and anticipating his death, Paul writes that he is ready for "the time of my departure. I have fought the good fight, I have finished the race, I have kept the faith" (2 Tim 4:6–7). Paul can understand death as a friend because he has lived a long, productive life. He has accomplished a lot, and he is ready to move on to the next life. Earlier, probably during a different imprisonment, he expressed his preference for dying and joining Jesus. He knew that he could render more service if he lived a while longer (Phil 1:21–26). We saw the same kind of readiness to die in the story of Barzillai in the chapter on aging. This elderly friend of David wanted to go home and die near his family (2 Sam 19:37).

Death is dead

Third, death is dead. This unusual phrase reflects Paul's teaching in 2 Timothy 1:10. Jesus, through his death and resurrection, "abolished death and brought life and immortality to light through the gospel." Although Christians still die physically, the sense of death as a primarily negative experience has ben transformed through Christ's death. In his discussion of Jesus' resurrection in 1 Corinthians 15, Paul insists that death no longer had its "sting" for Christians (1 Cor 15:54-57). When the Christians at Thessalonica are perplexed about the death of friends and family before Jesus returned, Paul reminds them that Christians "do not grieve as others do who have no hope" (1 Thess 4:13). Christians experience a grieving process over the loss of loved ones, but they have hope that their loved ones have moved on to be with God.

The Christian View of Death in a Broader Context

One way to see the significance of the Christian view of death is to compare it with rival views. For instance, C. S. Lewis compares the Christian view to two others. First, the "lofty view" of the ancient Stoics insists that death really does not matter, and we should be indifferent to death. Second, the "natural" view is that death is "the greatest of all evils." By contrast, Lewis states, the Christian view is that death is "Satan's great weapon and also God's great weapon: it is holy and unholy; our supreme disgrace and our only hope; the thing Christ came to conquer and the means by which He conquered."[6]

C. S. Lewis captures an important facet of the Christian hope in the conclusion to his children's story, *The Last Battle,* the last of the *Chronicles of Narnia* Aslan the lion, who represents Jesus in these stories, explains to some children that they and their parents had died in a wreck. He uses several word pictures to explain the Christian hope. "Your father and mother and all of you are—as you used to call it in the Shadowlands—dead. The term is over: the holidays have begun. The dream is ended: this is the morning."[7] Lewis's concluding comment adds another image: "All their life in this world and all their adventures in Narnia had only been the cover and the title page: now at last they were beginning Chapter One of the Great Story, which no one on earth has read: which goes on for ever: in which every chapter is better than the one before."[8]

JESUS WEPT

Christians who have a strong hope in God and the future he provides for them still grieve over the death of friends and family. The outpouring of grief over those killed in the 9/11 attacks in 2001, over the death of Princess Diana in 1997, and over the assassination of President Kennedy in 1963 reminds us that people even mourn the deaths of people they have never met personally.

Even though Christians affirm belief in resurrection and life after physical death, the grieving process can be very difficult. In the introductory chapter we looked at the grief C. S. Lewis experienced when his wife, Joy, died. Nicholas Wolterstorff recounts his personal anguish over the death of his son in a mountain climbing accident.[9] Hubert Locke discusses his grief over his parents's death.[10] Reading testimonies such as these books by Lewis, Wolterstorff, and Locke reminds us of the agony of losing a loved one. In this section we will look briefly at several examples of biblical grief. These stories will illustrate how deeply we suffer when we lose someone close to us.[11]

> **How should Christians react to death?**

The Death of a Friend

We grieve over the death of a close friend. One of the most revealing stories from Jesus' life is the death of Lazarus, the brother of Mary and Martha. The story is remarkable for a number of reasons. For instance, to visit Lazarus's home, Bethany, meant going near Jerusalem, where the leaders wanted to arrest Jesus. Thomas boldly proposes that they all go with Jesus, even if it means dying with him (John 11:16). More significantly, Jesus offers one of his famous "I am" sayings (11:25) in response to Lazarus's death: "I am the resurrection and the life. Those who believe in me, even though they die, will live." After affirming resurrection of the dead to Martha and Mary, Jesus raises Lazarus.

Snuck into the middle of this story is Jesus' emotional response to the death of his friend. Even though Jesus knows that he can and will raise Lazarus from the dead, Jesus still identifies emotionally with the immense grief felt by Lazarus's family and other friends. John's cryptic remark is amazing: "Jesus began to weep" (John 11:35; "Jesus wept" KJV).

Perhaps the most graphic story of grief over the death of a friend in the Old Testament is David's grief at the death of Jonathan. David and Jonathan became close friends when David served in the court of Saul, Jonathan's father. Although Samuel had already anointed David to be Saul's successor, Jonathan felt no jealousy. Jonathan protected David from Saul's attacks, and the two friends made a covenant to seal their friendship (1 Sam 18:1–4). When David learns that Jonathan has been killed in battle, his grief is intense: "I am distressed for you, my brother Jonathan; greatly loved were you to me; your love to me was wonderful, passing the love of women" (2 Sam 1:26).

The Death of a Child

David's grief over the death of Jonathan is matched by his sense of loss when his son Absalom dies. Absalom had led a rebellion against David and temporarily took control of Jerusalem. David fled from the city until Absalom was killed by David's men. When David learns of his son's death, he grieves loudly: "O my son Absalom, my son, my son Absalom! Would I had died instead of you, O Absalom, my son, my son!" (2 Sam 18:33). Joab confronts the king about his grief, saying that he is demoralizing his troops, and David regains some of his composure.

The Bible contains many stories about the death of a child. Perhaps because of the lack of medical care, younger children often die. Others were adult children, such as Absalom, who died in war.

Several children die, for instance, when King Herod orders the slaughter of the young boys in Bethlehem after the visit of the Magi (Matt 2:16-18). Matthew interprets the "slaughter of the innocents" as the fulfillment of Jeremiah 31:15, reflecting the weeping of Rachel for her children. Rachel had been Jacob's favorite wife, but she died giving birth to Benjamin (Gen 35:16-20).[12]

Two of Jesus' revivifications of the dead involve children. Jairus, a ruler of the synagogue, approaches Jesus while his daughter is "at the point of death" (Mark 5:23). Jesus' journey with Jairus is interrupted by the women with the flow of blood, and Jairus's daughter is dead when Jesus arrives at his house. Professional mourners had already stared grieving loudly, but Jesus raises the girl from the dead. Jesus also raises the widow of Nain's son from the dead (Luke 7:11-17). As his body is being carried to the grave, Jesus has compassion on the widow and tells her not to cry. He then raises her only son from the dead.

Although these two stories do not report the details of the parent's grief, Jesus' response reflects his concern for a parent's loss of a child. Just as God intervenes to keep Abraham from losing his son Isaac, so Jesus intervenes to rescue these two parents from their grief.

The Death of a Spouse

Another face of grief is the bereavement caused by the death of a spouse. Probably the most detailed biblical story is Abraham's response to the death of Sarah. We do not know exactly how long they had been married, although Abraham was seventy-five and she was sixty-five when they left Haran (Gen 12:4). Sarah died when she was 127 years old (Gen 23:1), so they had been married over sixty years. Abraham mourns her death and seeks an appropriate burial site. The Hittites are so impressed with Abraham that they offer him their best grave, but Abraham insists on paying for Sarah's tomb. The prophet Ezekiel also loses his wife, although he is specifically instructed by God not to grieve over her death (Ezek 24:15-18).

More common than the death of a wife in the Bible is the death of a husband. As today, women in the ancient world outlived men, perhaps in some part because of numerous deaths in battle.

Predictably, the Bible includes several references to widows. Two of the most remarkable widows in the Bible are Naomi and Ruth, her daughter-in-law. Naomi and her husband had moved to Moab to find food during a famine. While living there their two sons married Moabite women. Eventually all three men die, leaving three widows, Naomi, Ruth, and Orpah. Naomi encourages her daughters-in-law to remain in Moab. Although the book of Ruth does not dwell on the widows' grief, Naomi recognizes that young widows often want to remarry. Orpah does stay in Moab, but Ruth travels with Naomi to find a new life in Bethlehem.

The plight of widows was often desperate in biblical times, and God's people were encouraged to provide for their welfare. Earlier we saw that the custom of levirate marriage was designed to provide a husband and children for a widow. Tamar, Onan's widow, resorts to desperate measures when her father-in-law will not enforce this custom (Gen 38). The first conflict in the early church involves a discussion about the distribution to the widows in the Jerusalem church (Acts 6:1–6). James includes attention to widows as part of his definition of religion (James 1:27). Paul tells Timothy that widows should be supported by their family and the church (1 Tim 5:5–13).

The Death of a Parent

Several Bible passages briefly mention the death of parents. The biblical authors do not always dwell on the details of children's bereavement. After the death of Sarah, for instance, Abraham seeks a wife for his son, Isaac. When Isaac marries Rebekah, he "is comforted after his mother's death" (Gen 24:67). This cryptic remark hints that the death of his mother affects Isaac deeply. When Jacob dies, Joseph's grief is highlighted by the biblical author. "Then Joseph threw himself on his father's face, and wept over him and kissed him" (Gen 50:1).

Suicide

Another kind of grief occurs when a close friend or family member commits suicide.[13] The Bible mentions several suicides, with the most famous being the deaths of Saul, Samson, and Judas. The clearest statement of grief over a suicide is David's reaction to Saul's death. Although Saul had tried to kill David, David sincerely grieves over his death as well as Jonathan's (2 Sam 1:11-27). A messenger tells David that he has killed Saul, but the account in 1 Samuel 31:1-4 clearly presents Saul's death as a suicide.

People commit suicide for a variety of reasons.[14] Some, like Saul who was mortally wounded on the battlefield, experience such severe pain or limitations due to a chronic or life-threatening illness that they want to escape their frustration. Others, such as Samson who had been captured and blinded by his enemies, want to escape torture or punishment. Samson pulls a building down, killing himself and his enemies, perhaps to avoid further humiliation.

Although relatively few suicides are reported in the Bible, some biblical figures experience the kind of despair that might lead to suicide. Job, for example, suffers so much that he wishes he had never been born or had died at birth. If he had known he would suffer so much, he would have chosen not to exist at all. "Why did I not die at birth, come forth from the womb and expire?" (Job 3:11) is a typical expression of his early anguish at his immense suffering. Qoheleth, the Teacher in Ecclesiastes, tries to find some meaning in life. When his early efforts produce no satisfaction, he concludes "So I hated life, because what is done under the sun was grievous to me; for all is vanity and a chasing after wind" (Eccl 2:17). Jeremiah's "confessions" also reflect depression or despair at times. Like Job, he wishes he had never been born: "Cursed be the day on which I was born!" (Jer 20:14).[15] When Jezebel seeks to kill Elijah, he asks God to take his life (1 Kings 19:4). Jonah is ready to die after the people of Nineveh repent (Jonah 4:3). None of these sufferers commit suicide, but their sense of hopelessness is consistent with the feeling that motivates some suicide attempts.

Physical and emotional suffering might provoke a suicide attempt, and the family and friends of those who commit suicide also suffer. "What could I have done to prevent this?" is a common response to suicide. Christians can receive training in noticing signals that may indicate someone is potentially suicidal, and Christians can assist in social and church programs such as hot-lines that seek to counsel hurting people considering suicide. Sometimes the best help for a depressed person is a sense of the presence of God. A pastor friend of mine talks about the "ministry of showing up," meaning that Christians can help by being sensitive to the needs of others and being physically present with them.

RESURRECTION

In chapter four I mentioned the story of Frank Tupper, a seminary professor whose wife was dying of cancer. A few months before she died, Betty asked Frank, "Do you believe in resurrection?"[16] He had studied with a famous German theologian, Wolfhart Pannenberg, who wrote extensively about Jesus' resurrection. When Professor Tupper started to give an abstract, theoretical answer to Betty's question, reflecting his academic study, Betty repeated her question: "I asked you, 'Do you believe in resurrection?' Today. Now."[17] He answered her more pointed and personal question, "Yes." He realized that she faced the prospect of death and life after death.[18]

> **How does the Bible envision resurrection?**

Jesus' Resurrection

The basis for Christian hope is Jesus' resurrection.[19] The Apostle Paul insists that our faith is futile unless God has really raised Jesus from the dead (1 Cor 15:13-19). Paul assembles a list of witnesses of the risen Jesus, including Jesus' appearance to him on the road to Damascus. Paul affirms the reality of our future resurrection as well, but he realizes the difficulty of the subject. For example, when someone asks about the nature of our resurrection body, he replies, "Fool!" (1 Cor 15:36). Paul tries to explain what we will experience in the resurrection through a series of comparisons. For example, drawing on agriculture, he says "It is sown a physical body, it is raised a spiritual body. If there is a physical body, there is also a spiritual body" (1 Cor 15:44). He admits, however, that he is dealing in the realm of mystery. Somehow we will be transformed. We will have bodies, but they will be somehow different from the ones we possess now (1 Cor 15:51–54).

Heaven

The ultimate destiny of God's resurrected people is heaven. Although heaven is often discussed by Christians, occasionally the news media study popular opinion about heaven. For example, the cover story for *Time* magazine for March 24, 1997 was "Does Heaven Exist?" According to that survey, 81 percent of Americans believe in heaven, and 61 percent believe that they will go directly to heaven.[20] The cover story for *Newsweek* for August 12, 2002 was "Visions of Heaven." In 2003 Mitch Albom published a best-selling novel on *The Five People You Meet in Heaven* which in 2004 was made into a movie.[21]

Christians generally affirm the existence of heaven and hell, but questions about the details of heavenly existence abound.[22] For instance, will you recognize family and friends who are in heaven with you? Will you know what is happening on earth while history continues? Will there be levels or degrees of rewards in heaven? Will you remember your earthly life in heaven? Will you change or develop in heaven?

The amount of biblical evidence that is relevant to these questions is limited, so some believers speculate a lot. For example, I have heard Christians insist that everyone in heaven will be thirty-three years old, since that is the perfect age. Jesus, they note, was thirty-three when he died.

Characteristics of heaven

The Bible is clearer on some general characteristics of heaven. Christians will experience the presence of God. They will receive relief from suffering and death. They will be rewarded. They will have fellowship with God's people.[23] Perhaps the best short statement on heavenly existence is John's report: God "will wipe away every tear from their eyes. Death will be no more; mourning and crying and pain will be no more, for the former things have passed away" (Rev 21:4). C. S. Lewis notes that we experience some pleasures in this life, but we will always have a sense of longing for something more. "If I find in myself a desire which no experience in this world can satisfy, the most probable explanation is that I was made for another world. If none of my earthly pleasures satisfy it, that does not prove that the universe is a fraud. Probably earthly pleasures were never meant to satisfy it, but only to arouse it, to suggest the real thing."[24]

Children in heaven

Before we leave the topics of death and resurrection, one other topic needs some attention. Some parents whose young children have died struggle over their child's eternal destiny. Most parents believe that infants and young children go to heaven. One relevant Bible text is David's response to the death of the child conceived in adultery with Bathsheba. As the child approaches death, David fasts and prays, but when the child dies, David returns to his normal routine. He explains, "Can I bring him back again? I shall go to him, but he will not return to me" (2 Sam 12:23). It is important to note, however, that David's efforts to return to normalcy so quickly after the death of his child is not something God directs him to do. Rather it is his own personal response to his child's death and not something we should expect from other parents.

Several key Christian doctrines relate to the subject of an infant's destiny.[25] Groups that affirm the biological inheritance of sin and guilt from Adam and Eve often practice infant baptism, partly to avoid the problem of unsaved infants. Other Christians propose that a child is innocent until he or she reaches an age of accountability.[26] Most Christians correctly trust a loving God to bring these innocent children to him. The parents of dead children can move on more easily when we assure them that their children are with God.

Chapter Thirteen

ANIMAL SUFFERING

One of the most anguished questions a parent can hear from her child is "Will my dog go to heaven?" When a child's favorite pet dies, the child often wonders if the pet will experience an afterlife similar to human postmortem existence. I often tell my theology students that children's questions are the hardest theological questions, partly because they need to be answered on a level suitable for the child. Such questions are also challenging because the parent wants to comfort the child. Answering "yes," will console the child, but can the parent in good conscience affirm animal immortality? The child's question about animal immortality is also difficult because it is often neglected by academic theologians. Discussing the Trinity or some other theological question with a child might be easier than tackling animal immortality, since Christians have written children's books on some of these topics.

If questions of animal suffering and immortality are mentioned at all in studies of theodicy, providence, and theology of suffering, these topics are usually treated briefly.[1] Although they do

> **Do all dogs go to heaven?**

not fit easily into the womb to tomb scheme I have followed for most of Part Two, the issues are intriguing to many Christians and deserve serious attention.

In this chapter I will examine the treatment of animal suffering and immortality by two academic theologians, C. S. Lewis and Stephen Webb. Their discussions will help us reflect on this perennial question. Renewed interested by Christians in ecology provides the larger context for our study of animal immortality. After a brief glance at that trend, we will look in more depth at animal suffering and its relation to animal immortality. In these later sections of this chapter, I will interact primarily with the ideas of C. S. Lewis, whose discussion of these two interrelated topics in *The Problem of Pain* has intrigued and frustrated several of his readers. Although Lewis's discussion of animal immortality predates the recent interest in ecotheology, he provides a classic discussion of this topic. I will also briefly look at the more recent view of Stephen Webb, who also affirms the possibility of animal immortality.[2]

THE GREENING OF THEOLOGY

A Brief History of Christian Ecology

Ecology has gained national exposure in this country at least since the first Earth Day celebration in April 1970. Rachel Carson's *Silent Spring* alerted many people to the problem of pollution of the environment, and concerned citizens began to mobilize to bring about changes in public policy on the environment. Some concerned Christians began to notice Bible passages such as Isaiah 24:4-5: "The earth dries up and withers, the world languishes and withers; the heavens languish together with the earth. The earth lies polluted, under its inhabitants; for they have transgressed laws, violated the statutes, broken the everlasting covenant." Interpreting apocalyptic texts such as this is always difficult, but Isaiah seemed to envision a planet afflicted by ecological problems due to human sin. A certain comic strip echoes Isaiah's warning as it shows our planet with the following narration: "In the beginning God created the earth, the air, the water, the trees, and the animals. Then he created man." The last picture shows a globe engulfed by pollution with the caption: "Enough said."

> **How are we to have "dominion over the earth"?**

In the early days of the ecology movement not all Christians were ready to jump on the environmental bandwagon or to endorse the need for a "green theology."[3] Some were convinced that the

Bible stressed the status and value of humanity in God's plan. God sent his Son to save humans, not whales. Some evangelical Christians were, in fact, critical of environmentalism as a New Age strategy that challenged traditional Christian priorities.[4]

In recent years, however, Christians from across the theological spectrum have begun to see the necessity of a Christian concern for ecology. Evangelical scholar Ebbie Smith offers four reasons for Christian concern about the environment that seem representative of a growing ecumenical consensus.[5] First, the ecological crisis is real. Although scholars debate how large the threat of global warming or nuclear winter might be in the foreseeable future, most agree ecological crisis is genuine. Second, Christianity has been accused of being a major cause of ecological crisis. Lynn White's famous essay insists that God's assignment of "dominion" over the earth to humans has led to ecological disaster as people have exploited natural resources.[6] Christians need to offer a responsible interpretation of this theme in order to respond to White and others. Third, evangelical Christianity has been accused of a false dualism that contributes to environmental problems. Christian otherworldliness, for instance, discourages concern with this world. As the old saying suggests, "Christians are so heavenly minded that they are of no earthly good." Fourth, ecological concern is a valid expression of Christian stewardship. Stewardship is not limited to tithing or pledging at church.[7] Stewardship ideals should also govern how Christians treat their physical bodies, the physical world, animals, and all creatures.

Christian Ecological Activism

Increasingly, even conservative Christians have seen the validity of ecological activism.[8] Evangelicals have realized that God's instruction to "have dominion" and to "subdue" the earth do not support irresponsible actions (Gen 1:26, 28). Responsible stewardship includes all of life, and how we use our God-given resources, such as air and water, concern God. Tony Campolo, for instance, acknowledges that some people have accused him of being "an evangelist who was out to save whales."[9] Campolo responds that his primary obligation is to witness to humans but that God is also concerned about whales.[10]

Some Christians have pushed for a radical rethinking of the relationship of God and the world. Sallie McFague, for example, has devoted considerable attention to the dangers of a dualistic, monarchical world view typical of Christian theism. She recommends an organic model for the God-world relationship. Such a theology of nature should lead to more ecological concern among Christians. Christians should, she argues, love nature.[11]

The familiar words from John 3:16, "For God so loved the world," are usually interpreted to mean that God loves all humans. Certainly the rest of Jesus' comments to Nicodemus relate primarily to his need to become a disciple and be born again. Other biblical passages, however, clearly point to God's concern for all of his created world. God's covenant with Noah after the flood includes all living creatures, not just humans (Gen 9:8-11). Jesus, for instance, advises us not to be anxious about life's necessities because God is concerned for the birds and flowers (Matt 6:25-33). God is more concerned about humans than these other creatures, but God is concerned about them as well.

Some Christians wonder if the traditional commitment to anthropocentrism, or a human-centered approach to theology and ethics, is not a dangerous form of speciesism. Speciesism is the elevation of one species over other species. For example, Andrew Linzey asks is "Christianity destined to remain irredeemably speciesist?"[12] More traditional Christians affirm that humanity is the crown of God's creation but that as the crown we should care for all creatures as God does.

This brief glance at recent Christian interest in ecology provides the general context for my study of animal immortality. Although a child's question about animal afterlife may be more personal, many adult Christians, such as my college students, wonder about how the topic of animal immortality fits into their developing views of creation, God, and salvation.

C. S. LEWIS AND "OUR DOCTRINE OF BEASTS"

The Bible mentions many species of animals.[13] One clue to the biblical view of these creatures is that the term *nephesh*, sometimes translated "soul," is used both for humans (Gen 2:7) and other creatures (Gen 1:20, 21, 24, 30). Originally both humans and animals ate vegetables rather than meat (Gen 1:29–30; 2:16), but after the flood humans are allowed to eat animals (Gen 9:1–3). God's concern for the welfare of animals is occasionally noted in the Bible. For example, God concludes his conversation with Jonah by asking "Should I not be concerned about Nineveh, that great city, in which there are more than a hundred and twenty thousand persons who do not know their right hand from their left, and also many animals?" (Jonah 4:11).

> **Do animals have souls?**

Although scholars puzzle over the reference to animals, one interpretation is that God is concerned about what happens to the animals in Nineveh as well as the sinful humans.

Attention to what Andrew Linzey calls "animal theology," or what C. S. Lewis terms "our doctrine of beasts," entails exploring a wide range of ethical and theological issues.[14] Linzey, for instance, in *Animal Theology* devotes chapter length discussions to topics such as animal rights, experimentation with animals, hunting for recreation, and vegetarianism. Tony Campolo discusses the question "Is hunting a sin?" in his *20 Hot Potatoes Christians Are Afraid to Touch*.[15] A few years ago Tim Stafford reviewed recent thinking on animal rights for conservative Christians.[16]

The topic of animal pain or suffering has been addressed by scientists, philosophers, and a few theologians.[17] Probably the most famous and accessible Christian treatment of animal suffering and animal immortality is C. S. Lewis's chapter in *The Problem of Pain*. Lewis admits that his discussion must be speculative, since the Bible does not deal with this issue at length.

Types of Animal Suffering

First, Lewis raises the question of what kind of suffering animals might experience. He begins by distinguishing sentience from consciousness. Sentience is a basic awareness of and responsiveness to the outside world. Consciousness is a higher cognitive capacity involving the ability to have a "perception of succession" of experiences, not just a succession of individual, unconnected perceptions.[18] The higher animals, he suggests, have consciousness, something like a self or a soul. Although Lewis argues that these higher animals can experience pain and suffering, he is aware of the "pathetic fallacy," the projection of human-like experiences onto non-human creatures. An extreme form of this projection is demonstrated in the predisposition some humans have to anthropomorphize their pets, treating them as smaller versions of humans.[19] Some people who resist the topic of animal suffering argue that our sentimentality has overridden our reason when we discuss animal pain.

Causes of Animal Suffering

Second, Lewis discusses the possible origin of animal suffering. Earlier he had rejected the view that animals can sin, thereby eliminating pain as a penalty for their sins.[20] He also dismisses the view that the fall of Adam and Eve causes animal suffering. Although some Christians trace the genesis of natural evil—a category that might include animal suffering—to the "thorns and thistles" of Genesis 3:18, Lewis notes that animals attacked and ate each other before Adam and Eve sinned.

Lewis proposes as a better explanation of animal suffering, the fall of Satan.[21] As an evangelical thinker, Lewis affirms the existence of Satan and suggests Satan could have corrupted the world, including animals, before Adam and Eve sinned. One of humanity's roles might be "to restore peace to the animal world."[22]

Responses to Animal Suffering

How you respond to Lewis's discussion may depend on at least two factors: 1) your willingness to speculate beyond explicit biblical teaching and 2) your relationship with animals, especially pets. First, the Bible briefly treats animal suffering without giving many details about it. For example, Paul describes the universe as "groaning" (Rom 8:22) in its current state, which perhaps includes animal suffering. The Bible devotes much more attention to human suffering and divine suffering than to animal suffering. If, some would argue, the Bible slights a subject, why do we need to think about it? A recent book on animals, however, devotes two chapters to the relation of Jesus to animals.[23] Second, if you are close to pets or other animals, you can easily imagine a good Creator God being concerned about the pain felt by any of his creatures. The issue of animal suffering is probably more meaningful to people with pets than other Christians.

> **How can Christians treat animals justly?**

A theory that Lewis does not develop at length in his chapter is the effect of human sin on animals. Animal rights advocates argue that much animal suffering outside of the wild is due to human experimentation, hunting, and abuse. Lewis is concerned about these issues, as he demonstrates in his essay criticizing vivisection.[24] In a similar vein, Dr. Seuss's story about the Lorax stresses the disastrous consequences on the environment resulting from human greed. Cutting down all of the trees leads to an ecological disaster affecting several species in this children's tale.

C. S. LEWIS AND A "DERIVATIVE IMMORTALITY" FOR ANIMALS

Lewis also addresses the topic of justice as it relates to animals.[25] Here he broaches the issue of animal immortality, a subject often neglected in Christian theology, at least among academic theologians. Stephen Webb notes that many theologians find the issue "unnerving."[26] An exception to this neglect was John Wesley, who advocated animal immortality, as well as some other writers have dealt seriously with the issue.[27]

Lewis realizes he might be ridiculed for his views on animal immortality, and he acknowledges the "complete silence of Scripture and Christian tradition on animal immortality" is a serious objection to his view.[28] He still, however, argues for the possibility of a "derivative immortality" for some animals.[29]

Animal Immortality

Lewis suggests that some higher animals, especially those with close relations with humans, almost become an extension of the human's personality. God's instruction to humans to have "dominion" includes the domestication of some animals:

> The tame animal is therefore, in the deepest sense, the only "natural" animal—the only one we see occupying the place it was made to occupy, and it is on the tame animal that we must base all our doctrine of beasts.[30]

In other words, an animal might gain immortality through its relationship with a human being.

Lewis explains his view of animal immortality in relation to human resurrection in a letter written on November 26, 1962, commenting on *The Problem of Pain*:

> I ventured the supposal—it could be nothing more—that as we are raised *in* Christ, so at least some animals are raised *in* us. Who knows, indeed, that a great deal even of the inanimate creation is raised *in* the redeemed souls who have, during this life, taken its beauty into themselves?[31]

Objections to Animal Immortality

In *The Problem of Pain* Lewis acknowledges two possible objections to this view.[32] First, some Christians resist the notion of animals having souls; humans are qualitatively different from animals. Another evangelical, Tony Campolo, seems to support the objection Lewis anticipates. Campolo endorses the traditional "chain of being" concept: "there is a hierarchy in nature, and humans are placed above all else in God's creation. There is a spirituality to humans that is unique, and it is primarily for our salvation that Christ went to the cross."[33] Lewis seems to agree that humans are superior to non-human animals, but for him being "saved" is not the key concept. Animals might be in heaven because of their close relation to humans, not because they sinned and were somehow "saved" through Jesus' death.

The second objection Lewis addresses is that animal immortality might be a compensation for the miserable existence of animals now. God is not, contends Lewis, making up for allowing animal suffering within history. They are immortal because of their relation to humans.

Without going into all of the details of Lewis's position, it will be obvious that he mounts a serious, albeit somewhat speculative, case for animal immortality. If you have children whose pet has died, or you are close to animals, you may have wondered about this issue. Billy Graham, for example, has answered questions about animals being in heaven in his newspaper column. To one correspondent Graham replied: "God knows what we will need to be perfectly happy in heaven, and if he knows animals are necessary, he will have them there."[34] Graham mentions that some people take the peaceable kingdom passages, such as Isaiah 65:25 or 11:6-9, literally. Animals that are natural enemies are pictured in these texts living together peacefully and some see this as a vision of heaven.

Some who reject animal immortality cite the Bible as well. For example, some people point to Revelation 22:15 as a rejection of animals in heaven: "Outside are the dogs. . . ." Many commentators insist that the word *dogs* here is symbolic, as Paul uses the term for his opponents in Philippians 3:2 ("Beware of the dogs").[35] Others with reservations about animal immortality might point to Ecclesiastes 3:19-21, which suggests that humans and animals have a similar fate. This passage seems to reject any afterlife for animals or humans.

STEPHEN WEBB AND GOD'S GRACE

Stephen Webb, a more recent theologian, has also advocated animal immortality. Webb has dealt with the topic in two books, *On*

God and Dogs and *Good Eating*. I will focus especially on the latter book. His work fits more clearly into the context of green theology than does Lewis's. Although they both affirm animal immortality, Webb argues to that conclusion from a different standpoint.

Animals in the Bible

In *On God and Dogs* Webb sketches out the biblical witness on animals and gives a summary of Christian tradition before reviewing contemporary Christian theories about animals.[36] In *Good Eating* Webb presents a biblical theology of animals as the context for his reflections on animal immortality.[37] He notes three main points in this biblical theology.

> **Does God's grace extend to animals?**

First, although animals have their own integrity and dignity, they are not equal to humans. Second, humans have a God-given power over animals; humans should exercise that power according to God's intentions. Third, the world today is not what it was meant to be. Eventually God will restore the world to its original peace and harmony.

Animal Afterlife

When Webb moves to the subject of animal afterlife, he sets the discussion in the context of contemporary views of heaven. Webb acknowledges that many contemporary people are reluctant to talk about heaven at all, much less consider the possibility of animals in heaven. Webb notes two major objections to discussions of heaven.[38] First, an epistemological concern is that we really cannot know anything about the afterlife. As a result, theologians are often reluctant to sound too literalistic in their depictions of heaven. Webb responds that many in our culture are curious about the afterlife and want to hear discussions of what it will be like. Webb insists "The language that puts animals in heaven . . . is true and trustworthy language. It refers to a reality that will indeed be all-inclusive."[39] Second, some have a moral objection to affirmations about heaven. More liberal theologians worry about belief in heaven encouraging greed or selfishness. People might do good deeds for selfish reasons, earning a place in heaven. For more conservative theologians the pleasures in heaven need to be minimized in our theology. Heaven is about God, not human pleasure; heaven is radically different from our world today.

Webb bases his affirmation of animal immortality primarily on his understanding of God. God's love and power are essential to his animal theology. "God is full of grace" he notes, so neither humans nor animals really deserve heaven.[40] Webb criticizes C. S. Lewis for limiting animal immortality to domestic animals, such as pets, that are connected to humans. Webb insists that "heaven is for all creatures who have suffered, so that not only pampered dogs will be there."[41] Both humans and animals will be in heaven because of God's love and power to redeem his creation. Since humans have free will, they can choose not to be in heaven, but animals, Webb suggests, have a moral innocence humans do not possess.

Webb also responds to a traditional objection to animal immortality, namely, that animals do not have souls. Webb notes that God will redeem the total human person, not just the soul. "The Christian idea is that the afterlife, just as with this life, is a gift of God's grace. This gift can include animals because God intends to put all of creation right in the end."[42]

ANIMAL IMMORTALITY AND COSMIC ESCHATOLOGY

Whether you find Webb's arguments for animal immortality compelling or not, he has at least touched on a neglected theme in academic theology. The larger context for this presentation could be what theologians call cosmic eschatology. Although Christians usually focus on personal eschatology (death and afterlife) or corporate eschatology (what will happen to human beings at the end of time), cosmic eschatology includes God's transformation of the entire world (cosmos) at the end of time.[43] Apocalyptic texts such as Isaiah's peaceable kingdom (Isa 11:6–9) hint at this transformation.

Isaiah also notes that God will "create new heavens and a new earth" (Isa 65:17). John echoes this theme in Revelation 21.

Some Bible students see an emphasis on cosmic redemption in passages such as Colossians 1:20 and Ephesians 1:9-10. Since animals do not sin and carry the burden of guilt as humans do, they do not need salvation in the strict sense of forgiveness of sins. These two texts by Paul, however, present the entire world as taken up in God's redemptive process. God has a plan to "gather up all things" in Christ (Eph 1:10). Like-

> **Will the lion really lie down with the lamb?**

wise, God intends through Christ "to reconcile to himself all things whether on earth or in heaven, by making peace through the blood of his cross" (Col 1:20). By placing animal immortality within the context of cosmic eschatology, Webb offers a position that is more theocentric or cosmocentric that Lewis's position. As a result, he explores how Christians can move from "the passion of the canophile," meaning our love for our dogs and other companion animals, to "a zoophilic compassion for all animals."[44]

Although Lewis and Webb both affirm at least the possibility of animal immortality, they differ in significant ways. For instance, Lewis is more anthropocentric in his approach, suggesting that pets might be in heaven because of their relationship to humans. Webb is more theocentric than Lewis when he argues that animals might be in heaven because of God's grace, not merely because of their relation to humans.

SENTIMENTALITY OR SYSTEMATIC THEOLOGY?

A recent opinion poll indicates that Americans have a divided mind about animal immortality. When asked "Do pets go to heaven?" 43 percent answered "yes," 40 percent said "no," and 17 percent said they had no opinion. Even pet owners were only slightly more positive, with 47 percent saying "yes."[45] Some people worry that those who affirm animal immortality are motivated more by wishful thinking than logical or theological reflection. A pet owner's affection for his pet might incline him to hope his dog would be in heaven with him. Since the Bible and tradition are relatively silent on this issue, are we left with mere speculation?

Questions for Further Reflection

Both Lewis and Webb tackle this issue as Christian theologians, although Lewis is more of a lay theologian. Both raise many of the issues that a systematic theologian would need to investigate to reach a conclusion about animal immortality. Any Christian who wants to think seriously about animal immortality would need to consider these as well. Although Webb stresses cosmic eschatology in his discussion of animal immortality, he also notes that Christian theologians typically discuss animals in relation to three topics: creation, humanity, and the problem of evil.[46] C. S. Lewis, for instance, treats animal immortality in the context of his theodicy. Here I will briefly mention four basic issues as a good starting point for further systematic reflection.

Is animal immortality wishful thinking?

First, the character of God is crucial to any discussion of animal immortality. Webb's argument that all animals may be included in God's future plans is based on his view of God as concerned with the entirety of his creation. Webb's overall argument is more theocentric than Lewis's. Lewis's argument that domestic animals may go to heaven because of their relationship to human beings is more anthropocentric than Webb's view.

Second, our view of human nature is basic to the discussion. For example, how do humans differ from non-human animals? Most theologians stress the image of God as what distinguishes humans, but many lay people focus on whether or not animals have souls.

Third, do animals need salvation? Some Christians see heaven as part of God's answer to the human predicament of sin. Do animals have free will? If not, how can they sin? Webb notes that animals do not sin, but they need God's grace. "Redemption is not from sin alone. It is from everything that distorts fulfillment, including pain and premature loss of life."[47]

Fourth, how do animals relate to the cosmic Christ theme of the Bible? Webb devotes a section in his earlier book to this neglected topic.[48] While some theologians highlight the specificity of Jesus' incarnation, others note the cosmic dimensions of his role, which could affect one's view of animals.

Questions such as these four and others need serious consideration for a full-scale theological response to the question of animal immortality. Webb and Lewis have given us some preliminary explorations into this field.

Christian Responsibility for Animals

If Lewis's and Webb's views on animal suffering and animal immortality have merit, how should Christians react? Christians might respond by examining other animal related issues. For example, some Christians are concerned about animal rights and the use of animals in experimentation. Also, some Christians have advocated vegetarianism as the proper diet for God's people. For instance, Webb's latest discussion of animal immortality is part of a book promoting vegetarianism. Andrew Linzey notes, "Of all the ethical challenges arising from animal theology, vegetarianism can arguably claim to have the strongest support."[49] Christian vegetarians note that God allows the eating of meat after the flood, but in the Garden of Eden and in the period before the flood, the ideal diet was meatless. Critics of vegetarianism note that Paul identifies vegetarianism as a view held by "weak" Christians, meaning less liberated or less mature in the faith (Rom 14:1–2). Tony Campolo offers a mediating position. "In this hierarchy of life, there is nothing wrong with sacrificing lower forms of life in order to sustain higher forms of life. Vegetarianism may be a good idea, but it is not a biblical mandate for this present age."[50]

Those convinced that animal suffering is a serious issue for Christians will look for other concrete applications of this view.

Hunting for recreation, animal experimentation, puppy mills, and other issues may deserve careful attention. Political action, prayer, education, and other responses are appropriate ways to respond to animal suffering as well as human suffering. Your view of creation, stewardship, and the relation of humans to the entire non-human world are involved in any serious decision making in this arena.

Chapter Fourteen

A THEODICY FOR LIVING IN THE REAL WORLD

Human life is the dialogue between expectation and experience."[1] With those words, Douglas John Hall captures the source of much suffering in this world. We expect life, God, or other people to treat us fairly, but we soon learn from living in the real world that life is tough. "Life is difficult . . . Life is a series of problems" states a famous counselor.[2] Many survivors of the proverbial school of hard knocks have also concluded that life is not fair.

Since I am a college teacher, I am familiar with the traditional distinction between the academic world, or the so-called ivory tower, and the real world. According to this distinction, college students might somehow be exempt from the struggles of real life. I'm not sure this distinction is accurate, however, since some of my students have seen parents die from cancer, had best friends betray them, helped in disaster

> **How do we live in a world in which we suffer?**

relief, seen poverty firsthand on mission trips to other countries, and encountered racial and gender discrimination. The academic world seems very real at times to my students and to me!

People in the so-called real world and in the academic world often ask "Where is the God of justice?" (Mal 2:17). Although the people quoted by Malachi may have been more sarcastic than sincere in asking this question, their question epitomizes the concern of many suffering people. The issue of theodicy summed up in the question "Is God just?" is a perennial concern for God's people who suffer in the real world.

PRACTICAL RELEVANCE OF OUR STUDY

My focus in this book has been on concrete examples of human suffering, with brief attention to divine suffering and animal suffering as well. Generally, I have followed the womb to tomb journey of the human life span, looking at types of suffering typical of each part of human life. So, we have already been doing a theodicy for life in the real world. In other words, this book has been an attempt to develop a theology of suffering for life in the real world.

In this concluding chapter I want to reinforce the practical relevance of what we have studied so far. Some books on evil and suffering are very theoretical. The theological and philosophical issues related to evil and suffering are complex and deserve a Christian's best, clearest thinking. Sometimes, however, writers on theodicy forget to demonstrate the practical relevance of a clearer understanding of God and suffering.[3] One writer critiques "the evil of theodicy," suggesting that some philosophical and theological studies do more harm than good. Past attempts to provide a rational solution to the "problem of evil" have often silenced the voices of suffering people.[4] By highlighting concrete suffering situations, I hope to have avoided the "evil" of theodicy.[5]

THREE SUGGESTIONS

Be Practical

Theodicy as an intellectual enterprise often dwells on the issue of the origin of suffering. Is suffering caused by God, the devil, natural forces, human sin, or some mysterious cause? Although we glanced at such issues along the way, our focus has also been on how Christians can respond to their own suffering and the suffering experienced by others in light of the Bible. Above all, we do not want to become like Job's unwelcome friends. James Cone, a leading theologian, states that Christians need to focus their energies on responding practically to suffering and not worry too much about its source. "The weight of the biblical view of suffering in not on the *origin* of evil but on what God in Christ has done about evil. According to the New Testament, God became human in Jesus Christ, and defeated decisively the power of sin, death, and Satan, thereby bestowing upon us the freedom to struggle against suffering which destroys humanity."[6]

Ask Clear Questions

German theologian Jürgen Moltmann has struggled with the issue of God's relation to suffering since the bombing of his hometown in World War II and his three years as a prisoner of war.[7] He helpfully distinguishes two kinds of questions about suffering. The first question is a theoretical question, the onlooker's question, the question of theodicy: Why did God let this happen? The second question is a more existential question, the question of a sufferer: Does God suffer with me?[8] As a sufferer, Moltmann wants to know if God cares about his situation. This study has dealt with both kinds of questions, but I have tried to be especially sensitive to the latter existential question.

> **What are the practical implications of this study of suffering?**

Know Your Needs

In a similar vein, Daniel Simundson notes that people respond to suffering on two levels, the intellectual and the survival levels. In terms of this helpful distinction, our study has been primarily on the survival level: "The *survival level* is concerned with the 'how' rather than the 'why' of suffering."[9] Although I believe our ideas and our actions are interdependent, I agree that some people respond more to the intellectual difficulties of belief in a good God in the face of crises and others attend more directly to practical concerns.

In this concluding chapter, then, I will direct our attention to some biblical examples of faithful responses to suffering. These stories will illustrate how people of faith living in the real world have dealt with life's difficulties. There are still no simple, easy answers to the theodicy issue, but these biblical people remind us how we should live in our world, a world still interrupted by life's problems.

REVERENT CREATIVITY

God's people respond in a variety of ways to life's problems. Two stories illustrate an approach I call reverent creativity. Rather than being permanently overwhelmed by their problems or resigning themselves to their situations, these people creatively respond from the resources of their faith in God.

How Reverent Creativity Saved Moses

First, let's look at the way Moses' parents respond to persecution by the Egyptians. The oppression of the Hebrews illustrates again the problem of moral evil, or people's inhumanity to each other as it has often been labeled. Moses' birth must have caused mixed feelings for his parents, identified as Amram and Jochebed later in the story (Exod 6:20). Mingling with their joy at the birth of a child was the awareness that the Pharaoh had ordered the killing of all Hebrew male infants. The new Pharaoh is concerned at the fertility of the Hebrews. The males resulting from this Hebrew population explosion might eventually join Egypt's enemies and revolt against Egypt (Exod 1:10). The Hebrews are forced to work on Egyptian building projects, but they still manage to reproduce. Eventually the Pharaoh orders the Hebrew midwives to kill the baby boys they deliver.

Civil disobedience

How could a Hebrew family respond to this injustice? They could follow the king's orders, but more likely they considered other options. One such option is civil disobedience. [10] The two midwives disobey the Pharaoh's edict by secretly refusing to throw the male children they deliver into the Nile. Like later Christian advocates of civil disobedience, they could have argued that the Pharaoh's policy was immoral. In the chapter on violence, we looked at Martin Luther King's endorsement of civil disobedience as a strategy for social change. God does not expect the Hebrews to obey human law when it conflicts with God's commands. Although the ten commandments had not yet been given, the Hebrews know that killing an innocent person is wrong (Gen 9:6).

Lying to save a life

Another option is deception. A Hebrew family might lie about the arrival of a new baby boy. The midwives tell the Egyptians that the Hebrew women are so "vigorous" that they deliver their babies before the midwives can arrive (Exod 1:19). Like the families in World War II that hid Jews from the Nazis, these Hebrews might argue that lying to save life is a valid exemption to the usual policy of truth telling.

Fleeing

Flight is another response to injustice. Some Hebrews might have considered trying to escape Egypt. Would the Egyptians try to track down every missing slave family? Maybe the Hebrews could try to establish a kind of underground railroad like the one that helped slaves escape the South in the 19th century. Flight is sometimes the best response to a bad situation. Mary and Joseph take the baby Jesus to Egypt to escape Herod's slaughter of baby boys in Bethlehem. David flees when Saul tries to kill him, and David flees the city of Jerusalem when Absalom leads a political coup. Today, victims of spouse abuse often seek a safe haven from further verbal and physical abuse. People flee to safe rooms or storm shelters when tornadoes threaten. Flight does not necessarily reflect a lack of faith in God or his ability to do miracles.

Miriam's reverent creativity

We do not know what options Amram and Jochebed consider, but their daughter Miriam takes her baby brother and places him in a small basket in the Nile River. The family had hidden the baby boy as long as was feasible, but a new plan was needed. Miriam watches the basket "to know what would happen to him" (Exod 2:4). Speculation can be dangerous, but I wonder if Miriam and the rest of the family had researched this section of the Nile. Perhaps they knew that Pharaoh's daughter often bathed here. Perhaps they hoped she would be less cruel than her father.

When Pharaoh's daughter discovers the baby, she soon realizes the boy is Hebrew. Rather than report her discovery to her father or any other official, she protects the boy. Miriam approaches the king's daughter and offers to find a nurse for the presumed orphan. Miriam does not lie directly, but she creatively does not tell all she knows. With the princess's permission Miriam finds a nurse— Moses' own mother! Jochebed is able to nurse her son for awhile before he joins the princess.

Miriam's actions might raise ethical concerns for some moral purists. For example, is withholding part of the truth the same as lying? Should Miriam have told the Pharaoh's daughter the whole story, hoping Moses would still be safe? One commentator notes that one lesson we can learn from this story is to trust God and act responsibly.[11] For some Christians, trusting God suggests total passivity or quietism. "Let go and let God" could be dangerous when someone evil is using violence to wipe out others.

We do not know all the factors that entered into Miriam's decision making process, but she followed the strategy I call reverent creativity. Lewis Smedes writes that when we cannot be sure about the right moral decision, we can still be responsible.[12] Perhaps Miriam and her parents would endorse Jesus' later advice to his followers as they entered a hostile situation: "See, I am sending you out like sheep into the midst of wolves; so be wise as serpents and innocent as doves" (Matt 10:16). Those who advocate a policy of Christian non-violence especially look for creative ways to respond to physical and verbal attack.[13]

The reverent creativity of Ruth and Naomi

Another example of this reverent resourcefulness can be found in the story of Ruth and Naomi. Naomi suffers so much that we might fairly call her the female Job. We are not told about a heavenly discussion between God and Satan as in the case of Job, but Naomi suffers in several ways. The famine that drives her and her family from Bethlehem to Moab will illustrate again what the scholars call natural evil. The famine is not presented as divine punishment for Hebrew sin. Famines and droughts occurred naturally then, as they do now. Naomi later attributes all of her problems to God's action, just as Job assumes God is behind his suffering. Besides the famine, Naomi suffers the loss of her husband and her two sons.

When the famine is over, Naomi is ready to return to Bethlehem. Although she urges her two daughters-in-law to stay in Moab, Ruth insists on going with Naomi. When the two widows arrive in Bethlehem, Naomi changes her own name from Naomi, meaning "pleasant," to Mara, meaning "bitter," for, she states, "the Almighty has dealt bitterly with me. I went away full, and the Lord has brought me back empty; why call me Naomi, when the Lord has dealt harshly with me, and the Almighty has brought calamity upon me?" (Ruth 1:20-21).

If we did not know the rest of this story, we might assume that Naomi lived a life consumed with bitterness about her misfortune. You and I know people that have maintained that kind of bitter attitude, soured on life in general and angry at God. The story actually takes a different turn because of the actions of Ruth. This younger widow offers to work in the fields to support them. Apparently the Moabite Ruth knows enough about Hebrew law and custom to realize that a farmer should leave some leftovers for the poor and needy to glean (Lev 19:9-10).

The Hebrew storyteller might have expected the reader to smile at the transitional statement "As it happened, she came to the part of the field belonging to Boaz," a relative of Naomi's family (Ruth 2:3). What seems like chance or happenstance is a turning point for Ruth and Naomi. Boaz protects Ruth and provides food for her and Naomi.

The growing relationship between Ruth and Boaz can be read several ways, but I suspect they were falling in love. When Naomi learns these two have met each other, she plays the role of self-appointed matchmaker. Eventually, Naomi tells Ruth to present herself to Boaz one night.

Both Ruth and Boaz are aware of the legal practice of the kinsman redeemer. Although another man is closer kin to Ruth's dead husband, he does not want to redeem Ruth. Ruth and Boaz are soon married and produce a child that is in the family tree of King David and Jesus.

The actions of Ruth and Naomi both illustrate reverent creativity in response to life's problems. Rather than waiting on someone else to help them, Ruth is proactive, going into the fields to find food. Naomi demonstrates her resourcefulness by encouraging a relationship that will gain Ruth a new husband and support the family economically as well.

Where is God while Naomi's family suffers? As in the story of Miriam and Moses' infancy, God performs no miracles. God again is in the background more than the foreground of the story. Naomi blames God for her misfortunes, but she prays that God will be kind to her two daughters-in-law (Ruth 1:8–9). Naomi feels that God's hand has been against her (1:13), but her underlying conviction in God's goodness is not totally shaken. Indeed, Ruth is so impressed with Naomi's faith in God that she wants to follow him too, turning her back on her culture and her Moabite religion.

Reverent Creativity Today

How do we practice reverent creativity today? Christians can respond to suffering in a number of ways. First, they can pray for God's guidance in their decision making. As we saw earlier in our study, however, prayer and problem solving are not mutually exclusive approaches to suffering. If we face a serious illness, we faithfully pray for healing, but we also seek out the best medical care we can find. Miriam probably prayed about the fate of baby Moses, but she used human ingenuity to reduce the risk of his death. If our suffering today is infertility, for instance, we might attempt technological assistance in reproduction as an expression of reverent creativity. Such technological advances may be a God-given way of solving a problem rather than playing God in the medical arena.

Some Christians today follow the strategy of reverent resource-fulness in other arenas as well. For example, some work diligently through the political process to alleviate sources of suffering. Jürgen Moltmann, for example, encourages a political hermeneutic of the gospel.[14] The good news about Jesus has political implications. Without striving for a theocracy, Christians can tackle issues such as racial discrimination, sexism, war, spouse abuse, and ageism. Molt-mann quotes the social gospel theologian Walter Rauschenbusch to support his emphasis on social action: "Ascetic Christianity called the world evil *and left it.* Humanity is waiting for a revolutionary Christianity which will call the world evil *and change it.*"[15] Without endorsing the excesses of the social gospel, we can be politically ac-tive, working for the improvement of our society.

Reverent creativity recognizes that the total elimination of suf-fering will be God's prerogative at the end of time. In the meantime, however, Christians can wisely tackle many kinds of suffering. Prayer, political activism, medical technology, and other forms of Christian response to human suffering fit under the umbrella of rev-erent creativity.

Reverent creativity can be both reactive and proactive. When a tornado strikes, many government agencies and private groups react by springing into action to respond to the destruction brought by the tornado. Other actions might be proactive. Dietrich Bonhoeffer is re-ported to have said that "it is not only my task to look after the victims of madmen who drive a motorcar in a crowded street, but to do all in my

> **How do we practice reverent creativity today?**

power to stop their driving at all."[16] Scientists and meteorologists can develop ways to track tornadoes more successfully, thereby pre-venting the loss of life.

Reverent creativity and creation stewardship

Reverent creativity might be understood as a case study in the doctrines of creation and stewardship. In the Genesis 1 account of creation, God tells humans that they have "dominion" over the created world. The development of science and technology can be seen as legitimate expressions of the divine assignment. To borrow an example from earlier in our study, my eye glasses solve my eye problems. God enabled someone to develop the technology that allows me to read and write more easily. That technology is not playing God but is, rather, a responsible use of God's dominion task for humanity.

Stewardship involves a grateful response to God's goodness and a wise appropriation of his gifts. To respond with total passivity in the face of suffering is poor stewardship of the talents God has given us. Although stewardship encompasses more than money, stewardship can involve the way we use our financial resources. We help alleviate human suffering when we support humanitarian organizations such as Habitat for Humanity with our funds. Money given for medical research on the causes and treatment of life-threatening and debilitating diseases is another helpful response to suffering. Our concern for suffering can also affect our career choices. I often encourage my college students to investigate the helping professions; they may not offer as much financial reward, yet they help suffering people.

Overcoming evil with good

The Apostle Paul encourages Christians to respond to evil with good. "Do not be overcome by evil, but overcome evil with good" (Rom 12:21). Reverent creativity is one expression of Paul's overall strategy for dealing with everything negative in the real world.

One helpful way to classify practical Christian attempts to overcome evil with good is to divide them into pastoral and political responses. By "pastoral" responses I do not mean actions limited to what the pastor of a church might perform. Rather, I mean actions such as praying with and for suffering people. A pastoral response includes being sensitive to the stages of suffering, discussed in the introductory chapter. What we say, if anything, to a suffering person may depend on where they are in the stages of suffering. When they first learn of the death of a loved one, suffering people may not need to hear any words of comfort or advice. A hug might be enough reassurance for a grieving person.[17]

"Political" responses to suffering include traditional political actions such as lobbying, legislation, and running for office. I would also include volunteering for humanitarian groups such as the Red Cross and other social service agencies. According to Richard Bauckham and Trevor Hart, concerned Christians need to find the middle way between quietism and prometheanism: "Christian hope is thus neither promethean nor quietist. It neither attempts what can only come from God nor neglects what is humanly possible. Sustained by the hope of everything from God, it attempts what is possible within the limits of each present."[18] This perspective displays what I have called reverent creativity. Christians should not be guilty of quietism, or doing nothing, in the face of human suffering. Neither should Christians practice prometheanism assuming we can eliminate all suffering through our actions. Instead, we should strive to follow God's lead in alleviating suffering whenever we can.

GROPING FOR GOD

One of the most gripping accounts of suffering I read as I researched this book was a small work by Hubert G. Locke. Like many of us, he has suffered in several ways. The three events or experiences that triggered his reflections were the deaths of his parents, his academic research on the Holocaust, and his experiences as a black man suffering racial prejudice. Like many sufferers, he identifies with the plea of the man who wants Jesus to heal his son: "I believe; help my unbelief" (Mark 9:24).[19] Locke's reflections remind us that doubt is often an essential component or dimension in authentic faith. Locke also identifies his experience as "groping for God," a phrase he borrows from Acts 17:26-27. The Apostle Paul at the Areopagus in Athens describes the Gentiles as people who "search for God and grope for him." Locke concludes, "Groping for

God is what we find we must do, after we have discovered that nothing else in this world is worth the effort."[20]

Asking Questions

For Christians who struggle with suffering, asking questions
about God's justice and goodness may sometimes feel awkward.
Questioning God may seem sinful or, at least, theologically inappro-
priate. Locke and many other Christians have learned that doubt
can be "a supreme act of faith and devotion."[21] Some doubt leads to
a denial of God, but, as we saw in the experience of C. S. Lewis, a sufferer may doubt the goodness of God for a while.

Another powerful account of suffering is Nicholas Wolterstorff's *Lament for a Son*, in which he records his grief over the death of
his son, Eric, in a mountain climbing accident. A professor emeritus
of philosophical theology at Yale Divinity School, Wolterstorff experienced a wide range of emotions and thoughts as he grieved. He
had studied some of the theodicies that tried to explain suffering,
but he found them unsatisfactory. "To the most agonized question I
have ever asked I do not know the answer. I do not know why God
would watch him fall. I do not know why God would watch me
wounded. I cannot even guess . . . My wound is an unanswered question."[22] Wolterstorff did not lose his faith in God, but he could not
find answers to this doubts. Later in his reflections he found some
help in the notion of God suffering with him.[23]

Humans may be programmed to ask questions. Daniel Boorstin describes humans as seekers: "But we are *all* Seekers. We all
want to know *why*. Man is the asking animal."[24] In Willie Morris's
novel *Taps*, a boy is troubled by pastors that are dogmatic in their approach to theology. A friend tells the boy, "They don't have any question marks . . . Ain't life itself a question mark?"[25] As we have seen
throughout this study, the Bible rarely gives us simple or simplistic
answers. Many people in the Bible are groping for God as they
struggle to find answers to their questions.

Many Christians have learned that asking questions of God is
a crucial component of faith. Doubt in the sense of refusing to believe is unhealthy, but doubt in the sense of asking honest questions

is essential to our relationship with God. Paul Tillich in a classic study denoted several kinds of doubt. The kind of doubt experienced by C. S. Lewis, Hubert Locke, Nicholas Wolterstorff, and many other sufferers is existential doubt. As Tillich notes: "If doubt appears, it should not be considered the negation of faith, but as an element which was always and will always be present in the act of faith. Existential doubt and faith are poles of the same reality, the state of ultimate concern."[26] Sufferers often ask God questions. Many will eventually find some help through their study of the Bible, conversations with mature Christian friends, and prayer. Their asking questions such as "Is God just?" will be part of their pilgrimage of faith.

I suggested in the introductory chapter that in this life we will learn only partial answers to our questions about God and suffering. Here I agree with British theologian Paul Fiddes: "There cannot be a totally satisfactory theodicy, in the literal sense of the word, which is an intellectual 'justification of God' ... But I believe that we can at least work towards a theodicy with the more modest aim of thinking of God and suffering together."[27] This book has been an effort at "thinking of God and suffering together," a theology of suffering rather than a philosophical justification of God.

> **Is doubt okay?**

Summary of God's Relation to Suffering

Some of the partial, provisional perspectives about God's relation to suffering dealt with in this book can be summarized briefly. These perspectives are rooted in the Bible, and they provide believers some insight into suffering. First, some suffering is the result of human sin. Sin, such as rape or racial discrimination, inflicts suffering on other people. Sin can also lead to suffering for the sinner. A drug addict, for example, suffers long-term consequences from her addiction. We looked at the doctrine of retribution earlier and learned that it is not a comprehensive explanation of suffering. Some suffering seems innocent or undeserved, although it could be caused by the sinful actions of other people.

Second, traditional Christians acknowledge the reality of Satan, who can play a role in causing suffering. Giving the devil too much credit, however, might lead to a non-biblical form of dualism. The Book of Job is a key text for seeing how God allows Satan to cause some suffering.

Third, God allows some suffering as a test of our faith. As a result of our suffering we might gain a deeper understanding of ourselves and of God. Late in his reflections on his grief for his son, Nicholas Wolterstorff comments: "In the valley of suffering, despair and bitterness are brewed. But there also character is made. The valley of suffering is the vale of soul-making."[28]

Fourth, suffering can be redemptive. The supreme example of this perspective is Jesus. Isaiah's songs about the suffering servant, especially Isaiah 52–53, are understood by Christians to foreshadow Jesus' innocent, vicarious suffering for sinners. Sometimes our suffering can be redemptive or sacrificial, at least in the popular sense that we suffer for the good of others.

Fifth, some suffering is due to natural forces producing tornadoes, hurricanes, and floods. Rather than call these "acts of God," many Christians suggest that the physical world has been fallen since the sin of Adam and Eve. Other Christians propose that sinful actions today contribute to global warming and other environmental concerns. Others suggest that Satan influenced the world even before the sin of the first humans.

Can humans be free without suffering?

Sixth, many Christians, especially those who grope for God, consider mystery the best biblical perspective. They resist all glib, overly pious answers. They look forward to a time and place when God will explain why bad things happened to them and those they loved.

Seventh, biblical perspectives about the relation of God and suffering reflect your view of God. Does God cause suffering? The view I have suggested throughout this study is that God is not necessarily the direct cause of suffering. God created a world in which bad things can happen, but a monergistic view of God creates many theological difficulties. Although the Bible affirms God's sovereignty over his creation, the Bible also consistently teaches that God loves and cares for us. The next section will explore a theology, a doctrine of God, that I have found helpful in my struggles with the question, Is God just?

THE GOD WHO WOOS

Suffering prompts questions about God's character. Some sufferers may lose their faith in God's power, but many struggle more with God's goodness. The attitude of many people today, inside and outside of the church, is captured in C. S. Lewis's famous phrase, "God in the dock." Lewis notes that people in the ancient world generally understood they were sinners on trial before God. Now people envision a different scene:

> For the modern man the roles are reversed. He is the judge: God is in the dock. He is a quite kindly judge: if God should have a reasonable defence for being the god who permits war, poverty and disease, he is ready to listen to it. The trial may even end in God's acquittal. But the important thing is that Man is on the Bench and God in the Dock.[29]

God Cannot Ravish

My goal in this section is not to develop a full-scale doctrine of God. Sufferers often question either God's goodness or his power. One of the most helpful insights in my own pilgrimage of faith comes from C. S. Lewis. In Lewis's *Screwtape Letters* the senior devil says humans sometimes wonder why God never reveals himself more directly. Surely people would quickly acknowledge him if his reality were more obvious. God, however, refuses to override human freedom the devil says wisely: "But you now see that the Irresistible and the Indisputable are the two weapons which the very nature of His scheme forbids Him to use . . . He cannot ravish. He can only woo."[30] Throughout our study we have seen that sufferers struggle with their experience of God's absence in their lives. Where is the God of justice? Why doesn't God answer my prayers? How could God let this happen? What didn't God stop this? My God, my God, why have you forsaken me? Questions such as these reflect a sense of the absence of God or of his lack of concern for our suffering.

People often expect an all-powerful, loving God to exempt them from all pain and suffering. Yet suffering happens to most of us. The ongoing "dialogue between expectation and experience," to return to Douglas John Hall's apt description of life, makes us wonder about God. We hope that our problems will go away, that our lives will be free from pain and free from trouble.

The Centrality of the Incarnation

A distinctively Christian theology of suffering, such as C. S. Lewis suggests in the quotation from The Screwtape Letters, is rooted and grounded in Christology. Our view of God must be defined in light of God's revelation in the life, death, and resurrection of Jesus. Too often the problem of theodicy is discussed in light of an abstract notion of God, a kind of theoretical monotheism. Jürgen Moltmann and many other contemporary theologians have reminded us that our theology must be distinctively Trinitarian and Christocentric.[31]

We need to define God's power and love in light of God's revelation in Jesus. The Apostle Paul points to this reversal of traditional notions of divine power: "For God's foolishness is wiser than human wisdom, and God's weakness is stronger than human strength" (1 Cor 1:25). For some theologians this move to a more distinctively Christian understanding of God's power involves the retrieval of a theology of the cross.[32]

Many contemporary theologians stress the special relationship between Christology and theodicy. Thomas Oden, for instance, affirms that "A high Christology is the key to a deep-going theodicy. . . . The best Christian theodicy flows directly out of the cross."[33] In other words, a genuinely Christian theodicy needs to be based on the story of Jesus, including his death and resurrection.

Rest from suffering

One of the most famous sayings from Jesus' teachings can help us see how we can deal with our suffering when God's presence does not seem obvious to us. Jesus states:

Come to me, all you who labor and are carrying heavy burdens, and I will give you rest. Take my yoke upon you, and learn from me; for I am gentle and humble in heart, and you will find rest for your souls. For my yoke is easy, and my burden is light. (Matt 11:28-30)

The picture alongside this text in the Good News Bible depicts a person carrying a large box, a person with a cane, a person on crutches, a person seated with his head down, and a woman with several children. The artist tries to help readers envision the kinds of burdens people bear in the real world. Physical limitations, depression, and heavy responsibilities might be what Jesus has in mind. Some scholars suggest Jesus is primarily concerned with the burden of legalism imposed by the religious leaders of his day. Eugene Peterson renders part of this text "Are you tired? Worn out? Burned out on religion?"[34]

Whatever burdens or troubles us, Jesus offers us rest. I admit that when I think of "rest" I imagine the total lack of activity. Rest, to me, suggests a playful, relaxing vacation. Rest might mean total escape from life's problems. Sometimes God does miraculously eliminate our problems. For example God parts the waters of the Red Sea so the Hebrews can leave Egypt. I like the comment in a comic strip several years ago. A heavenly voice tells the Hebrews, "This is a one time opportunity, not an entitlement." Miracles are rare, and most of the time we trust in God while we respond actively to our problems.

Surprisingly, the "rest" Jesus offers us includes a yoke, a large object placed on oxen and cattle in order to lead them. How could wearing a yoke be compatible with rest? Bible scholars note that a well-fitted yoke does not oppress an animal. The animal can accomplish its task without injury. A relationship with Jesus does not guarantee a pain-free existence, but Jesus promises that he will make our tasks bearable.

Discipleship

Above all, Jesus invites us to become his student. We can learn from him if we commit to being his disciples. Jesus consistently teaches the original disciples that suffering is essential to his messiahship and that his followers will suffer in this life. Even the first disciples have trouble accepting this view of Jesus, since it contradicts their preference for a trouble-free life. Simon Peter, for instance, later rebukes Jesus for predicting his crucifixion (Matt 16:22). Jesus considers a passionless messiahship as another satanic temptation.

Instead of the total elimination of our troubles in this life, Jesus offers us a new relationship. Rather than the fantasy of a restful vacation, Jesus calls his followers to the vocation of discipleship. In his service we will still face cancer, discrimination, and tornadoes, but we can respond to them with reverent creativity. Our relationship to Jesus should lead to Christian action in the world to alleviate suffering.

> There is no christology without christopraxis, no knowledge of Christ without the practice of Christ. We cannot grasp Christ merely with out heads or our hearts. We come to understand him through a total, all-embracing practice of living; and that means discipleship.[35]

God's Wooing Love

The God who woos us does not give us a subpoena. Hosea describes God's patient, forgiving response to the sinful Hebrew nations as a wooing process. Israel is like an unfaithful wife, but God tries to win her back. "I will woo her, I will go with her into the wilderness and comfort her" (Hosea 2:14 NEB). The God whose essence is love (1 John 4:8) voluntarily limits the exercise of his power for the sake of relationship. Wooing epitomizes a loving relationship. God suffers when his people disobey him, and they sometimes experience his tough love. Ultimately, God woos his people back to him.

The Jesus who offers his disciples an easy yoke later tells the church at Laodicea that he is knocking on their door. He will not knock the door down; he knocks requesting permission to enter his own church again. The God who woos will not ravish, according to Lewis, but he works in and through his people to alleviate suffering in this world. At the end of time all suffering will disappear. The old hymn "Wonderful Words of Life" suggests that Jesus' words are "wooing us to heaven."[36] In the meantime, we must live faithfully in the real world. We are called both to a relationship with God's Son and to the task of reverent creativity.

One of the best short statements of a Christian approach to suffering, which incorporates both belief and behavior, comes from S. Paul Schilling: "The Christian stance toward evil is therefore two-faceted: it involves trust in a power that far exceeds our highest human capacities, a power that can be relied on because God is ultimately and supremely good; and it arouses in those who have this trust a commitment to become co-laborers with God in the struggle against the negativities of existence."[37] The task of being "co-laborers with God" is central to the strategy I have called reverent creativity.

NOTES

PREFACE

1. All Bible references are from the New Revised Standard Version unless otherwise noted.

2. For example, Pamela J. Scalise, "To Fear or Not to Fear: Questions of Reward and Punishment in Malachi 2:17–4:3," *RevExp* 84 (1987): 410. For a more full study of suffering in Malachi, see John Oswalt, *Where Are You, God? Malachi's Perspectives on Injustice and Suffering* (Nappanee, Ind.: Evangel Publishing House, 1999).

3. Peter Kreeft, *Making Sense Out of Suffering* (Ann Arbor, Mich.: Servant, 1986), 16.

4. Warren McWilliams, *When You Walk Through the Fire* (Nashville: Broadman, 1986).

5. Shirley C. Guthrie, *Christian Doctrine* (rev. ed.; Louisville: Westminster John Knox, 1994), 167.

INTRODUCTION: IS GOD JUST?

1. Joyce G. Baldwin, *Haggai, Zechariah, Malachi* (TOTC 24; Downers Grove, Ill.: InterVarsity, 1972), 241–42.

2. For a short, recent treatment of God's justice, see Jürgen Moltmann, *In the End–The Beginning: The Life of Hope* (trans. Margaret Kohl; Minneapolis: Fortress, 2004), 53–78.

3. For a study that follows a canonical approach to the Bible see Warren McWilliams, *When You Walk Through the Fire* (Nashville: Broadman, 1986).

4. Walter Brueggemann, *Theology of the Old Testament: Testimony, Dispute, Advocacy* (Minneapolis: Fortress, 1997), 739. For a collection of

classic discussions, see James L. Crenshaw, *Theodicy in the Old Testament* (Philadelphia: Fortress, 1983).

5. John E. Thiel, *God, Evil, and Innocent Suffering: A Theological Reflection* (New York: Crossroad Publishing, 2002), ix, highlights these two different approaches.

6. For example, John G. Stackhouse, *Can God Be Trusted? Faith and the Challenge of Evil* (New York: Oxford University Press, 1998), 11, cites Epicurus and then David Hume as sources; Ted M. Dorman, *A Faith for All Seasons* (2d ed.; Nashville: Broadman & Holman, 2001), 88, cites Epicurus as the source of this trilemma. For an excellent recent collection of essays, see Peter van Inwagen, ed., *Christian Faith and the Problem of Evil* (Grand Rapids: Eerdmans, 2004).

7. For example, Daniel L. Migliore, *Faith Seeking Understanding* (Grand Rapids: Eerdmans, 1991), 119.

8. Kenneth Surin, *Theology and the Problem of Evil* (New York: Blackwell, 1986).

9. Ibid., 101–4. For a more full analysis, see Stackhouse, *Can God Be Trusted?* 34–44, and S. Paul Schilling, *God and Human Anguish* (Nashville: Abingdon, 1977), 24–28.

10. Langdon Gilkey, *Shantung Compound: The Story of Men and Women Under Pressure* (New York: Harper & Row, 1966).

11. Migliore, *Faith Seeking Understanding,* 107; more broadly see 104–14.

12. A classic overview of the history of theodicy is John Hick, *Evil and the God of Love* (London: Collins, 1968). For a history from the perspective of process theology, see David Ray Griffin, *God, Power, and Evil: A Process Theodicy* (Philadelphia: Fortress, 1976). For a short overview, see John Bowker, *Problems of Suffering in Religions of the World* (London: Cambridge University Press, 1970), 81–98.

13. For a good overview of recent literature, see Dan R. Stiver, "The Problem of Theodicy," *RevExp* 93 (1996): 507–17. For more popular theodicies, see David Nelson Duke, "Theodicy at the Turn of Another Century, an Introduction," *PRSt* 26 (1999): 241–51.

14. Lucien Richard, *What Are They Saying About the Theology of Suffering?* (New York: Paulist, 1992). Richard included chapters on Walter Brueggemann, Edward Schillebeeckx, Jürgen Moltmann, Johannes B. Metz, Dorothee Soelle, Gustavo Gutierrez, and Stanley Hauerwas.

15. For short introductions to the doctrine of providence, see Roger E. Olson, *The Mosaic of Christian Belief* (Downers Grove, Ill.:

InterVarsity, 2002), 177-97, and Alister E. McGrath, *Christian Theology: An Introduction* (3d ed.; Oxford: Blackwell, 2001), 284-95. For fuller treatments see Georgia Harkness, *The Providence of God* (New York: Abingdon, 1960); Terrance Tiessen, *Providence & Prayer* (Downers Grove, Ill.: InterVarsity, 2000); and John Sanders, *The God Who Risks: A Theology of Providence* (Downers Grove, Ill.: InterVarsity, 1998).

16. Paul S. Fiddes, *Participating in God: A Pastoral Doctrine of the Trinity* (Louisville: Westminster John Knox, 2000), 7-8, explains pastoral theology. Suffering is the focus of his chapter five.

17. Lewis Joseph Sherrill, *The Struggle of the Soul* (New York: Macmillan, 1951).

18. Gail Sheehy, *Passages: Predictable Crises of Adult Life* (New York: Bantam, 1977).

19. William Shakespeare, "As You Like It," Act II, Scene 7.

20. For a short introduction to narrative theology, see Stanley J. Grenz and Roger E. Olson, *Twentieth-Century Theology: God and World in a Transitional Age* (Downers Grove, Ill.: InterVarsity, 1992), 271-85.

21. Jürgen Moltmann, *In the End—The Beginning*. For a more strictly chronological review, see Richard Dayringer, *Life Cycle: Psychological and Theological Perspectives* (Binghampton, N.Y.: Haworth Press, 2000).

22. David Keck, *Forgetting Whose We Are: Alzheimer's Disease and the Love of God* (Nashville: Abingdon, 1996) and John Goldingay, *Walk On: Life, Loss, Trust, and Other Realities* (Grand Rapids: Baker Academic, 2002).

23. For a sympathetic treatment of Lewis' life, see Roger Lancelyn Green and Walter Hooper, *C. S. Lewis, A Biography* (New York: Harcourt Brace Jovanovich, 1974).

24. C. S. Lewis, *The Problem of Pain* (New York: Macmillan, 1962), 9.

25. Ibid., 10.

26. Ibid., 28.

27. Ibid., 42-46.

28. Ibid., 10.

29. George Sayer, *Jack: C. S. Lewis and His Times* (San Francisco: Harper & Row, 1988), 168-74.

30. Douglas John Hall, *God and Human Suffering: An Exercise in the Theology of the Cross* (Minneapolis: Augsburg, 1986), 168.

31. John Beversluis, *C. S. Lewis and the Search for Rational Religion* (Grand Rapids: Eerdmans, 1985), 163. For another study of Lewis'

reaction, see Richard L. Purtill, "Did C. S. Lewis Lose His Faith?" in *A Christian for All Christians* (ed. Andrew Walker and James Patrick; London: Hodder & Stoughton, 1990), 27-62.

32. C. S. Lewis, *A Grief Observed* (New York: Bantam, 1976), 4-5.

33. Ibid., 35.

34. Ibid., 44.

35. Ibid., 5. See the helpful comparison of Lewis and Sigmund Freud in Armand M. Nicholi, Jr., *The Question of God: C. S. Lewis and Sigmund Freud Debate God, Love, Sex, and the Meaning of Life* (New York: Free Press, 2002), 187-215.

36. William Nicholson, *Shadowlands* (New York: Plume, 1991).

37. Elizabeth Kubler-Ross, *On Death and Dying* (New York: Macmillan, 1969), 34-121.

38. A. N. Wilson, *C. S. Lewis: A Biography* (New York: W. W. Norton, 1990), 283. See Wayne E. Oates, *Grief, Transition, and Loss: A Pastor's Practical Guide* (Minneapolis: Fortress, 1997), 40-42.

39. Dorothee Soelle, *Suffering* (trans. Everett R. Kalin; Philadelphia: Fortress, 1975), 61-86. Richard F. Vieth, *Holy Power, Human Pain* (Bloomington, Ind.: Meyer Stone, 1988), 114-22, offers a similar scheme. For a scheme of eight stages, see Erika Schuchardt, *Why Is This Happening to Me?* (Minneapolis: Augsburg, 1989). Some experts suggest communities pass through similar stages after a disaster. See Karen Klinka, "Bomb's Emotional Scars Heal at Different Rates, Experts Say," *The Sunday Oklahoman*, 30 April 1995, 17.

40. Lewis, *A Grief Observed*, 5.

41. See Migliore, 111-12 for a brief overview.

42. Lewis, *A Grief Observed*, 38.

43. Ibid., 41.

44. C. S. Lewis, *The Screwtape Letters* (New York: Macmillan, 1978), 36.

45. C. S. Lewis, *Mere Christianity* (New York: Macmillan, 1952), 123.

46. For the quotation, see Warren W. Wiersbe, *From Worry to Worship: Studies in Habakkuk* (Wheaton, Ill.: Victor, 1983).

47. Quoted in R. B. Y. Scott, *The Way of Wisdom in the Old Testament* (New York: Macmillan, 1971), 140-41.

48. Peter Kreeft, *Making Sense Out of Suffering* (Ann Arbor, Mich.: Servant, 1986).

49. D. A. Carson, *How Long, O Lord? Reflections on Suffering and Evil* (Grand Rapids: Baker, 1990).

50. The literature on Job is extensive. *RevExp* 99 (Fall 2002) is a theme issue on Job. Also helpful are the popular studies by Dick and Sue Rader, *A Road Beyond the Suffering: An Experiential Journey through the Book of Job* (Franklin, Tenn.: Providence House, 1997) and Bill Thomason, *God on Trial: The Book of Job and Human Suffering* (Collegeville, Minn.: Liturgical Press, 1997).

51. Austin Farrer, *A Faith of Our Own* (Cleveland: World, 1960), 34.

52. John Sanders, *The God Who Risks: A Theology of Providence* (Downers Grove, Ill.: InterVarsity, 1998), 90.

53. E. Frank Tupper, *A Scandalous Providence: The Jesus Story of the Compassion of God* (Macon, Ga.: Mercer University Press, 1995), 3.

54. John R. Claypool, *Tracks of a Fellow Struggler* (rev. ed.; New Orleans: Insight, 1995), 61-77.

55. *Hymnbook for Christian Worship* (St. Louis: Bethany Press, 1970), number 46, verse 1.

1. IS SUFFERING A PUNISHMENT FOR SIN?

1. Daniel J. Simundson, *Where Is God in My Suffering? Biblical Responses to Seven Searching Questions* (Minneapolis: Augsburg, 1983). His first question, "Do I Deserve This?" relates to this chapter's topic.

2. Warren McWilliams, *When You Walk Through the Fire* (Nashville: Broadman, 1986), 47.

3. Daniel J. Simundson, *Faith Under Fire: Biblical Interpretations of Suffering* (Minneapolis: Augsburg, 1980), 17-41. Simundson offers a careful analysis of this theme and presents others in the Bible as well.

4. For a classic study, see Klaus Koch, "Is There a Doctrine of Retribution in the Old Testament?" in *Theodicy in the Old Testament* (ed. James L. Crenshaw; Philadelphia: Fortress, 1983), 57-87. For a study set in a the larger context of the Old Testament's "theodic settlement" see Walter Brueggemann, "Some Aspects of Theodicy in Old Testament Faith," *PRSt* 26 (1999): 253-68.

5. For example, see C. K. Barrett, *The Gospel According to John* (2d ed.; Philadelphia: Westminster, 1978), 356.

6. See W. Sibley Towner, *How God Deals with Evil* (Philadelphia: Westminster, 1976), 22. Towner puts retribution within the larger context of God's redemptive purpose in history.

7. For my earlier reflections on this issue, see Warren McWilliams, "Is Suffering a Punishment for Sin?" *Search* 19 (Winter 1989): 7-10.

8. See James L. Crenshaw, *A Whirlpool of Torment: Israelite Traditions of God as an Oppressive Presence* (Philadelphia: Fortress, 1984), 93-109.

9. For non-technical discussions of Job, see Dick and Sue Rader, *A Road Beyond the Suffering: An Experiential Journey through the Book of Job* (Franklin, Tenn.: Providence House, 1997), and Bill Thomason, *God on Trial: The Book of Job and Human Suffering* (Collegeville, Minn.: Liturgical Press, 1997).

10. Arthur Ashe and Arnold Rampersad, *Days of Grace: A Memoir* (New York: Ballentine, 1993) is Ashe's autobiography.

11. William Powell Tuck, *Getting Past the Pain: Making Sense of Life's Darkness* (Macon, Ga.: Peake Road, 1997), 55-70; Carson, *How Long, O Lord?* 253-64.

12. Adapted from John Paterson, *The Book That Is Alive: Studies in Old Testament Life and Thought as Set Forth by the Hebrew Sages* (New York: Charles Scribner's Sons, 1954), 90-91.

13. Lewis, *Problem of Pain*, 8.

2. DOES GOD CAUSE TORNADOES?

1. Pat Gilliland, "No Simple Answers in Dealing with Ordeal, Ministers Say," *Daily Oklahoman*, 5 May 1999, 23.

2. Brenda J. Sanders, "Why Does God Allow Disasters to Happen?" *The Baptist Messenger*, 8 October 1992, 13.

3. Cited in Leslie D. Weatherhead, *Why Do Men Suffer?* (7th ed.; London: Student Christian Movement Press, 1947), 114.

4. Cited in S. Paul Schilling, *God and Human Anguish* (Nashville: Abingdon, 1977), 131-32.

5. For an overview of the topic, see Weatherhead, *Why Do Men Suffer?* 100-119, and George Arthur Buttrick, *God, Pain, and Evil* (Nashville: Abingdon, 1966), 38-55. For a more technical discussion, see D. K. Chester, "The Theodicy of Natural Disasters," *SJT* 51 (1998): 485-504.

6. Chester, "The Theodicy of Natural Disasters," 485-87. For a recent study that highlights apocalyptic, see David C. Toole, "Divine Ecology and the Apocalypse: A Theological Description of Natural Disasters and the Environmental Crisis," *ThTo* 55 (January 1999): 547-61.

7. David Nelson Duke, "Theodicy at the Turn of Another Century, An Introduction," *PRSt* 26 (Fall 1999): 242-48.

8. See Gary Harbaugh, *Act of God/Active God: Recovering from Natural Disasters* (Minneapolis: Fortress, 2001) for a pastoral perspective based on lengthy service with the Lutheran Disaster Response program.

9. See the observation of A. J. Conyers, "After the Hurricane," *Christianity Today* 9 (1992): 34-36, about the public reaction to hurricane Hugo.

10. L. B. Miller, Jr., "Disappointing Answer," *Baptist Message*, 22 October 1992, 2.

11. For a good overview, see Duane A. Garrett, *Angels and the New Spirituality* (Nashville: Broadman & Holman, 1995), especially 27-49 on Satan. See also Marvin E. Tate, "Satan in the Old Testament," *RevExp* 89 (Fall 1992): 461-74. For a more full treatment, see Elaine Pagels, *The Origin of Satan* (New York: Random House, 1995).

12. Fiddes, *Participating in God*, 116-24, summarizes and critiques this view of God's actions.

13. Richard F. Vieth, *Holy Power, Human Pain* (Bloomington, Ind.: Meyer Stone, 1988), 27; Kreeft, *Making Sense of Suffering*, 38.

14. Douglas John Hall, *God & Human Suffering: An Exercise in the Theology of the Cross* (Minneapolis: Augsburg, 1986), 62. See also, Schilling, 95-118, for a review of several types of dualism.

15. For a recent evangelical defense of the role of Satan and evil spirits highlighting the problem of evil, see Gregory A. Boyd, *Is God to Blame? Beyond Pat Answers to the Problem of Suffering* (Downers Grove, Ill.: InterVarsity, 2003), 17-19. Boyd earlier developed this warfare worldview in his *God at War: The Bible and Spiritual Conflict* (Downers Grove, Ill.: InterVarsity, 1997) and *Satan and the Problem of Evil* (Downers Grove, Ill.: InterVarsity, 2001). In *Satan and the Problem of Evil*, 242-318, Boyd devotes three chapters to alternative views of natural evil and his own view.

16. For example, Wayne Grudem, *Bible Doctrine: Essential Teachings of the Christian Faith* (ed. Jeff Purswell; Grand Rapids: Zondervan, 1999), 349.

17. Elizabeth Achtemeier, *Nature, God, and Pulpit* (Grand Rapids: Eerdmans, 1992), 112.

18. B. W. Woods, *Christians in Pain* (Grand Rapids: Baker, 1974), 37.

19. Sallie McFague, *Life Abundant: Rethinking Theology and Economy for a Planet in Peril* (Minneapolis: Fortress, 2001), 153.

20. "Legislators Strike Religious Phrase," *Dallas Morning News*, 27 March 1997, 35A.

21. John Sanders, *The God Who Risks: A Theology of Providence* (Downers Grove, Ill.: InterVarsity, 1998), 81–87.

22. Ibid., 59–61.

23. Sanders, *The God Who Risks*, 213–17.

24. Donald G. Bloesch, *Essentials of Evangelical Theology, Volume 1* (New York: Harper & Row, 1982 reprint), 28.

25. Sanders, *The God Who Risks*, 81, 87.

26. Georgia Harkness, *The Providence of God* (New York: Abingdon, 1960), 89.

27. Weatherhead, *Why Do Men Suffer?* 120–37. On the will of God, see also Leslie D. Weatherhead, *The Will of God* (New York: Abingdon-Cokesbury, 1944), Morris Ashcraft, *The Will of God* (Nashville: Broadman, 1980), and Garry Friesen with J. Robin Maxson, *Decision Making & the Will of God: A Biblical Alternative to the Traditional View* (Portland, Ore.: Multnomah, 1980).

28. John Calvin, *Institutes of the Christian Religion* (trans. Ford Lewis Battles; Philadelphia: Westminster, 1960), 1:198–99; for a good overview, see Ted M. Dorman, *A Faith for All Seasons* (2d ed.; Nashville: Broadman & Holman, 2001), 90–95.

29. Sanders, *The God Who Risks*, 227, prefers divine restraint to self-limitation.

30. Ibid., 160.

31. For a brief analysis of belief in a finite God, see Millard J. Erickson, *Christian Theology, Volume 1* (Grand Rapids: Baker, 1983), 414–17.

32. Harkness, *The Providence of God*, 105.

33. Harold S. Kushner, *When Bad Things Happen to Good People* (New York: Avon, 1983 reprint), 113.

34. Ibid., 134.

35. Dorman, *A Faith for All Seasons*, 115–16.

36. Hall, *God and Human Suffering*, 154–55.

37. Warren McWilliams, *When You Walk Through the Fire* (Nashville: Broadman, 1986), 158.

3. DOES GOD SUFFER?

1. Elie Wiesel, *Night* (trans. Stella Rodway; New York: Avon, 1969), 76.

2. Jürgen Moltmann, *The Crucified God* (trans. R. A. Wilson and John Bowden; New York: Harper & Row, 1974), 274. Moltmann has been one of the main advocates of divine suffering in contemporary theology. For short analyses of his view, see Warren McWilliams, *The Passion of God: Divine Suffering in Contemporary Protestant Theology* (Macon, Ga.: Mercer University Press, 1985), 25-49, Vieth, *Holy Power, Human Pain*, 99-104, and Lucien Richard, *What Are They Saying About the Theology of Suffering?* (Mahwah, N.J.: Paulist, 1992), 42-57.

3. Ronald Goetz, "The Suffering God: The Rise of a New Orthodoxy," *Christian Century* 16 (April 1986): 385-89.

4. Dennis Ngien, "The God Who Suffers," *Christianity Today*, 3 February 1997, 38-42.

5. Joni Eareckson and Steven Estes, *When God Weeps: Why Our Sufferings Matter to the Almighty* (Grand Rapids: Zondervan, 1997).

6. Thomas G. Weinandy, *Does God Suffer?* (Notre Dame: University of Notre Dame Press, 2000) offers a traditional rejection of divine suffering.

7. Dietrich Bonhoeffer, *Letters and Papers from Prison* (rev. and enl. ed.; New York: Macmillan, 1967), 188.

8. For brief studies, see McWilliams, *The Passion of God*, 10-16, and Alister E. McGrath, *Christian Theology: An Introduction* (3d ed.; Cambridge, Mass.: Blackwell, 1997), 274-75. For fuller analyses, see H. Wheeler Robinson, *Suffering Human and Divine* (New York: Macmillan, 1939), 139-200, and George Arthur Buttrick, *God, Pain, and Evil* (Nashville: Abingdon, 1966), 84-97.

9. Moltmann, *The Crucified God*, 267-70.

10. Paul S. Fiddes, *The Creative Suffering of God* (Oxford: Clarendon, 1988), 16-45.

11. Fiddes, *The Creative Suffering of God*, 40. For a short study of a process theologian on divine suffering, see, McWilliams, *The Passion of God*, 119-46, on Daniel Day Williams.

12. McGrath, *Christian Theology*, 276-77.

13. For a recent exploration, see Douglas John Hall, *The Cross in Our Context: Jesus and the Suffering World* (Minneapolis: Fortress, 2003).

14. Abraham J. Heschel, *The Prophets, Part II* (New York: Harper & Row, 1975 reprint), 56.

15. Terence E. Fretheim, *The Suffering of God: An Old Testament Perspective*, (OBT; Philadelphia: Fortress, 1984).

16. For insightful short studies, see Vieth, *Holy Power, Human Pain*, 86-109, and D. A. Carson, *How Long, O Lord?* (Grand Rapids: Baker Book House, 1990), 179-95.

17. Fretheim, *The Suffering of God*, 120.

18. For an excellent study, see Diane Bergant, "Compassion in the Bible," in *Compassionate Ministry* (ed. Gary L. Sapp; Birmingham, Ala.: Religious Education Press, 1993), 9-34.

19. Ibid., 130-36.

20. Ibid., 136.

21. Ibid., 138.

22. Fiddes, *The Creative Suffering of God*, 12-13; McGrath, *Christian Theology*, 252. For a specialized study, see Dennis Ngien, *The Suffering of God According to Martin Luther's 'Theologia Crucis'* (New York: Peter Lang, 1995).

23. Carson, *How Long, O Lord?* 187-88.

24. John R. W. Stott, *The Cross of Christ* (Downers Grove, Ill.: InterVarsity, 1986), 329-37.

25. Ibid., 331.

26. Moltmann, *The Crucified God*, 192.

27. For example, see Jürgen Moltmann and Elisabeth Moltmann-Wendel, *Passion for God: Theology in Two Voices* (Louisville: Westminster John Knox, 2003), 69-85, for his reaffirmation of his thinking thirty years after the publication of *The Crucified God*.

28. S. Paul Schilling, *God and Human Anguish* (Nashville: Abingdon, 1977), 235.

29. For an earlier version of my thinking, see *The Passion of God*, 173-91.

30. T. B. Maston, *Biblical Ethics: A Survey* (Waco, Tex.: Word, 1967), 282.

31. William Barclay, *New Testament Words* (Philadelphia: Westminster, 1974), 276. For a provocative study of the Hebrew word for

compassion, see Phyllis Trible, *God and the Rhetoric of Sexuality* (OBT; Philadelphia: Fortress, 1978), 38-56.

32. For a good introduction, see T. B. Maston, *To Walk as He Walked* (Nashville: Broadman, 1985), 113-27.

33. Wayne Whitson Floyd Jr., "Compassion in Theology," in *Compassionate Ministry*, 48.

34. James H. Cone, *God of the Oppressed* (New York: Seabury, 1975), 177.

4. HOW LONG, O LORD?

1. E. Frank Tupper, *A Scandalous Providence: The Jesus Story of the Compassion of God* (Macon, Ga.: Mercer University Press, 1995), 435.

2. Vieth, *Holy Power, Human Pain*, 114.

3. For a recent overview, see Hans Schwarz, *Eschatology* (Grand Rapids: Eerdmans, 2000).

4. For example, Stanley J. Grenz, *Theology for the Community of God* (Nashville: Broadman & Holman, 1994), 743-846. Jürgen Moltmann, *The Coming of God: Christian Eschatology* (trans. Margaret Kohl; Minneapolis: Fortress, 1996), 321-39, treats a fourth category, "Glory: Divine Eschatology."

5. For contemporary treatments of the theology of history, see Langdon Gilkey, *Reaping the Whirlwind: A Christian Interpretation of History* (New York: Seabury, 1976) and Eric C. Rust, *Towards a Theological Understanding of History* (New York: Oxford University Press, 1963).

6. For a nice overview of major "Images of Hope," see Richard Bauckham and Trevor Hart, *Hope Against Hope: Christian Eschatology at the Turn of the Millennium* (Grand Rapids: Eerdmans, 1999), 109-73.

7. Peter DeVries, *The Blood of the Lamb* (New York: Popular Library, 1961).

8. For a good introduction, see Simundson, *Faith Under Fire*, 43-61.

9. James L. Crenshaw, *A Whirlpool of Torment* (Philadelphia: Fortress, 1984), 31-56, examines Jeremiah's confessions.

10. Simundson, *Where Is God in My Suffering*, 21.

11. Bernhard W. Anderson, *Out of the Depths: The Psalms Speak for Us Today* (rev. and exp. ed., Philadelphia: Westminster, 1983), 76-77.

For the laments outside of the Psalms, see Samuel E. Balentine, *Prayer in the Hebrew Bible: The Drama of Divine-Human Dialogue* (OBT; Minneapolis: Fortress, 1993), 146-98.

12. For a brief discussion, see Jürgen Moltmann, *Jesus Christ for Today's World* (trans. Margaret Kohl; Minneapolis: Fortress, 1994), 34-36.

13. Walter Brueggemann, *The Message of the Psalms: A Theological Commentary* (Minneapolis: Augsburg, 1984), 19.

14. Simundson, *Faith Under Fire*, 44-50.

15. Simundson, *Where Is God in My Suffering?* 26.

16. Shirley C. Guthrie, *Christian Doctrine* (rev. ed.; Louisville: Westminster John Knox, 1994), 385.

17. Harold Kushner, *When All You've Ever Wanted Isn't Enough* (New York: Pocket Books, 1987), 34.

18. For example, James L. Crenshaw, *Old Testament Wisdom: An Introduction* (Atlanta: John Knox, 1981), 129-33, on "Death Cancels Everything."

19. Simundson, *Faith Under Fire*, 113.

20. Richard Bauckham, *The Theology of the Book of Revelation* (Cambridge: Cambridge University Press, 1993), 8.

21. Ibid., 121.

22. D. A. Carson, *How Long, O Lord? Reflections on Suffering and Evil* (Grand Rapids: Baker Book House, 1990), 136, says this tension between the already and the not yet of God's kingdom is "a commonplace of biblical thought."

23. Oscar Cullmann, *Christ and Time* (trans. Floyd Filson, rev. ed.; Philadelphia: Westminster, 1964), 84-85. For a short introduction to contemporary eschatology, especially views of the kingdom of God, see A. J. Conyers, *A Basic Christian Theology* (Nashville: Broadman & Holman, 1995), 203-30.

24. James C. Peterson, *Genetic Turning Points: The Ethics of Human Genetic Intervention* (Grand Rapids: Eerdmans, 2001), 349, acknowledges that genetic intervention can improve our lives but will not "bring heaven or a utopia."

25. Grenz, *Theology for the Community of God*, 855.

26. Ibid., 857.

27. Keillor's program is *A Prairie Home Companion* on National Public Radio.

5. INFERTILITY

1. Sallie McFague, *Life Abundant: Rethinking Theology and Economy for a Planet in Peril* (Minneapolis: Fortress, 2001), 178. McFague was commenting on Annie Dillard's views.

2. Lynda Rutledge Stephenson, *Give Us a Child: Coping with the Personal Crisis of Infertility* (San Francisco: Harper & Row, 1987), 168-88.

3. Stanley Grenz, *Sexual Ethics: A Biblical Perspective* (Dallas: Word, 1990), 147-48.

4. Ibid., 147.

5. Gilbert Meilaender, *Bioethics: A Primer for Christians* (Grand Rapids: Eerdmans, 1996), 25.

6. For a good review of "Reproductive Technologies," see Scott B. Rae, *Moral Choices: An Introduction to Ethics* (Grand Rapids: Zondervan, 1995), 137-59. For several relevant essays, see Stephen E. Lammers and Allen Verhey, *On Moral Medicine: Theological Perspectives in Medical Ethics* (Grand Rapids: Eerdmans, 1987), 331-45.

7. Meilaender, *Bioethics*, 22.

8. For an earlier exploration, based on theological principles, see Warren McWilliams, "*In vitro* Fertilization: An Exercise in Biotheology," *Search* 21 (Winter 1992): 29-36.

9. Stanley Hauerwas, *Suffering Presence: Theological Reflections on Medicine, the Mentally Handicapped, and the Church* (Notre Dame, Ind.: University of Notre Dame Press, 1986), 145.

10. Raymond C. Van Leeuwen, "Breeding Stock or Lords of Creation," *Christianity Today* (Nov. 11, 1991): 36.

11. Pamela J. Scalise, " 'I Have Produced a Man with the LORD': God as Provider of Offspring in Old Testament Theology," *RevExp* 91 (Fall 1994): 579-81.

12. Hauerwas, *Suffering Presence*, 145.

13. Daniel B. McGee, "Issues of Life and Death," in *Understanding Christian Ethics: An Interpretive Approach* (ed. William M. Tillman Jr.; Nashville: Broadman, 1988), 231-33.

14. David C. Thomasma, *Human Life in the Balance* (Louisville: Westminster John Knox, 1990), 82-89.

15. Grenz, *Sexual Ethics*, 144.

16. Henlee H. Barnette, *Exploring Medical Ethics* (Macon, Ga.: Mercer University Press, 1982), 88-89.

17. McGee, "Issues of Life and Death," 229.

18. Grenz, *Sexual Ethics*, 150.

19. Robertson McQuilkin, *An Introduction to Biblical Ethics* (Wheaton, Ill.: Tyndale House, 1989), 240.

20. Grenz, *Sexual Ethics*, 153-54.

21. Meilaender, *Bioethics*, 12.

22. Hauerwas, *Suffering Presence*, 143.

23. Ibid., 148. For a similar view of the family and children, see William H. Willimon, *The Service of God: How Worship and Ethics Are Related* (Nashville: Abingdon, 1983), 170-86.

24. Thomas D. Lea, *1, 2 Timothy, Titus* (NAC 34; Nashville: Broadman, 1992), 102.

25. Meilaender, *Bioethics*, 24.

26. Lewis Smedes, *Forgive and Forget: Healing the Hurts We Don't Deserve* (San Francisco: Harper & Row, 1981), 91.

6. ILLNESS AND DISABILITY

1. For a helpful collection of essays on how different types of suffering impact children, see Andrew D. Lester, ed., *When Children Suffer: A Sourcebook for Ministry with Children in Crisis* (Philadelphia: Westminster, 1987). Relevant to this chapter are essays on children who are hospitalized, terminally ill, chronically ill, disabled, or who experience learning disabilities.

2. Edwin Hui, "Sickness," in *The Complete Book of Everyday Christianity* (ed. Robert Banks and R. Paul Stevens; Downers Grove, Ill.: InterVarsity, 1997), 894-95.

3. Mitch Albom, *Tuesdays with Morrie: An Old Man, a Young Man, and Life's Greatest Lesson* (New York: Doubleday, 1997).

4. Harold S. Kushner, *When Bad Things Happen to Good People* (New York: Avon Books, 1981), 2.

5. John Goldingay, *Walk On: Life, Loss, Trust, and Other Realities* (Grand Rapids: Baker Academic, 2002).

6. Frances Young, *Face to Face: A Narrative Essay in the Theology of Suffering* (Edinburgh: T&T Clark, 1990), 22.

7. Jürgen Moltmann, *The Source of Life: The Holy Spirit and the Theology of Life* (trans. Margaret Kohl; Minneapolis, Fortress, 1997), 66-68.

See also, Moltmann, "Liberate Yourselves by Accepting One Another," in *Human Disability and the Service of God* (ed. Nancy L. Eisland and Don E. Saliers; Nashville: Abingdon, 1998), 105-22. For further discussion, see Nancy L. Eisland, *The Disabled God* (Nashville: Abingdon, 1994).

8. For example, see Barbara Milligan, *Desperate Hope: Experiencing God in the Midst of Breast Cancer* (Downers Grove, Ill.: InterVarsity, 1999) and Mac N. and Anne Shaw Turnage, *Grace Keeps You Going: Spiritual Wisdom from Cancer Survivors* (Louisville: Westminster John Knox, 2001).

9. Elizabeth T. Hall, *Caring for a Loved One with Alzheimer's Disease: A Christian Perspective* (New York: Haworth Pastoral Press, 2000), 40.

10. David Keck, *Forgetting Whose We Are: Alzheimer's Disease and the Love of God* (Nashville: Abingdon, 1996), 13-20.

11. Robertson McQuilkin, *A Promise Kept* (Wheaton, Ill.: Tyndale House, 1998).

12. Archibald D. Hart, "Depression," in *The Complete Book of Everyday Christianity* (Robert Banks and R. Paul Stevens, eds.; Downers Grove, Ill.: InterVarsity, 1997), 287-91).

13. For a classic study, see Wayne E. Oates, *Behind the Masks: Personality Disorders in Religious Behavior* (Philadelphia: Westminster, 1987). For several essays on psychiatric issues, see Stephen E. Lammers and Allen Verhey, eds., *On Moral Medicine* (2d ed.; Grand Rapids: Eerdmans, 1998), 817-82.

14. For several essays about the mentally handicapped, see Hauerwas, *Suffering Presence,* 159-217.

15. For fuller discussions of the biblical data, see Michael L. Brown, *Israel's Divine Healer* (Grand Rapids: Zondervan, 1995), and Klaus Seybold and Ulrich B. Mueller, *Sickness & Healing* (trans. Douglas W. Stott; Nashville: Abingdon, 1981). For shorter treatments, see Erhard S. Gerstenberger and Wolfgang Schrage, *Suffering* (trans. John E. Steely; Nashville: Abingdon, 1980), 34-41, 159-61, and Allen Verhey, *Remembering Jesus: Christian Community, Scripture, and the Moral Life* (Grand Rapids: Eerdmans, 2002), 79-154.

16. Seybold and Mueller, *Sickness & Healing,* 67-74.

17. Brown, *Israel's Divine Healer,* 99.

18. Ibid., 221, 227-29.

19. Ibid., 47-53.

20. Seybold and Mueller, *Sickness & Healing,* 24-34.

21. Seybold and Mueller, *Sickness & Healing,* 35.

22. See the brief treatment in Roy Porter, *The Greatest Benefit to Mankind: A Medical History of Humanity* (New York: W. W. Norton, 1997), 87–88.

23. Daniel J. Simundson, "Health and Healing in the Bible," *WW* 2 (Fall 1982): 335–36.

24. For example, Larry Dossey, *Prayer Is Good Medicine: How to Reap the Benefits of Prayer* (San Francisco: HarperSanFrancisco, 1996).

25. Dallas Willard, *The Divine Conspiracy: Rediscovering Our Hidden Life in God* (San Francisco: HarperSanFrancisco, 1998), 247–50.

26. C. S. Lewis, *Miracles: A Preliminary Study* (New York: Macmillan, 1960), 5.

27. For a good introduction to biblical and theological issues, see Colin Brown, *That You May Believe: Miracles and Faith Then and Now* (Grand Rapids: Eerdmans, 1985).

28. Nancy Gibbs, "The Message of Miracles," *Time* 10 April 1995, 65.

29. Dana Blanton, "More Believe in God than Heaven," n.p. [cited 1 June 2004]. Online: http://www.foxnews.com/printer_friendly_story/0,3566,99945.00.html.

30. Dan Wakefield, *Expect a Miracle: The Miraculous Things that Happen to Ordinary People* (San Francisco: HarperSanFrancisco, 1995).

31. Adapted from Wayne A. Grudem, *Are Miraculous Gifts for Today? Four Views* (Grand Rapids: Zondervan, 1996). I have combined the third wave and pentecostal/charismatic categories. For a fuller typology, see John N. Newport, *Life's Ultimate Questions: A Contemporary Philosophy of Religion* (Dallas: Word, 1989), 170–83, on miracles, providence, and intercessory prayer.

32. For brief introductions, see David L. Smith, *A Handbook of Contemporary Theology* (Wheaton, Ill.: Bridgepoint, 1992), 227–40, and Carson, *How Long, O Lord?* 123–26.

33. Grudem, *Are Miraculous Gifts for Today?* 12–13.

34. C. S. Lewis, *Christian Reflections* (ed. Walter Hooper; Grand Rapids: Eerdmans, 1967), 142–51.

35. Ibid., 150.

36. Simundson, "Health and Healing in the Bible," 330.

37. Ibid.

38. Gerstenberger and Schrage, *Suffering*, 152–55.

39. Brown, *Israel's Divine Healer*, 30.

40. Simundson, "Health and Healing in the Bible," 336.

41. Ibid., 337.

42. T. B. Maston, *God Speaks Through Suffering* (Waco, Tex.: Word, 1977), 63.

7. BETRAYAL OF TRUST

1. Stanley J. Grenz and Roy D. Bell, *Betrayal of Trust: Sexual Misconduct in the Pastorate* (Downers Grove, Ill.: InterVarsity, 1995).

2. See two popular books by Lewis B. Smedes, *The Art of Forgiving: When You Need to Forgive and Don't Know How* (Nashville: Moorings, 1996) and *Forgive and Forget: Healing the Hurts We Don't Deserve* (San Francisco: Harper & Row, 1984). A little more academic is L. Gregory Jones, *Embodying Forgiveness: A Theological Analysis* (Grand Rapids: Eerdmans, 1995). *Christian Reflection* (2001) has an excellent theme issue on forgiveness.

3. *Anchor Bible Dictionary* (1992).

4. For a collection of excerpts on friendship, see Eudora Welty and Ronald A. Sharp, eds., *The Norton Book of Friendship* (New York: Norton, 1991).

5. William J. Ireland, Jr., "Friend, Friendship," *HoBD*, 515; see also S. H. Blank, "Friend, Friendship," *IDB* 2:325 and Stephen J. Andrews, "Friendship," *MDB*, 310. For a good discussion of biblical and historical materials, see R. Paul Stevens, "Friendship," in *The Complete Book of Everyday Christianity* (ed. Robert Banks and R. Paul Sevens; Downers Grove, Ill.: InterVarsity Press, 1997), 435-42.

6. For a recent exploration of this theme, see Sallie McFague, *Models of God: Theology for an Ecological, Nuclear Age* (Philadelphia: Fortress, 1987), 157-80.

7. C. S. Lewis, *The Four Loves* (New York: Harcourt Brace Jovanovich, 1960), 88. For a valuable study of friendship, see Gilbert Meilaender, *Friendship: A Study in Theological Ethics* (South Bend, Ind.: University of Notre Dame Press, 1985).

8. Lewis, *Four Loves*, 91.

9. C. S. Lewis, *Letters to Malcolm: Chiefly on Prayer* (New York: Harcourt Brace Jovanovich, 1964), 106.

10. Phyllis Trible, *Texts of Terror: Literary-Feminist Readings of Biblical Narratives* (OBT; Philadelphia: Fortress, 1984), 93–116.

11. John Gray, *Men Are from Mars, Women Are from Venus* (New York: HarperCollins, 1992).

12. For a provocative study of the way promiscuous wives were depicted in Hosea, Jeremiah, and Ezekiel, see Renita J. Weems, *Battered Love: Marriage, Sex, and Violence in the Hebrew Prophets* (Minneapolis: Fortress, 1995).

13. Lewis B. Smedes, *Mere Morality: What God Expects from Ordinary People* (Grand Rapids: Eerdmans, 1983), 169–72.

14. Richard J. Foster, *Money, Sex & Power: The Challenge of the Disciplined Life* (San Francisco: Harper & Row, 1985), 162.

15. For good reviews of the key issues, see Glen H. Stassen and David P. Gushee, *Kingdom Ethics: Following Jesus in Contemporary Context* (Downers Grove, Ill.: InterVarsity, 2003), 271–87; Richard B. Hays, *The Moral Vision of the New Testament* (San Francisco: HarperSanFrancisco, 1996), 347–78; David Instone-Brewer, *Divorce and Remarriage in the Bible: The Social and Literary Context* (Grand Rapids: Eerdmans, 2002); Grenz, *Sexual Ethics*, 99–125; and Diana R. Garland, "The Church and Divorce," *RevExp* 92 (1995): 419–34.

16. H. Wayne House, ed., *Divorce and Remarriage: Four Christian Views* (Downers Grove, Ill.: InterVarsity, 1990).

17. Craig S. Keener, *And Marries Another: Divorce and Remarriage in the Teaching of the New Testament* (Peabody, Mass.: Hendrickson, 1991), 104–10.

18. The title of a fine theological study: John G. Stackhouse, *Can God Be Trusted? Faith and the Challenge of Evil* (New York: Oxford University Press, 1998).

19. Philip Yancey, *Disappointment with God: Three Questions No One Asks Aloud* (Grand Rapids: Zondervan, 1988), 35–36.

20. For a classic study of these kinds of texts, see James L. Crenshaw, *A Whirlpool of Torment: Israelite Traditions of God as an Oppressive Presence* (OBT; Philadelphia: Fortress, 1984).

8. VIOLENCE

1. For example, Stanley Hauerwas and Frank Lentricchia, eds., *Dissent from the Homeland: Essays after September 11* (Durham, N.C.: Duke

University Press, 2003) collects essays from several perspectives. For a collection of essays, sermons, interviews, and other reflections, see Donald B. Kraybill and Linda Gehman Peachey, eds., *Where Was God on September 11? Seeds of Faith and Hope* (Scottdale, Pa.: Herald, 2002.) For a short discussion of terrorism, see Edward LeRoy Long, Jr., *Facing Terrorism: Responding as Christians* (Louisville: Westminster John Knox, 2004).

2. For example, the work of Rene Girard on violence has evoked some theological responses. Ted Peters, "Atonement and the Final Scapegoat," *PRSt* 19 (Summer 1992): 151-81, discusses Girard's view that Jesus was a scapegoat. See also Daniel L. Migliore, *Faith Seeking Understanding: An Introduction to Christian Theology* (Grand Rapids: Eerdmans, 1991), 158-61.

3. For a classic study of Jesus' teaching on non-retaliation, see Ronald J. Sider, *Christ and Violence* (Scottdale, Pa.: Herald, 1979).

4. S. J. Mikolaski, "Violence," *Encyclopedia of Biblical and Christian Ethics,* 428-29. This brief article identifies ten contemporary forms of violence.

5. David K. Clark and Robert V. Rakestraw, eds., *Readings in Christian Ethics: Volume 2* (Grand Rapids: Baker, 1996), 493.

6. For a brief treatment of torture, see Jürgen Moltmann, *Jesus Christ for Today's World* (trans. Margaret Kohl; Minneapolis: Fortress, 1994), 58-70.

7. For essays on a wide range of topics see the theme issue on "Christian Responses to Violence," *RevExp* 93 (1996). For an intriguing review of Bible texts, mainly from the Old Testament, see Patricia M. McDonald, *God and Violence: Biblical Resources for Living in a Small World* (Scottdale, Pa.: Herald, 2004).

8. Oscar Hijuelos, *Mr. Ives' Christmas* (New York: HarperCollins, 1995), 8.

9. Dallas Willard, *The Divine Conspiracy: Rediscovering Our Hidden Life in God* (San Francisco: HarperSanFrancisco, 1998), 159.

10. For example, see Glen H. Stassen, "Biblical Teaching on Capital Punishment," *RevExp* 93 (Fall 1996): 485-96; Stassen and Gushee, *Kingdom Ethics,* 194-214; and Christopher D. Marshall, *Beyond Retribution: A New Testament Vision for Justice, Crime, and Punishment* (Grand Rapids: Eerdmans, 2001).

11. Carol J. Adams, *Woman-Battering* (Minneapolis: Fortress, 1994), especially 103-14 on "Suffering and Theology." See also, Betty Coble

Lawther and Jenny Potzler, "The Church's Role in the Healing Process of Abused Women," *RevExp* 98 (2001): 225-41.

12. For a recent study, see Kristen J. Leslie, *When Violence Is No Stranger: Pastoral Counseling with Survivors of Acquaintance Rape* (Minneapolis: Fortress, 2003), especially 99-131 on "A Pastoral Theological Framework."

13. The other famous story is the rape of Dinah (Gen 34).

14. For a good recent study, see Trible, *Texts of Terror*, 37-63.

15. Ibid., 65-91, is a valuable study.

16. John Macquarrie, *The Concept of Peace* (New York: Harper & Row, 1973), 19.

17. Walter Brueggemann, *Peace* (St. Louis: Chalice, 2001) is a valuable shorter study.

18. For a good overview, see Ronald D. Sisk, "World Peace," in *Understanding Christian Ethics: An Interpretive Approach* (ed. William M. Tillman, Jr.; Nashville: Broadman, 1988), 208-14. A classic statement is Roland H. Bainton, *Christian Attitudes Toward War and Peace* (Nashville: Abingdon, 1960). Also, John A. Wood, *Perspectives on War in the Bible* (Macon, Ga.: Mercer University Press, 1998) and Robert G. Clouse, ed., *War: Four Christian Views* (Downers Grove, Ill.: InterVarsity, 1981).

19. Jeph Holloway, "The Ethical Dilemma of Holy War," *SwJT* 51 (Fall 1998): 44-69.

20. Dr. Seuss, *The Butter Battle Book* (New York: Random House, 1984).

21. See the helpful discussion of "The Politics of Providence" in E. Frank Tupper, *A Scandalous Providence: The Jesus Story of the Compassion of God* (Macon, Ga.: Mercer University Press, 1995), 215-67. He includes brief biographical sketches of Christians involved in politics.

22. Cited in Larry Rasmussen, ed., *Reinhold Niebuhr: Theologian of Public Life* (Minneapolis: Fortress, 1991), 15.

9. POVERTY AND HUNGER

1. Gustavo Gutierrez, *A Theology of Liberation: History, Politics and Salvation* (trans. Sister Caridad Inda and John Eagleson; New York: Orbis, 1973), 91-91.

2. Ibid., 108-9. See Stanley J. Grenz and Roger E. Olson, *20th Century Theology: God & the World in a Transitional Age* (Downers Grove, Ill.: InterVarsity, 1992), 211-12, for a brief introduction to Latin American liberation theology.

3. Richard J. Foster, *Money, Sex & Power: The Challenge of the Disciplined Life* (San Francisco: Harper & Row, 1985), 33.

4. W. David Sapp, "The Church and Economic Life," in *Understanding Christian Ethics: An Interpretive Approach* (ed. William M. Tillman, Jr.; Nashville: Broadman, 1988), 169-70.

5. Carson, *How Long, O Lord?* 55-65.

6. Cited in Fiddes, *The Creative Suffering of God*, 108.

7. Ronald J. Sider, *Just Generosity: A New Vision for Overcoming Poverty in America* (Grand Rapids: Baker, 1999), 34-42.

8. Bruce M. Metzger, *The New Testament: Its Background, Growth, and Content* (Nashville: Abingdon, 1965), 221.

9. For a recent review of biblical teaching on economics, see Stassen and Gushee, *Kingdom Ethics*, 409-26.

10. Foster, *Money, Sex & Power*, 19-50.

11. Sapp, *The Church and Economic Life*, 166-67.

12. For a fuller discussion of this commandment, see Lewis B. Smedes, *Mere Morality: What God Expects from Ordinary People* (Grand Rapids: Eerdmans, 1983), 183-209.

13. David Briggs, "Poor Americans Most Likely to Count Blessings, Survey Finds," *Shawnee News-Star*, 28 January 1995, 15.

14. F. F. Bruce, *Paul: Apostle of the Heart Set Free* (Grand Rapids: Eerdmans, 1996 reprint), 142.

15. Rodney Clapp, ed., *The Consuming Passion: Christianity & the Consumer Culture* (Downers Grove, Ill.: InterVarsity, 1998).

16. Sallie McFague, *Life Abundant: Rethinking Theology and Economy for a Planet in Peril* (Minneapolis: Fortress, 2001), 112.

17. For a popular overview, see Randy Petersen, "Modern Voices: The Christian and Money," *Christian History* 6, no. 2 (1987): 28-33. For a recent evangelical defense of capitalism in the context of globalization, see John R. Schneider, *The Good of Affluence: Seeking God in a Culture of Wealth* (Grand Rapids: Eerdmans, 2002).

18. Richard J. Foster, *Freedom of Simplicity* (San Francisco: Harper & Row, 1981).

19. Ronald J. Sider, *Rich Christians in an Age of Hunger: A Biblical Study* (Downers Grove, Ill.: InterVarsity, 1977), 175-78.

20. McFague, *Life Abundant*, 116.
21. Sapp, *The Church and Economic Life*, 169–70.

10. DISCRIMINATION

1. Bruce M. Metzger, *The New Testament: Its Background, Growth, and Content* (Nashville: Abingdon, 1965), 41.

2. The literature on homosexuality is voluminous. Good recent studies include Stanley J. Grenz, *Welcoming but Not Affirming: An Evangelical Response to Homosexuality* (Louisville: Westminster John Knox, 1998), Willard M. Swartley, *Homosexuality: Biblical Interpretation and Moral Discernment* (Scottdale, Pa.: Herald, 2003), and Robert J. Gagnon, *The Bible and Homosexual Practices: Texts and Hermeneutics* (Nashville: Abingdon, 2001).

3. Dr. Seuss, *The Sneetches, and Other Stories* (New York: Random House, 1961).

4. 1. Mary Magdalene, Mary the mother of James, Joanna, Salome, and other women; 2. Deborah; 3. Miriam; 4. Phoebe; 5. Hagar; 6. Ruth, Esther; 7. Anna.

5. Two older, conservative studies are Edith Deen, *All the Women of the Bible* (Edison, N.J.: Castle Books reprint; 1955 original) and Herbert Lockyer, *All the Women of the Bible* (Grand Rapids: Zondervan, n.d.). More recent studies include Audra and Joe Trull, eds., *Putting Women in Their Place: Moving Beyond Gender Stereotypes in Church and Home* (Macon, Ga.: Smyth & Helwys, 2003) and Alice Bach, ed., *Women in the Hebrew Bible: A Reader* (New York: Routledge, 1999).

6. For a good survey of recent views, see Randy Maddox, "The Word of God and Patriarchalism: A Typology of the Current Christian Debate," *PRSt* 14 (Fall 1987): 197–216.

7. Stanley J. Grenz with Denise Muir Kjesbo, *Women in the Church: A Biblical Theology of Women in Ministry* (Downers Grove, Ill.: InterVarsity, 1995), 17–18.

8. Richard N. Ostling, "The Second Reformation," *Time*, 23 November 1992, 53–58.

9. For example, see the theme issue "Women's Leadership in the Church," *RevExp* 95 (Summer 1998).

10. "The Baptist Faith and Message," article 6, "The Church."

11. For good introductions, see Linda Belleville, *Women Leaders and the Church* (Grand Rapids: Baker, 2000) and Bonnidell Clouse and Robert Clouse, eds., *Women in Ministry: Four Views* (Downers Grove, Ill.: InterVarsity, 1989).

12. For a powerful retelling of this tragic event, see Diane Glancy, *Pushing the Bear: A Novel of the Trail of Tears* (San Diego: Harvest Book, 1996).

13. For earlier statements of Indian concerns, see Vine Deloria Jr., *Custer Died for Your Sins, An Indian Manifesto* (New York: Macmillan, 1969) and *God Is Red* (New York: Grosset & Dunlap, 1973). For recent Indian theology, see Clara Sue Kidwell, Homer Noley, and George E. "Tink" Tinker, *A Native American Theology* (Maryknoll, N.Y.: Orbis, 2001).

14. Richard L. Rubenstein, *After Auschwitz: Radical Theology and Contemporary Judaism* (Indianapolis: Bobbs-Merrill, 1966).

15. William Scott Green, "Facing the One God Together," *PRSt* 26 (1999): 314-15.

16. For example, see Jürgen Moltmann, *Jesus Christ for Today's World* (trans. Margaret Kohl; Minneapolis: Fortress, 1994), 108-29; Richard B. Hays, *The Moral Vision of the New Testament* (San Francisco: HarperSanFrancisco, 1996), 407-43; Dan Cohn-Sherbok, ed., *Holocaust Theology: A Reader* (New York: New York University Press, 2002); Sarah Pinnock, *Beyond Theodicy: Jewish and Christian Continental Thinkers Respond to the Holocaust* (Albany: SUNY Press, 2002); and Hubert G. Locke, *Searching for God in Godforsaken Times and Places: Reflections on the Holocaust, Racism, and Death* (Grand Rapids: Eerdmans, 2003).

17. David P. Gushee, *The Righteous Gentiles: A Christian Interpretation* (Minneapolis: Fortress, 1994).

18. For example, see Scot McKnight, "Who Is Jesus? An Introduction to Jesus Studies," in *Jesus Under Fire* (ed. Michael J. Wilkins and J. P. Moreland; Grand Rapids: Zondervan, 1995), 55, and Shirley C. Guthrie, *Christian Doctrine* (rev. ed.; Louisville: Westminster John Knox, 1994), 238.

19. James H. Cone, *A Black Theology of Liberation* (Philadelphia: Lippincott, 1970), 61.

20. For a summary, see Richard Wightman Fox, *Jesus in America: Personal Savior, Cultural Hero, National Obsession* (San Francisco: HarperSanFrancisco, 2004), 361-62.

21. Ralph Ellison, *Invisible Man* (New York: Vintage, 1972 reprint), 3.

22. William Jones, *Is God a White Racist?* (Garden City, N.Y.: Doubleday, 1973).

23. James H. Cone, *God of the Oppressed* (New York: Seabury, 1975), 163-94. For a white theologian's sympathetic response to Cone, see Jürgen Moltmann, *Experiences in Theology: Ways and Forms of Christian Theology* (trans. Margaret Kohl; Minneapolis: Fortress, 2000), 189-216. For a short introduction to Cone's early thought, see Warren McWilliams, *The Passion of God: Divine Suffering in Contemporary Protestant Theology* (Macon, Ga.: Mercer University Press, 1985), 51-71.

24. Sid Smith, "Preparing for Multiethnic Ministry," in William M. Tillman, Jr., ed., *Understanding Christian Ethics: An Interpretive Approach* (Nashville: Broadman, 1988), 150.

25. For an excellent review of biblical material, see J. Daniel Hays, *From Every People and Nation: A Biblical Theology of Race* (Downers Grove, Ill.: InterVarsity, 2003).

26. Willard M. Swartley, *Slavery, Sabbath, War & Women: Case Issues in Biblical Interpretation* (Scottdale, Pa.: Herald, 1983), 31-64, surveys texts used for and against slavery.

27. For a good summary of relevant issues, see Joe E. Trull, *Walking in the Way: An Introduction to Christian Ethics* (Nashville: Broadman & Holman, 1997), 211-23.

28. For example, Timothy George, *Galatians* (NAC 30: Nashville: Broadman, 1994), 285.

29. *Hymns for the Family of God* (Nashville: Paragon, 1976), 15.

30. T. B. Maston, *Interracial Marriage* (Nashville: Christian Life Commission of the Southern Baptist Convention, 1974), 5.

31. Smith, "Preparing for Multiethnic Ministry," 154-56.

32. Donald McGavran, *Understanding Church Growth* (rev. ed.; Grand Rapids: Eerdmans, 1980), 95.

33. Martin Luther King Jr., *Why We Can't Wait* (New York: Mentor, 1964), 76-95.

34. Ibid., 91.

35. Martin Luther King Jr., "The American Dream," in *A Testament of Hope: The Essential Writings and Speeches of Martin Luther King Jr.* (ed. James M. Washington; San Francisco: HarperSanFrancisco, 1986), 213.

11. AGING

1. Gail Sheehy, *Passages: Predictable Crises of Adult Life* (New York: Bantam, 1977).

2. See the excellent collection of essays by Stanley Hauerwas, et al., eds., *Growing Old in Christ* (Grand Rapids: Eerdmans, 2003). For a good overview of issues by a retired pastor, see Robert E. Seymour, *Aging without Apology: Living the Senior Years with Integrity and Faith* (Valley Forge, Pa.: Judson, 1995).

3. Patricia Beattie Jung, "Differences Among the Elderly: Who Is on the Road to Bremen?" in Hauerwas, et al, *Growing Old in Christ,* 113.

4. For an intriguing study from the viewpoint of pastoral and practical theology, see Karen D. Scheib, *Challenging Invisibility: Practices of Care with Older Women* (St. Louis: Chalice, 2004).

5. For a brief treatment, see Stuart Barton Babbage, "Retirement," in *The Complete Book of Everyday Christianity,* 855-59. For a fuller overview, see Johnnie C. Godwin, *Life's Best Chapter: Retirement* (Birmingham: New Hope, 2000).

6. For example, Harold G. Koenig, *Aging and God: Spiritual Pathways to Mental Health in Midlife and Later Years* (New York: Haworth Pastoral Press, 1994); L. Eugene Thomas and Susan A. Eisenhandler, eds., *Religion, Belief, and Spirituality in Late Life* (New York: Springer Publishing Co., 1999); and Eugene C. Bianchi, *Aging as a Spiritual Journey* (New York: Crossroad, 1992).

7. Lewis Joseph Sherrill, *The Struggle of the Soul* (New York: Macmillan, 1963 reprint), 189-219.

8. Ibid., 190.

9. See the collection of essays on the theme of "The Graying of the Church," *RevExp* 88 (Summer 1991).

10. William L. Hendricks, *A Theology for Aging* (Nashville: Broadman, 1986).

11. J. Gordon Harris, *Biblical Perspectives on Aging: God and the Elderly* (Philadelphia: Fortress, 1987), 14.

12. Two outstanding studies are Harris, mentioned in note 11, and Frank Stagg, *The Bible Speaks on Aging* (Nashville: Broadman, 1981). Stagg follows the canonical sequence, while Harris gives a topical treatment.

13. Stagg regularly mentions this bias, preferring to spell it *agism* (e.g., 14, 21).

14. Edith Deen, *All the Women of the Bible* (Edison, N.J.: Castle Books, n.d., 1955 original), 27.

15. Stagg, *The Bible Speaks on Aging,* 58.

16. Donald J. Wiseman, *1 & 2 Kings* (TOTC 9; Downers Grove, Ill.: InterVarsity, 1993), 68 reports this view but does not affirm it.

17. F. F. Bruce, *Paul: Apostle of the Heart Set Free* (Grand Rapids: Eerdmans, 1977), 37.

18. Philip Sellew, "Paul, Martyrdom of," *ABD* 5:204-5.

19. Robert F. Stoops, Jr., "Peter and Paul, Passion of," *ABD* 5:264.

20. Harris, *Biblical Perspectives on Aging*, 105.

21. William Powell Tuck, *Getting Past the Pain: Making Sense of Life's Darkness* (Macon, Ga.: Peake Road, 1997), 102-3.

22. Hendricks, *A Theology for Aging*, 13.

23. Barton Babbage, "Aging," in *The Complete Book of Everyday Christianity* (ed. Robert Banks and R. Paul Stevens; Downers Grove, Ill.: InterVarsity, 1997), 30.

24. Jimmy Carter, *The Virtues of Aging* (New York: Ballantine, 1998).

25. W. H. Lewis, ed., *Letters of C. S. Lewis* (New York: Harcourt Brace Jovanovich, 1966), 308.

12. DEATH AND GRIEF

1. C. S. Lewis, "As One Oldster to Another," *Poems* (ed. Walter Hooper; San Diego: Harcourt Brace & Company, 1992 reprint), 41-42.

2. For a good discussion, see Amy Plantinga Pauw, "Dying Well" in *Practicing Our Faith: A Way of Life for a Searching People* (ed. Dorothy C. Bass; San Francisco: Jossey-Bass, 1997), 163-77.

3. Albom, *Tuesdays with Morrie*.

4. Arthur Ashe and Arnold Rampersad, *Days of Grace* (New York: Ballentine, 1994), 329-42. For a novel-length fictional letter from an aging man to his young son, see Marilynne Robinson, *Gilead* (New York: Farrar, Straus, and Giroux, 2004).

5. Dale Moody, *The Word of Truth: A Summary of Christian Doctrine Based on Biblical Revelation* (Grand Rapids: Eerdmans, 1981), 491-502, discusses two faces of death, destruction and departure.

6. C. S. Lewis, *Miracles: A Preliminary Study* (New York: Macmillan, 1978 reprint), 125. See also, Armand M. Nicholi, Jr., *The Question of God: C. S. Lewis and Sigmund Freud Debate God, Love, Sex, and the Meaning of Life* (New York: Free Press, 2002), 216-39.

7. C. S. Lewis, *The Last Battle* (New York: Collier, 1970 reprint), 183.

8. Ibid., 184.

9. Nicholas Wolterstorff, *Lament for a Son* (Grand Rapids: Eerdmans, 1987). For a collection of short accounts of responses to the death of a child, see Richard S. Hipps, ed., *When a Child Dies: Stories of Survival and Hope* (Macon, Ga.: Peake Road, 1996).

10. Hubert G. Locke, *Searching for God in Godforsaken Times and Places: Reflections on the Holocaust, Racism, and Death* (Grand Rapids: Eerdmans, 2003).

11. For a short introduction, E. S. Gerstenberger and W. Schrage, *Suffering* (trans. John E. Steely; Nashville: Abingdon, 1980), 29-31.

12. E. Frank Tupper, *A Scandalous Providence: The Jesus Story of the Compassion of God* (Macon, Ga.: Mercer University Press, 1995), 83-119, treats the slaughter of the innocents.

13. For a short study, see Lewis B. Smedes, *Mere Morality: What God Expects from Ordinary People* (Grand Rapids: Eerdmans, 1983), 111-18. For a fuller study, see Robert N. Wennberg, *Terminal Choices: Euthanasia, Suicide, and the Right to Die* (Grand Rapids: Eerdmans, 1989), 16-107. John H. Hewett, *After Suicide* (Philadelphia: Westminster, 1980), suggests using "attempted" suicides and "completed" suicides to avoid "a connotation of criminality" connected with the traditional term "commit" suicide. Hewett's book is a useful discussion of pastoral care for family and friends of those to complete suicide.

14. William Powell Tuck, *Getting Past the Pain: Making Sense of Life's Darkness* (Macon, Ga.: Peake Road, 1997), 74-77.

15. Robert Davidson, *The Courage to Doubt: Exploring an Old Testament Theme* (London: SCM, 1983), 121-39, offers a valuable study of these confessions.

16. Tupper, *A Scandalous Providence*, 435.

17. Ibid., 436.

18. See also the account of Gary R. Habermas, *The Risen Jesus & Future Hope* (Lanham, Md.: Rowman & Littlefield, 2003), 187-97, about his wife's death from stomach cancer and his belief in Jesus' resurrection.

19. For a classic study, see Oscar Cullmann, *Immortality of the Soul or Resurrection of the Dead? The Witness of the New Testament* (New York: Macmillan, 1958). Hans Schwarz, *Eschatology* (Grand Rapids:

Eerdmans, 2000), 247–307, discusses death, immortality, and resurrection. For a recent, massive study of Jesus' resurrection and its implications for Christian hope, see N. T. Wright, *The Resurrection of the Son of God* (Minneapolis: Fortress, 2003). For a recent overview of several theories, see Alan F. Segal, *Life After Death: A History of the Afterlife in the Religions of the World* (New York: Doubleday, 2004).

20. David Van Biema, "Does Heaven Exist?" *Time,* 24 March 1997, 73.

21. Mitch Albom, *The Five People You Meet in Heaven* (New York: Hyperion, 2003).

22. For a study of many of these issues, see John Gilmore, *Probing Heaven: Key Questions on the Hereafter* (Grand Rapids: Baker, 1989). For overviews of Christian belief in heaven, see Jerry L. Walls, *Heaven: The Logic of Eternal Joy* (Oxford: Oxford University Press, 2002); Jeffrey Burton Russell, *History of Heaven: The Singing Silence* (Princeton: Princeton University Press, 1997); and Alister McGrath, *A Brief History of Heaven* (Oxford: Blackwell, 2003).

23. For similar theses, see James Leo Garrett, Jr., *Systematic Theology: Biblical, Historical, and Evangelical, Volume 2* (Grand Rapids: Eerdmans, 1995), 816–20.

24. Lewis, *Mere Christianity,* 120.

25. For an excellent study, see John Sanders, *No Other Name: An Investigation into the Destiny of the Unevangelized* (Grand Rapids: Eerdmans, 1992), 287–305.

26. For a short statement by a Baptist theologian, see William L. Hendricks, *A Theology for Children* (Nashville: Broadman, 1980), 238–51.

13. ANIMAL SUFFERING

1. For example, in his classic study, John Hick devotes a few pages to the topic. See Hick, *Evil and the God of Love,* 91–93, 108–11, 345–53.

2. Lewis, *Problem of Pain,* 129–43. Lewis responded to one critique in *God in the Dock* (ed. Walter Hooper; Grand Rapids: Eerdmans, 1970), 161–71. Stephen Webb, *Good Eating* (Grand Rapids, Mich.: Brazos Press, 2001). For a good overview of the subject of animal suffering, see Robert N. Wennberg, *God, Humans, and Animals: An Invitation to Enlarge Our Moral Universe* (Grand Rapids: Eerdmans, 2003), 309–41.

3. For a review of pioneering pro-ecology theology, see Steven Bouma-Prediger, *The Greening of Theology: The Ecological Models of Rosemary Radford Ruether, Joseph Sittler, and Jürgen Moltmann* (Atlanta: Scholars Press, 1995). See also Warren McWilliams, "Christic Paradigm and Cosmic Christ: Ecological Christology in the Theologies of Sallie McFague and Jürgen Moltmann," *PRSt* 25 (Winter 1998), 341-55 for a comparison of two recent theologians.

4. Noted by Ronald J. Sider, *Living Like Jesus: Eleven Essentials for Growing a Genuine Faith* (Grand Rapids: Baker, 1996), 152.

5. Ebbie C. Smith, "Environlove: The Christian Approach to Ecology," *SwJT* 37 (Spring 1995): 25-26.

6. Lynn White, "The Historical Roots of Our Ecological Crisis," in *Ecology and Religion in History* (ed. David Spring and Eileen Spring; New York: Harper & Row, 1974), 15-31.

7. For a list of ten reasons, see Steven Bouma-Prediger, "Why Care for Creation: Prudence to Piety," *Christian Scholar's Review* 27 (Spring 1998): 277-97.

8. For example, Henlee H. Barnette, *The Church and the Ecological Crisis* (Grand Rapids: Eerdmans, 1972); Richard E. Land and Louis A. Moore, eds., *The Earth Is the Lord's* (Nashville: Broadman, 1992); the theme issue "Christianity and Environmentalism," *Christian Scholar's Review* 28 (Winter 1998).

9. Campolo, *Is Jesus a Republican or a Democrat?* 129.

10. For a fuller statement of his views, see Campolo, *How to Rescue the Earth without Worshiping Nature.*

11. See especially Sallie McFague, *The Body of God: An Ecological Theology* (Minneapolis: Fortress, 1993); *Super, Natural Christians: How We Should Love Nature* (Minneapolis: Fortress, 1997); *Life Abundant: Rethinking Theology and Economy for a Planet in Peril* (Minneapolis: Fortress, 2001).

12. Andrew Linzey, "Is Christianity Irredeemably Speciesist?" in *Animals on the Agenda: Questions about Animals for Theology and Ethics* (ed. Andrew Linzey and Dorothy Yamamoto; Urbana: University of Illinois Press, 1998), xviii.

13. Most Bible dictionaries have entries on animals, but note the extensive article by Edwin Firmage, "Zoology (Fauna)," *ABD* 6:1109-67.

14. Andrew Linzey, *Animal Theology* (Urbana: University of Chicago, 1995); Lewis, *Problem of Pain*, 139.

15. Tony Campolo, *20 Hot Potatoes Christians Are Afraid to Touch*, 133-40.

16. Tim Stafford, "Animal Lib," *Christianity Today*, 6 June 1990, 18-23.

17. See Stephen H. Webb, *On God and Dogs: A Christian Theology of Compassion for Animals* (New York: Oxford University Press, 1998) for a good introduction. Also see the unpublished essay by Steve Lemke, "On the Pain of Animals" (delivered at the Southwest regional meeting of the American Academy of Religion, March 1992) for a review of recent studies.

18. Lewis, *Problem of Pain*, 132.

19. Elizabeth Marshall Thomas, *The Hidden Life of Dogs* (New York: Pocket Books, 1995), ix-xxiii, addresses this issue in light of long-term observation of dogs.

20. Lewis, *Problem of Pain*, 129.

21. Ibid., 133-36.

22. Ibid., 136. For a summary of responses to Lewis's use of the fall of Satan, see Wennberg, *God Humans, and Animals*, 328-32.

23. Richard Bauckham, "Jesus and Animals I: What Did He Teach?" and "Jesus and Animals II: What Did He Practice?" in *Animals on the Agenda*, 33-60.

24. C. S. Lewis, "Vivisection," in *God in the Dock*, 224-28.

25. Lewis, *Problem of Pain*, 136-43.

26. Webb, *On God and Dogs*, 174.

27. John Wesley, "The General Deliverance," in *The Works of John Wesley* (ed. Albert C. Outler; Nashville: Abingdon, 1985), 2:436-50. See brief discussions in John Gilmore, *Probing Heaven: Key Questions on the Hereafter* (Grand Rapids: Baker, 1989), 130-33; Jay B. McDaniel, "Can Animal Suffering be Reconciled with Belief in an All-loving God?" in *Animals on the Agenda*, 161-70, especially 169-70; Webb, 171-80.

28. Ibid., 137.

29. Ibid., 141.

30. Ibid., 138-39.

31. C. S. Lewis, *Letters to an American Lady* (ed. Clyde S. Kilby; Grand Rapids: Eerdmans, 1978), 110.

32. Lewis, *Problem of Pain*, 140-41.

33. Campolo, *Is Jesus a Republican or a Democrat?*, 133. See also, Paul Badham, "Do Animals Have Immortal Souls?" in *Animals on the Agenda*, 181-89.

34. "Billy Graham," *Daily Oklahoman*, 8 December 1988, 18.

35. For example, John P. Newport, *The Lion and the Lamb: A Commentary on the Book of Revelation for Today* (Nashville: Broadman, 1986), 330.

36. Webb, *On God and Dogs*, 20-43.

37. Webb, *Good Eating*, 37.

38. Ibid., 163-69.

39. Ibid., 165.

40. Ibid., 170.

41. Ibid., 171.

42. Ibid., 173.

43. For this traditional classification, see Jürgen Moltmann, *The Coming of God: Christian Eschatology* (trans. Margaret Kohl; Minneapolis: Fortress, 1996).

44. Webb, *On God and Dogs*, 109.

45. "See Spot Go to Heaven? The Public's Not Sure" (ABC News/ Beliefnet Poll), www.beliefnet.com, accessed July 23, 2001.

46. Webb, *On God and Dogs*, 130.

47. Ibid., 173.

48. Ibid., 167-73.

49. Linzey, *Animal Theology*, 125.

50. Campolo, *Is Jesus a Republican or a Democrat?* 133.

14. A THEODICY FOR LIVING IN THE REAL WORLD

1. Douglas John Hall, *Lighten Our Darkness: Toward an Indigenous Theology of the Cross* (Philadelphia: Westminster, 1976), 19.

2. M. Scott Peck, *The Road Less Traveled* (New York: Touchstone, 1978), 15.

3. For a strong statement on the importance of both intellectual and practical aspects of the problem of evil, see S. Paul Schilling, *God and Human Anguish* (Nashville: Abingdon, 1977), 43-49.

4. Terrence W. Tilley, *The Evils of Theodicy* (Washington, D.C.: Georgetown University Press, 1991), 1-5.

5. Kenneth Surin, *Theology and the Problem of Evil* (New York: Basil Blackwell, 1986), 70-141, classifies theodicies into two categories, those that have theoretical emphases and those with practical emphases.

6. Cone, *God of the Oppressed*, 174.

7. Jürgen Moltmann, *Jesus Christ for Today's World* (trans. Margaret Kohl; Minneapolis: Fortress, 1994), 2.

8. Ibid., 30-31.

9. Simundson, *Faith Under Fire*, 15.

10. For a valuable study of civil disobedience, see Stephen Charles Mott, *Biblical Ethics and Social Change* (New York: Oxford University Press, 1982), 142-66.

11. Walter C. Kaiser, Jr., "Exodus," in *The Expositor's Bible Commentary* (ed. Frank E. Gaebelein; Grand Rapids: Regency, 1990), 309.

12. Smedes, *Choices*, 91-114.

13. For example, see the pacifist critique of physical self-defense in John H. Yoder, *What Would You Do?* (Scottdale, Pa.: Herald, 1983).

14. Jürgen Moltmann, *The Crucified God* (trans. R. A. Wilson and John Bowden; New York: Harper & Row, 1974), 317-40.

15. W. Rauschenbusch, *Christianizing the Social Order* (New York, 1912), quoted in Moltmann, *In the End–The Beginning*, 91.

16. Bonhoeffer, *The Cost of Discipleship*, 28.

17. See Wolterstorff, *Lament for a Son*, 34.

18. Richard Bauckham and Trevor Hart, *Hope Against Hope: Christian Eschatology at the Turn of the Millennium* (Grand Rapids: Eerdmans, 1999), 43.

19. Hubert G. Locke, *Searching for God in Godforsaken Times and Place: Reflections on the Holocaust, Racism, and Death* (Grand Rapids: Eerdmans, 2003), 87-95.

20. Ibid., 104.

21. Ibid., 55.

22. Wolterstorff, *Lament for a Son*, 68.

23. Ibid., 80-83.

24. Daniel J. Boorstin, *The Seekers: The Story of Man's Continuing Quest to Understand His World* (New York: Random House, 1998), xiii.

25. Willie Morris, *Taps: A Novel* (Boston: Houghton Mifflin, 2002), 24.

26. Paul Tillich, *Dynamics of Faith* (New York: Harper & Row, 1958), 22. For other good studies, see Alister McGrath, *The Sunnier Side of Doubt* (Grand Rapids: Academie Books, 1990), and Robert Davidson, *The Courage to Doubt: Exploring an Old Testament Theme* (Philadelphia: Trinity International Press, 1989).

27. Paul S. Fiddes, *Participating in the Life of God: A Pastoral Doctrine of the Trinity* (Louisville: Westminster John Knox, 2000), 153. Fiddes goes on to call this approach theodicy in a softer sense.

28. Wolterstorff, *Lament for a Son.* 97.

29. Lewis, *God in the Dock,* 244.

30. Lewis, *Screwtape Letters,* 38.

31. For a summary of Moltmann's contribution, see Stanley J. Grenz, *Rediscovering the Triune God: The Trinity in Contemporary Theology* (Minneapolis: Fortress, 2004), 73-88.

32. For example, Moltmann, *The Crucified God,* 65-75, and Hall, *God and Human Suffering,* 104-7.

33. Thomas C. Oden, *The Word of Life, Systematic Theology: Volume Two* (Peabody, Mass.: Prince Press, 1998), 414-15.

34. Eugene H. Peterson, *The Message: The New Testament in Contemporary Language* (Colorado Springs: NavPress, 1993), 36.

35. Moltmann, *Jesus Christ for Today's World,* 47.

36. *Baptist Hymnal* (Nashville: Convention Press, 1991), number 261.

37. Schilling, *God and Human Anguish,* 31.

WORKS CITED

NOTE: Readers looking for a few books to get started on the topic of evil and suffering should look for the ones marked with an asterisk. I have included overviews of the general subject as well as some novels and more autobiographical pieces.

Achtemeier, Elizabeth. *Nature, God, and Pulpit.* Grand Rapids, Mich.: Eerdmans, 1992.

Adams, Carol J. *Woman-Battering.* Minneapolis: Fortress, 1994.

Albom, Mitch. *The Five People You Meet in Heaven.* New York: Hyperion, 2003.

*———. *Tuesdays with Morrie: An Old Man, a Young Man, and Life's Greatest Lesson.* New York: Doubleday, 1997. A discussion between Albom and a former teacher, who is dying from ALS, or Lou Gehrig's disease. A best-seller for several years.

Anderson, Bernhard W. *Out of the Depths: The Psalms Speak for Us Today.* Rev and exp. ed. Philadelphia: Westminster, 1983.

Andrews, Stephen J. "Friendship." Page 310 in *Mercer Dictionary of the Bible.* Edited by Watson E. Mills. Macon, Ga.: Mercer University Press, 1990.

Ashcraft, Morris. *The Will of God.* Nashville: Broadman, 1980.

Ashe, Arthur and Arnold Rampersad. *Days of Grace: A Memoir.* New York: Ballentine, 1993.

Baggage, Stuart Barton. "Aging." Pages 30–32 in *The Complete Book of Everyday Christianity.* Edited by Robert Banks and R. Paul Stevens. Downers Grove, Ill.: InterVarsity, 1997.

———. "Retirement." Pages 855–59 in *The Complete Book of Everyday Christianity.* Edited by Robert Banks and R. Paul Stevens. Downers Grove, Ill.: InterVarsity, 1997.

Bach, Alice, ed. *Women in the Hebrew Bible: A Reader.* New York: Routledge, 1999.

Badham, Paul. "Do Animals Have Immortal Souls?" Pages 181–89 in *Animals on the Agenda: Questions about Animals for Theology and Ethics.* Edited by Andrew Linzey and Dorothy Yamamoto. Urbana: University of Illinois Press, 1998.

Bainton, Roland H. *Christian Attitudes Toward War and Peace.* Nashville: Abingdon, 1960.

Baldwin, Joyce G. *Haggai, Zechariah, Malachi.* Tyndale Old Testament Commentaries. Downers Grove, Ill.: InterVarsity, 1972.

Balentine, Samuel E. *Prayer in the Hebrew Bible: The Drama of Divine-Human Dialogue.* Minneapolis: Fortress, 1993.

"The Baptist Faith and Message." Nashville: LifeWay Christian Resources of the Southern Baptist Convention, 2000.

Baptist Hymnal. Nashville: Convention Press, 1991.

Barclay, William. *New Testament Words.* Philadelphia: Westminster, 1974.

Barnette, Henlee H. *The Church and the Ecological Crisis.* Grand Rapids, Mich.: Eerdmans, 1972.

———. *Exploring Medical Ethics.* Macon, Ga.: Mercer University Press, 1982.

Barrett, C. K. *The Gospel According to John.* 2d ed. Philadelphia: Westminster, 1978.

Bauckham, Richard. "Jesus and Animals, I: What Did He Teach?" Pages 33–60 in *Animals on the Agenda: Questions about Animals for Theology and Ethics.* Edited by Andrew Linzey and Dorothy Yamamoto. Urbana: University of Illinois Press, 1998.

———. *The Theology of the Book of Revelation.* Cambridge: Cambridge University Press, 1993.

Bauckham, Richard, and Trevor Hart. *Hope Against Hope: Christian Eschatology at the Turn of the Millennium.* Grand Rapids, Mich.: Eerdmans, 1999.

Belleville, Linda. *Women Leaders and the Church.* Grand Rapids, Mich.: Baker, 2000.

Bergant, Diane. "Compassion in the Bible." Pages 9–34 in *Compassionate Ministry.* Edited by Gary L. Sapp. Birmingham, Ala.: Religious Education, 1993.

Beversluis, John. *C. S. Lewis and the Search for Rational Religion.* Grand Rapids, Mich.: Eerdmans, 1985.

Bianchi, Eugene C. *Aging as a Spiritual Journey.* New York: Crossroad, 1992.

Bierma, David Van. "Does Heaven Exist?" *Time* (24 March 1997): 73.

"Billy Graham." *Daily Oklahoman* (8 December 1988): 18.

Blanton, Dana. "More Believe in God than Heaven." Cited 1 June 2004. Online: Http://www.foxnews.com/printer_friendly_story/0,3566,99945.00html.

Bloesch, Donald G. *Essentials of Evangelical Theology, Volume 1.* New York: Harper & Row, 1982 reprint.

Blomberg, Craig L. *Matthew.* New American Commentary. Nashville: Broadman, 1992.

Bonhoeffer, Dietrich. *The Cost of Discipleship.* Rev ed. New York: Macmillan, 1963.

———. *Letters and Papers from Prison.* Rev and enl. ed. New York: Macmillan, 1967.

Boorstin, Daniel J. *The Seekers: The Story of Man's Continuing Quest to Understand His World.* New York: Random House, 1998.

Bouma-Prediger, Steven. *The Greening of Theology: The Ecological Models of Rosemary Radford Ruether, Joseph Sittler, and Jürgen Moltmann.* Atlanta: Scholars, 1995.

———. "Why Care for Creation? Prudence to Piety." *Christian Scholar's Review* 27 (1988): 277–97.

*Bowker, John. *Problems of Suffering in Religions of the World.* London: Cambridge University Press, 1970. A useful summary of the approaches to suffering in the major world religions.

Boyd, Gregory A. *God at War: The Bible and Spiritual Conflict.* Downers Grove, Ill.: InterVarsity, 1997.

———. *Is God to Blame? Beyond Pat Answers to the Problem of Suffering.* Downers Grove, Ill.: InterVarsity, 2003.

———. *Satan and the Problem of Evil.* Downers Grove, Ill.: InterVarsity, 2001.

Briggs, David. "Poor Americans Most Likely to Count Blessings." *Shawnee News-Star* (28 January 1995): 15.

Brown, Colin. *That You May Believe: Miracles and Faith Then and Now.* Grand Rapids, Mich.: Eerdmans, 1985.

Brown, Michael L. *Israel's Divine Healer.* Grand Rapids, Mich.: Zondervan, 1995.

Bruce, F. F. *Apostle of the Heart Set Free.* Grand Rapids, Mich.: Eerdmans, 1996 reprint.

Brueggemann, Walter. *The Message of the Psalms: A Theological Commentary.* Minneapolis: Augsburg, 1984.

———. *Peace.* St. Louis: Chalice, 2001.

———. "Some Aspects of Theodicy in Old Testament Faith." *Perspectives in Religious Studies* 26 (1999): 253-68.

———. *Theology of the Old Testament: Testimony, Dispute, Advocacy.* Minneapolis: Fortress, 1997.

*Buttrick, George Arthur. *God, Pain, and Evil.* Nashville: Abingdon, 1966. A classic overview of the major theological issues in the problem of suffering.

Calvin, John. *Institutes of the Christian Religion.* Translated by Ford Lewis Battles. Philadelphia: Westminster, 1960.

Campolo, Tony. *How to Rescue the Earth Without Worshiping Nature.* Nashville: Thomas Nelson, 1992.

———. *Is Jesus a Republican or a Democrat? And 14 Other Polarizing Issues.* Dallas: Word, 1995.

———. *20 Hot Potatoes Christians Are Afraid to Touch.* Dallas: Word, 1988.

*Carson, D. A. *How Long, O Lord? Reflections on Suffering and Evil.* Grand Rapids, Mich.: Baker, 1990. Strong evangelical studies of several aspects of suffering by a noted Bible scholar.

———. "Matthew." Pages 3-599 in *The Expositor's Bible Commentary.* Edited by Frank E. Gaebelein. Grand Rapids, Mich.: Zondervan, 1984.

Carter, Jimmy. *The Virtues of Aging.* New York: Ballentine, 1998.

Chester, D. K. "The Theodicy of Natural Disasters." *Scottish Journal of Theology* 51 (1998): 485-504.

"Christian Responses to Violence" [theme issue]. *Review & Expositor* 93 (1996).

"Christianity and Environmentalism" [theme issue]. *Christian Scholar's Review* 28 (1998).

Clark, David K., and Robert V. Rakestraw, eds. *Readings in Christian Ethics: Volume 2.* Grand Rapids, Mich.: Baker, 1996.

Clapp, Rodney, *The Consuming Passion: Christianity & the Consumer Culture.* Downers Grove, Ill.: InterVarsity, 1998.

*Claypool, John R. *Tracks of a Fellow Struggler.* Rev ed. New Orleans: Insight, 1995. A series of candid sermons devoted to his daughter's diagnosis and eventual death from leukemia.

Clouse, Robert G., ed. *War: Four Christian Views.* Downers Grove, Ill.: InterVarsity, 1981.

Clouse, Bonnidell, and Robert Clouse, eds. *Women in Ministry: Four Views.* Downers Grove, Ill.: InterVarsity, 1989.

Cohn-Sherbok, Dan, ed. *Holocaust Theology: A Reader.* New York: New York University Press, 2002.

Cone, James H. *A Black Theology of Liberation.* Philadelphia: Lippincott, 1970.

———. *God of the Oppressed.* New York: Seabury, 1975.

Conyers, A. J. *A Basic Christian Theology.* Nashville: Broadman & Holman, 1995.

———. "After the Hurricane." *Christianity Today* (9 November 1992): 34–36.

Crenshaw, James L. *Old Testament Wisdom: An Introduction.* Atlanta: John Knox, 1981.

———, ed. *Theodicy in the Old Testament.* Philadelphia: Fortress, 1983.

———. *A Whirlpool of Torment: Israelite Traditions of God as an Oppressive Presence.* Philadelphia: Fortress, 1984.

Cullmann, Oscar. *Christ and Time.* Translated by Floyd Filson. Rev ed. Philadelphia: Westminster, 1964.

———. *Immortality of the Soul or Resurrection of the Dead? The Witness of the New Testament.* New York: Macmillan, 1958.

Davidson, Robert. *The Courage to Doubt: Exploring an Old Testament Theme.* London: SCM, 1983.

Dayringer, Richard. *Life Cycle: Psychological and Theological Perspectives.* Binghampton, N.Y.: Haworth, 2000.

Deen, Edith. *All the Women of the Bible*. Edison, N. J.: Castle Books reprint, 1955 original.

Deloria, Vine, Jr. *Custer Died for Your Sins, An Indian Manifesto*. New York: Macmillan, 1969.

———. *God Is Red*. New York: Grosset & Dunlap, 1973.

*DeVries, Peter. *The Blood of the Lamb*. New York: Popular Library, 1961. A powerful novel about a series of tragedies. Full of explicit discussion of God's character.

Dorman, Ted M. *A Faith for All Seasons*. 2d ed. Nashville: Broadman & Holman, 2001.

Dossey, Larry. *Prayer Is Good Medicine: How to Reap the Benefits of Prayer*. San Francisco: HarperSanFrancisco, 1996.

Duke, David Nelson. "Theodicy at the Turn of the Century, an Introduction." *Perspectives in Religious Studies* 26 (1999): 241-51.

Eareckson, Joni, and Steven Estes. *When God Weeps: Why Our Sufferings Matter to the Almighty*. Grand Rapids, Mich.: Zondervan, 1997.

Eisland, Nancy L. *The Disabled God*. Nashville: Abingdon, 1994.

Ellison, Ralph. *Invisible Man*. New York: Vantage, 1972 reprint.

Erickson, Millard J. *Christian Theology, Volume 1*. Grand Rapids, Mich.: Baker, 1983.

Farrer, Austin. *A Faith of Our Own*. Cleveland: World, 1960.

Fiddes, Paul S. *The Creative Suffering of God*. Oxford: Clarendon, 1988.

———. *Participating in God: A Pastoral Doctrine of the Trinity*. Louisville: Westminster John Knox, 2000.

Firmage, Edwin. "Zoology (Fauna)." Pages 1109-67 in vol. 6 of *The Anchor Bible Dictionary*. Edited by David Noel Freedman. 6 vol. New York: Doubleday, 1992.

Floyd, Wayne Whitson, Jr. "Compassion in Theology." Pages 35-63 in *Compassionate Ministry*. Edited by Gary L. Sapp. Birmingham, Ala.: Religious Education Press, 1993.

Foster, Richard J. *Freedom of Simplicity*. San Francisco: Harper & Row, 1981.

———. *Money, Sex & Power: The Challenge of the Disciplined Life*. San Francisco: Harper & Row, 1985.

Fox, Richard Wightman. *Jesus in America: Personal Savior, Cultural Hero, National Obsession*. San Francisco: HarperSanFrancisco, 2004.

*Fretheim, Terence E. *The Suffering of God: An Old Testament Perspective*. Overtures to Biblical Theology. Philadelphia: Fortress, 1984. A strong discussion of divine suffering developed from Old Testament texts. Often cited by other authors.

Friesen, Gary, and J. Robin Maxson. *Decision Making and the Will of God*. Portland: Multnomah, 1980.

Gagnon, Robert J. *The Bible and Homosexual Practices: Texts and Hermeneutics*. Nashville: Abingdon, 2001.

Garland, Diana R. "The Church and Divorce." *Review & Expositor* 92 (1995): 419-34.

Garrett, Duane A. *Angels and the New Spirituality*. Nashville: Broadman & Holman, 1995.

Garrett, James Leo, Jr. *Systematic Theology: Biblical, Historical, and Evangelical, Volume 2*. Grand Rapids, Mich.: Eerdmans, 1995.

George, Timothy. *Galatians*. New American Commentary. Nashville: Broadman, 1994.

*Gerstenberger, Erhard S., and Wolfgang Schrage. *Suffering*. Translated by John E. Steely. Nashville: Abingdon, 1980. A sweeping review of biblical texts on suffering, but not as readable as Simundson.

Gibbs, Nancy. "The Message of Miracles." *Time* (10 April 1995): 65.

Gilkey, Langdon. *Reaping the Whirlwind: A Christian Interpretation of History*. New York: Seabury, 1976.

*———. *Shantung Compound: The Story of Men and Women Under Pressure*. New York: Harper & Row, 1966. An autobiographical account of life in a prisoner of war camp during World War II by one of America's leading theologians.

Gilliand, Pat. "No Simple Answers in Dealing with the Ordeal, Ministers Say." *Daily Oklahoman* (5 May 1999): 23.

Gilmore, John. *Probing Heaven: Key Questions on the Hereafter*. Grand Rapids, Mich.: Baker, 1989.

Glancy, Diane. *Pushing the Bear: A Novel of the Trail of Tears*. San Diego: Harvest Book, 1996.

Godwin, Johnnie C. *Life's Best Chapter: Retirement.* Birmingham, Ala.: New Hope, 2000.

Goetz, Ronald. "The Suffering God: The Rise of a New Orthodoxy." *Christian Century* (16 April 1986): 385–89.

*Goldingay, John. *Walk On: Life, Loss, Trust, and Other Realities.* Grand Rapids, Mich.: Baker Academic, 2002. A series of reflections prompted by his wife's multiple sclerosis. The author is a Bible scholar.

Gray, John. *Men Are from Mars, Women Are from Venus.* New York: HarperCollins, 1992.

"The Graying of the Church" [theme issue]. *Review & Expositor* 88 (1991).

Green, Roger Lancelyn, and Walter Hooper. *C. S. Lewis, A Biography.* New York: Harcourt Brace Jovanovich, 1974.

Green, William Scott. "Facing the One God Together." *Perspectives in Religious Studies* 26 (1999): 303–15.

Grenz, Stanley J. *Rediscovering the Triune God: The Trinity in Contemporary Theology.* Minneapolis: Fortress, 2004.

———. *Sexual Ethics: A Biblical Perspective.* Dallas: Word, 1990.

———. *Theology for the Community of God.* Nashville: Broadman & Holman, 1994.

———. *Welcoming but Not Affirming: An Evangelical Response to Homosexuality.* Louisville: Westminster John Knox, 1998.

Grenz, Stanley J., and Roy D. Bell. *Betrayal of Trust: Sexual Misconduct in the Pastorate.* Downers Grove, Ill.: InterVarsity, 1995.

Grenz, Stanley J., and Denise Muir Kjesbo. *Women in the Church: A Biblical Theology of Women in Ministry.* Downers Grove, Ill.: InterVarsity, 1995.

Grenz, Stanley J., and Roger E. Olson. *20th-Century Theology: God and World in a Transitional Age.* Downers Grove, Ill.: InterVarsity, 1992.

Griffin, David Ray. *God, Power, and Evil: A Process Theodicy.* Philadelphia: Fortress, 1976.

Grudem, Wayne A., ed. *Are Miraculous Gifts for Today? Four Views.* Grand Rapids, Mich.: Zondervan, 1996.

———. *Bible Doctrine: Essential Teachings of the Christian Faith*. Edited by Jeff Purswell. Grand Rapids, Mich.: Zondervan, 1999.

Gushee, David P. *The Righteous Gentiles: A Christian Interpretation*. Minneapolis: Fortress, 1994.

Guthrie, Shirley. *Christian Doctrine*. Rev ed. Louisville: Westminster John Knox, 1994.

Gutierrez, Gustavo. *A Theology of Liberation: History, Politics and Salvation*. Translated by Sister Caridad Inda and John Eagleson. New York: Orbis, 1973.

Habermas, Gary R. *The Risen Jesus & Future Hope*. Lanham, Md.: Rowan & Littlefield, 2003.

Hall, Douglas John. *The Cross in Our Context: Jesus and the Suffering World*. Minneapolis: Fortress, 2003.

———. *God and Human Suffering: An Exercise in the Theology of the Cross*. Minneapolis: Augsburg, 1986.

———. *Lighten Our Darkness: Toward an Indigenous Theology of the Cross*. Philadelphia: Westminster, 1976.

Hall, Elizabeth T. *Caring for a Loved One with Alzheimer's Disease*. New York: Haworth Pastoral Press, 2000.

Harbaugh, Gary. *Act of God/Active God: Recovering from Natural Disasters*. Minneapolis: Fortress, 2001.

*Harkness, Georgia. *The Providence of God*. New York: Abingdon, 1960. A classic discussion of creation, prayer, miracles, and other issues related to providence. Very readable.

Harris, J. Gordon. *Biblical Perspectives on Aging: God and the Elderly*. Philadelphia: Fortress, 1987.

Hart, Archibald D. "Depression." Pages 287–91 in *The Complete Book of Everday Christianity*. Edited by Robert Banks and R. Paul Stevens. Downers Grove, Ill.: InterVarsity, 1997.

Hauerwas, Stanley, Carole Bailey, Stone King, Keith G. Meador, and David Cloutier, eds. *Growing Old in Christ*. Grand Rapids, Mich.: Eerdmans, 2003.

Hauerwas, Stanley. *Suffering Presence: Theological Reflections on Medicine, the Mentally Handicapped, and the Church*. Notre Dame: University of Notre Dame Press, 1986.

Hauerwas, Stanley, and Frank Lentricchia, eds. *Dissent from the Homeland: Essays after September 11.* Durham, N. C.: Duke University Press, 2003.

Hays, J. Daniel. *From Every People and Nation: A Biblical Theology of Race.* Downers Grove, Ill.: InterVarsity, 2003.

Hays, Richard B. *The Moral Vision of the New Testament.* San Francisco: HarperSanFrancisco, 1996.

Hendricks, William L. *A Theology for Aging.* Nashville: Broadman, 1986.

———. *A Theology for Children.* Nashville: Broadman, 1980.

Heschel, Abraham. *The Prophets, Part II.* New York: Harper & Row, 1975 reprint.

Hewett, John H. *After Suicide.* Philadelphia: Westminster, 1980.

*Hick, John. *Evil and the God of Love.* London: Collins, 1968. A pioneering study of theodicy that contrasts two major Christian approaches, the theodicies of Augustine and Irenaeus. Includes summaries of many major theologians on theodicy. Hick supports the Irenaean approach.

*Hijuelos, Oscar. *Mr. Ives' Christmas.* New York: HarperCollins, 1995. A compelling novel about a believer's response to his son's murder and the murderer.

*Hipps, Richard S., ed. *When a Child Dies: Stories of Survival and Hope.* Macon, Ga.: Peake Road, 1996. Several autobiographical accounts by people whose child died.

Holloway, Jeph. "The Ethical Dilemma of Holy War." *Southwestern Journal of Theology* 41 (1998): 44–69.

House, H. Wayne, ed. *Divorce and Remarriage: Four Christian Views.* Downers Grove, Ill.: InterVarsity, 1990.

Hui, Edwin. "Sickness." Pages 894–95 in *The Complete Book of Everyday Christianity.* Edited by Robert Banks and R. Paul Stevens. Downers Grove, Ill.: InterVarsity, 1997.

Hymnbook for Christian Worship. St. Louis: Bethany, 1970.

Hymns for the Family of God. Nashville: Paragon, 1976.

Instone-Brewer, David. *Divorce and Remarriage in the Bible: The Social and Literary Context.* Grand Rapids, Mich.: Eerdmans, 2002.

Inwagen, Peter van, ed. *Christian Faith and the Problem of Evil.* Grand Rapids: Eerdmans, 2004.

Ireland, William J., Jr. "Friend, Friendship." Page 515 in *Holman Bible Dictionary.* Edited by Trent C. Butler. Nashville: Holman, 1991.

"Job" [theme issue]. *Review & Expositor* 99 (2002).

Jones, L. Gregory. *Embodying Forgiveness: A Theological Analysis.* Grand Rapids, Mich.: Eerdmans, 1995.

Jones, William. *Is God a White Racist?* Garden City, N. Y.: Doubleday, 1973.

Jung, Patricia Beattie. "Differences among the Elderly: Who Is on the Road to Bremen?" Pages 112–28 in *Growing Old in Christ.* Edited by Stanley Hauerwas, Carole Bailey, Stone King, Keith G. Meador, and David Cloutier. Grand Rapids, Mich.: Eerdmans, 2003.

Kaiser, Walter C., Jr. "Exodus." Pages 287–497 in vol. 2 of *The Expositor's Bible Commentary, 6 vols.* Edited by Frank E. Gaebelein. Grand Rapids, Mich.: Regency, 1990.

*Keck, David. *Forgetting Whose We Are: Alzheimer's Disease and the Love of God.* Nashville: Abingdon, 1996. The son of a New Testament scholar writes about his mother's experience with Alzheimer's disease. Full of scholarly discussions of sin, the soul, and other theological issues.

Keener, Craig S. *And Marries Another: Divorce and Remarriage in the Teachings of the New Testament.* Peabody, Mass.: Hendrickson, 1991.

Kidwell, Clara Sue, Homer Noley, and George E. "Tink" Tinker. *A Native American Theology.* Maryknoll, N.Y.: Orbis, 2001.

King, Martin Luther, Jr. "The American Dream." Pages 208–16 in *A Testament of Hope: The Essential Writings and Speeches of Martin Luther King Jr.* Edited by James M. Washington. San Francisco: HarperSanFrancisco, 1986.

———. *Why We Can't Wait.* New York: Mentor, 1964.

Klinka, Karen. "Bomb's Emotional Scars Heal at Different Rates, Experts Say." *The Sunday Oklahoman* (30 October 1995), 17.

Koch, Klaus. "Is There a Doctrine of Retribution in the Old Testament?" Pages 57–87 in *Theodicy in the Old Testament*. Edited by James L. Crenshaw. Philadelphia: Fortress, 1983.

Koenig, Harold G. *Aging and God: Spiritual Pathways to Mental Health in Midlife and Later Years*. New York: Haworth Pastoral Press, 1994.

Kraybill, Donald B., and Linda Gehman Peachey, eds. *Where Was God on September 11? Seeds of Faith and Hope*. Scottdale, Penn.: Herald, 2002.

*Kreeft, Peter. *Making Sense Out of Suffering*. Ann Arbor, Mich.: Servant, 1986. A very readable study of the philosophical and theological aspects of suffering by a Roman Catholic apologist.

Kubler-Ross, Elizabeth. *On Death and Dying*. New York: Macmillan, 1969.

Kushner, Harold. *When All You've Ever Wanted Isn't Enough.* New York: Pocket Books, 1987.

*———. *When Bad Things Happen to Good People*. New York: Avon reprint, 1983. A popular study by a Jewish rabbi whose son died of progeria, or rapid aging. Some Christians criticize Kushner for advocating a finite God, or a God with limited power.

Lammers, Stephen E., and Allen Verhey, eds. *On Moral Medicine: Theological Perspectives in Medical Ethics*. 2d ed. Grand Rapids: Eerdmans, 1998.

Land, Richard E., and Louis A. Moore, eds. *The Earth Is the Lord's*. Nashville: Broadman, 1992.

Lawther, Betty Coble, and Jenny Potzler. "The Church's Role in the Healing Process of Abused Women." *Review & Expositor* 98 (2001): 225–41.

Lea, Thomas D. *1, 2 Timothy, Titus*. New American Commentary. Nashville: Broadman, 1992.

"Legislators Strike Religious Phrase." *Dallas Morning News* (27 March 1997): 35A.

Lemke, Steve. "On the Pain of Animals." Paper presented at the Southwest regional meeting of the American Academy of Religion, March 1992.

Leslie, Kristen J. *When Violence Is No Stranger: Pastoral Counseling with Survivors of Acquaintance Rape.* Minneapolis: Fortress, 2003.

Lester, Andrew D., ed. *When Children Suffer: A Sourcebook for Ministry with Children in Crisis.* Philadelphia: Westminster, 1987.

Lewis, C. S. "As One Oldster to Another." Pages 41–42 in *Poems.* Edited by Walter Hooper. San Diego: Harcourt Brace & Company, 1992 reprint.

———. *Christian Reflections.* Edited by Walter Hooper. Grand Rapids, Mich.: Eerdmans, 1967.

———. *The Four Loves.* New York: Harcourt Brace Jovanovich, 1960.

———. *God in the Dock.* Edited by Walter Hooper. Grand Rapids, Mich.: Eerdmans, 1970.

*———. *A Grief Observed.* New York: Bantam, 1976. Lewis's famous account of his grief over the death of his wife, Joy. Very candid about his struggle with the character of God. The basis for the drama and movie *Shadowlands.*

———. *The Last Battle.* New York: Collier, 1970 reprint.

———. *Letters to an American Lady.* Edited by Clyde S. Kilby. Grand Rapids, Mich.: Eerdmans, 1978.

———. *Letters to Malcolm: Chiefly on Prayer.* New York: Harcourt Brace Jovanovich, 1964.

———. *Mere Christianity.* New York: Macmillan, 1952.

———. *Miracles: A Preliminary Study.* New York: Macmillan, 1960.

*———. *The Problem of Pain.* New York: Macmillan, 1962. His classic discussion of the God's power, God's goodness, sin, animal suffering, and heaven. Written several years before the death of his wife.

———. *The Screwtape Letters.* New York: Macmillan, 1978.

Lewis, W. H., ed. *Letters of C. S. Lewis.* New York: Harcourt Brace Jovanovich, 1966.

Linzey, Andrew. *Animal Theology.* Urbana: University of Chicago Press, 1995.

———. "Is Christianity Irredeemably Speciesist?" Pages xi–xx in *Animals on the Agenda: Questions about Animals for Theology and Ethics.* Edited by Andrew Linzey and Dorothy Yamamoto. Urbana: University of Illinois Press, 1998.

*Locke, Herbert G. *Searching for God in Godforsaken Times and Places: Reflections on the Holocaust, Racism, and Death.* Grand Rapids, Mich.: Eerdmans, 2003. An intriguing study of three forms of suffering. Prompted by his parent's death, his scholarly study of the Holocaust, and his experience as a black man.

Lockyer, Herbert. *All the Women of the Bible.* Grand Rapids, Mich.: Zondervan, n.d.

Long, Edward LeRoy, Jr. *Facing Terrorism: Responding as Christians.* Louisville: Westminster John Knox, 2004.

Macquarrie, John. *The Concept of Peace.* New York: Harper & Row, 1973.

Maddox, Randy. "The Word of God and Patriarchalism: A Typology of the Current Christian Debate." *Perspectives in Religious Studies* 14 (1987): 197-216.

Marshall, Christopher D. *Beyond Retribution: A New Testament Vision for Justice, Crime, and Punishment.* Grand Rapids, Mich.: Eerdmans, 2001.

Maston, T. B. *Biblical Ethics: A Survey.* Waco, Tex.: Word, 1967.

*———. *God Speaks Through Suffering.* Waco, Tex.: Word, 1977. A very accessible study of sin, suffering, the will of God, miracles, and other theological subjects by the father of a disabled man. Maston was a Baptist seminary professor of ethics.

———. *Interracial Marriage.* Nashville: Christian Life Commission of the Southern Baptist Convention, 1974.

———. *To Walk as He Walked.* Nashville: Broadman, 1985.

McDaniel, Jay B. "Can Animal Suffering be Reconciled with Belief in an All-loving God?" Pages 161-70 in *Animals on the Agenda: Questions about Animals for Theology and Ethics.* Edited by Andrew Linzey and Dorothy Yamamoto. Urbana: University of Illinois Press, 1998.

McDonald, Patrician M. *God and Violence: Biblical Resources for Living in a Small World.* Scottdale, Penn.: Herald, 2004.

McFague, Sallie. *The Body of God: An Ecological Theology.* Minneapolis: Fortress, 1993.

———. *Life Abundant: Rethinking Theology and Economy for a Planet in Peril.* Minneapolis: Fortress, 2001.

———. *Models of God: Theology for an Ecological, Nuclear Age.* Philadelphia: Fortress, 1987.

———. *Super, Natural Christians: How We Should Love Nature.* Minneapolis: Fortress, 1997.

McGavran, Donald. *Understanding Church Growth.* Rev ed. Grand Rapids, Mich.: Eerdmans, 1980.

McGee, Daniel B. "Issues of Life and Death." Pages 227–48 in *Understanding Christian Ethics: An Interpretive Approach.* Edited by William M. Tillman. Nashville: Broadman, 1988.

McGrath, Alister E. *A Brief History of Heaven.* Oxford: Blackwell, 2003.

———. *Christian Theology: An Introduction.* 3d ed. Oxford: Blackwell, 2001.

———. *The Sunnier Side of Doubt.* Grand Rapids, Mich.: Academie Books, 1990.

McKnight, Scot. "Who Is Jesus? An Introduction to Jesus Studies." Pages 51–72 in *Jesus Under Fire.* Edited by Michael J. Wilkins and J. P. Moreland. Grand Rapids, Mich.: Zondervan, 1995.

McQuilkin, Robertson. *An Introduction to Biblical Ethics.* Wheaton, Ill.: Tyndale House, 1989.

*———. *A Promise Kept.* Wheaton, Ill.: Tyndale House, 1998. A moving account by a seminary president who cared for his wife, who suffered from Alzheimer's disease.

McWilliams, Warren. "Christic Paradigm and Cosmic Christ: Ecological Christology in the Theologies of Sallie McFague and Jürgen Moltmann." *Perspectives in Religious Studies* 25 (1998): 341-55.

———. "*In vitro* Fertilization: An Exercise in Biotheology." *Search* 21 (1992): 29-36.

———. "Is Suffering a Punishment for Sin?" *Search* 19 (Winter 1989): 7-10.

———. *The Passion of God: Divine Suffering in Contemporary Protestant Theology.* Macon, Ga.: Mercer University Press, 1985.

*———. *When You Walk Through the Fire.* Nashville: Broadman, 1986. A layman's level summary of biblical teaching on suffering.

Organized canonically (e.g., suffering in the prophets, suffering in the gospels).

Meilaender, Gilbert. *Bioethics: A Primer for Christians.* Grand Rapids, Mich.: Eerdmans, 1996.

———. *Friendship: A Study in Theological Ethics.* South Bend, Ind.: University of Notre Dame Press, 1985.

Metzger, Bruce M. *The New Testament: Its Background, Growth, and Content.* Nashville: Abingdon, 1965.

Migliore, Daniel L. *Faith Seeking Understanding.* Grand Rapids, Mich.: Eerdmans, 1991.

Mikolaski, S. J. "Violence." Pages 428–29 in *Encyclopedia of Biblical and Christian Ethics.* Edited by R. K. Harrison. Nashville: Thomas Nelson, 1987.

Miller, L. B., Jr. "Disappointing Answer." *Baptist Message* (22 October 1992): 2.

Milligan, Barbara. *Desperate Hope: Experiencing God in the Midst of Breast Cancer.* Downers Grove, Ill.: InterVarsity, 1999.

Moltmann, Jürgen. *The Coming of God: Christian Eschatology.* Translated by Margaret Kohl. Minneapolis: Fortress, 1996.

———. *The Crucified God.* Translated by R. A. Wilson and John Bowden. New York: Harper & Row, 1974.

———. *Experiences in Theology: Ways and Forms of Christian Theology.* Translated by Margaret Kohl. Minneapolis: Fortress, 2000.

———. *In the End–The Beginning: The Life of Hope.* Translated by Margaret Kohl. Minneapolis: Fortress, 2004.

———. *Jesus Christ for Today's World.* Translated by Margaret Kohl. Minneapolis: Fortress, 1994.

———. "Liberate Yourselves by Accepting One Another." Pages 105–22 in *Human Disability and the Service of God.* Edited by Nancy L. Eisland and Don E. Saliers. Nashville: Abingdon, 1998.

———. *The Source of Life: The Holy Spirit and the Theology of Life.* Translated by Margaret Kohl. Minneapolis: Fortress, 1997.

Moltmann, Jürgen, and Elisabeth Moltmann-Wendel. *Passion for God: Theology in Two Voices.* Louisville: Westminster John Knox, 2003.

Moody, Dale. *The Word of Truth: A Summary of Christian Doctrine Based on Biblical Revelation.* Grand Rapids, Mich.: Eerdmans, 1981.

Morris, Willie. *Taps: A Novel.* Boston: Houghton Mifflin, 2002.

Mott, Stephen Charles. *Biblical Ethics and Social Change.* New York: Oxford University Press, 1982.

Newport, John P. *Life's Ultimate Questions: A Contemporary Philosophy of Religion.* Dallas: Word, 1989.

———. *The Lion and the Lamb: A Commentary on the Book of Revelation for Today.* Nashville: Broadman, 1986.

Ngien, Dennis. "The God Who Suffers." *Christianity Today* (3 February 1997): 38-42.

———. *The Suffering of God According to Martin Luther's "Theologia Crucis."* New York: Peter Lang, 1995.

Nicholi, Armand M., Jr. *The Question of God: C. S. Lewis and Sigmund Freud Debate God, Love, Sex, and the Meaning of Life.* New York: Free Press, 2002.

Nicholson, William. *Shadowlands.* New York: Plume, 1991.

Oates, Wayne E. *Behind the Masks: Personality Disorders in Religious Behavior.* Philadelphia: Westminster, 1987.

———. *Grief, Transition, and Loss: A Pastor's Practical Guide.* Minneapolis: Fortress, 1997.

Oden, Thomas C. *The Word of Life, Systematic Theology: Volume Two.* Peabody, Mass.: Prince Press, 1998.

Olson, Roger E. *The Mosaic of Christian Belief.* Downers Grove, Ill.: InterVarsity, 2002.

Ostling, Richard N. "The Second Reformation." *Time* (23 November 1992): 53-58.

Oswalt, John. *Where Are You God? Malachi's Perspectives on Injustice and Suffering.* Nappanee, Ind.: Evangel, 1999.

Pagels, Elaine. *The Origin of Satan.* New York: Random House, 1995.

Paterson, John. *The Book That Is Alive: Studies in Old Testament Life and Thought as Set Forth by the Hebrew Sages.* New York: Charles Scribner's Sons, 1954.

Pauw, Amy Plantinga. "Dying Well." Pages 163-77 in *Practicing Our Faith: A Way of Life for a Searching People.* Ed. Dorothy C. Bass. San Francisco: Jossey-Bass, 1997.

Peck, M. Scott. *The Road Less Traveled.* New York: Touchstone, 1978.

Peters, Ted. "Atonement and the Final Scapegoat." *Perspectives in Religious Studies* 19 (1992): 151–81.

Petersen, Randy. "Modern Voices: The Christian and Money." *Christian History* 6 (1987): 28–33.

Peterson, Eugene H. *The Message: The New Testament in Contemporary Language.* Colorado Springs: NavPress, 1993.

Peterson, James C. *Genetic Turning Points: The Ethics of Human Genetic Intervention.* Grand Rapids, Mich.: Eerdmans, 2001.

Pinnock, Sarah. *Beyond Theodicy: Jewish and Christian Continental Thinkers Respond to the Holocaust.* Albany: SUNY Press, 2002.

Porter, Roy. *The Greatest Benefit to Mankind: A Medical History of Humanity.* New York: W. W. Norton, 1997.

Purtill, Richard L. "Did C. S. Lewis Lose His Faith?" Pages 27–62 in *A Christian for All Christians.* Edited by Andrew Walker and James Patrick. London: Hodder & Stoughton, 1990.

*Rader, Dick and Sue. *A Road Beyond the Suffering: An Experiential Journey through the Book of Job.* Franklin, Tenn.: Providence House, 1997. A series of candid, thoughtful letters between a husband and wife. The wife had experienced medical problems on the mission field. The husband later died from cancer.

Rae, Scott. *Moral Choices: An Introduction to Ethics.* Grand Rapids, Mich.: Zondervan, 1995.

Rasmussen, Larry, ed. *Reinhold Niebuhr: Theologian of Public Life.* Minneapolis: Fortress, 1991.

Rauschenbusch, Walter. *Christianizing the Social Order.* New York: n.p., 1912.

*Richard, Lucien. *What Are They Saying About the Theology of Suffering?* New York: Paulist, 1992. A helpful overview of several scholars on biblical and theological responses to the problem of evil and suffering.

Robinson, H. Wheeler. *Suffering Human and Divine.* New York: Macmillan, 1939.

Robinson, Marilynne. *Gilead.* New York: Farrar, Straus, and Giroux, 2004.

Rubenstein, Richard L. *After Auschwitz: Radical Theology and Contemporary Judaism.* Indianapolis: Bobbs-Merrill, 1966.

Russell, Jeffrey Burton. *History of Heaven: The Singing Silence.* Princeton: Princeton University Press, 1997.

Rust, Eric C. *Towards a Theological Understanding of History.* New York: Oxford University Press, 1963.

Sanders, Brenda J. "Why Does God Allow Disasters to Happen?" *The Baptist Messenger* (8 October 1992): 13.

Sanders, John. *The God Who Risks: A Theology of Providence.* Downers Grove, Ill.: InterVarsity, 1998.

———. *No Other Name: An Investigation into the Destiny of the Unevangelized.* Grand Rapids, Mich.: Eerdmans, 1992.

Sapp, W. David. "The Church and Economic Life." Pages 163–83 in *Understanding Christian Ethics: An Interpretive Approach.* Edited by William M. Tillman, Jr. Nashville: Broadman, 1988.

Sayer, George. *Jack: C. S. Lewis and His Times.* San Francisco: Harper & Row, 1988.

Scalise, Pamela J. "I Have Produced a Man with the LORD: God as Provider of Offspring in Old Testament Theology." *Review & Expositor* 91 (1994): 577–89.

———. "To Fear or Not to Fear: Questions of Reward and Punishment in Malachi 2:17–4:3." *Review & Expositor* 84 (1987): 409–18.

Scheib, Karen D. *Challenging Invisibility: Practices of Care with Older Women.* St. Louis: Chalice, 2004.

*Schilling, S. Paul. *God and Human Anguish.* Nashville: Abingdon, 1977. An excellent academic study of theodicy sprinkled with illustrations from life and literature.

Schneider, John R. *The Gospel of Affluence: Seeking God in a Culture of Wealth.* Grand Rapids, Mich.: Eerdmans, 2002.

Schuchardt, Erika. *Why Is This Happening to Me?* Minneapolis: Augsburg, 1989.

Schwarz, Hans. *Eschatology.* Grand Rapids, Mich.: Eerdmans, 2000.

Scott, R. B. Y. *The Way of Wisdom in the Old Testament.* New York: Macmillan, 1971.

"See Spot Go to Heaven? The Public's Not Sure." ABC News/Beliefnet Poll. Accessed July 23, 2001 at www.beliefnet.com.

Segal, Alan F. *Life After Death: A History of the Afterlife in the Religions of the World.* New York: Doubleday, 2004.

Sellew, Philip. "Paul, Martyrdom of." Pages 204–5 in vol. 5 of *The Anchor Bible Dictionary*. 6 vols. Edited by David Noel Freedman. New York: Doubleday, 1992.

Seuss, Dr. *The Butter Battle Book*. New York: Random House, 1984.

——. *The Sneetches, and Other Stories*. New York: Random House, 1961.

Seybold, Klaus, and Ulrich B. Mueller. *Sickness & Healing*. Translated by Douglas W. Stott. Nashville: Abingdon, 1981.

Seymour, Robert E. *Aging Without Apology: Living the Senior Years with Integrity and Faith*. Valley Forge, Penn.: Judson, 1995.

Shakespeare, William. *As You Like It*.

Sheehy, Gail. *Passages: Predictable Crises of Adult Life*. New York: Bantam, 1977.

Sherrill, Lewis Joseph. *The Struggles of the Soul*. New York: Macmillan, 1951.

Sider, Ronald J. *Christ and Violence*. Scottdale, Penn.: Herald, 1979.

——. *Just Generosity: A New Vision for Overcoming Poverty*. Grand Rapids, Mich.: Baker, 1999.

——. *Living Like Jesus: Eleven Essentials for Growing a Genuine Faith*. Grand Rapids, Mich.: Baker, 1996.

——. *Rich Christians in an Age of Hunger: A Biblical Study*. Downers Grove, Ill.: InterVarsity, 1977.

*Simundson, Daniel J. *Faith Under Fire: Biblical Interpretations of Suffering*. Minneapolis: Augsburg, 1980. An accessible study of biblical teaching on suffering. Focuses on key texts such as Job and Isaiah, with less attention given to the New Testament.

——. "Health and Healing in the Bible." *Word and World* 2 (1982): 330–39.

——. *Where Is God in My Suffering? Biblical Responses to Seven Searching Questions*. Minneapolis: Augsburg, 1983.

Sisk, Ronald D. "World Peace." Pages 208–14 in *Understanding Christian Ethics: An Interpretive Approach*. Edited by William M. Tillman Jr. Nashville: Broadman, 1988.

Smedes, Lewis B. *Choices: Making Right Decisions in a Complex World*. San Francisco: Harper & Row, 1986.

———. *The Art of Forgiving: When You Need to Forgive and Don't Know How.* Nashville: Moorings, 1996.

———. *Forgive and Forget: Healing the Hurts We Don't Deserve.* San Francisco: Harper & Row, 1981.

———. *Mere Morality: What God Expects from Ordinary People.* Grand Rapids, Mich.: Eerdmans, 1983.

Smith, David L. *A Handbook of Contemporary Theology.* Wheaton, Ill.: Bridgepoint, 1992.

Smith, Ebbie C. "Environlove: The Christian Approach to Ecology." *Southwestern Journal of Theology* 37 (1995): 23-31.

Smith, Sid. "Preparing for Multiethnic Ministry." Pages 145-61 in *Understanding Christian Ethics: An Interpretive Approach.* Edited by William M. Tillman, Jr. Nashville: Broadman, 1988.

Soelle, Dorothee. *Suffering.* Translated by Everett R. Kalin. Philadelphia: Fortress, 1975.

*Stackhouse, John G. *Can God Be Trusted? Faith and the Challenge of Evil.* New York: Oxford University Press, 1998. An outstanding study of the theological issues surrounding suffering. Scholarly yet readable.

Stafford, Tim. "Animal Lib." *Christianity Today* (6 June 1990): 18-23.

Stagg, Frank. *The Bible Speaks on Aging.* Nashville: Broadman, 1981.

Stassen, Glen H. "Biblical Teaching on Capital Punishment." *Review & Expositor* 93 (1996): 485-96.

Stassen, Glen H., and David P. Gushee. *Kingdom Ethics: Following Jesus in Contemporary Context.* Downers Grove, Ill.: InterVarsity, 2003.

Stephenson, Lynda Rutledge. *Give Us a Child: Coping with the Personal Crisis of Infertility.* San Francisco: Harper & Row, 1987.

Stevens, R. Paul. "Friendship." Pages 435-42 in *The Complete Book of Everyday Christianity.* Edited by Robert Banks and R. Paul Stevens. Downers Grove, Ill.: InterVarsity, 1997.

Stiver, Dan R. "The Problem of Theodicy." *Review & Expositor* 93 (1996): 507-17.

Stoops, Robert F., Jr. "Peter and Paul, Passion of." Page 264 in vol. 5 of *The Anchor Bible Dictionary.* 6 vols. Edited by David Noel Freedman. New York: Doubleday, 1992.

Stott, John R. W. *The Cross of Christ.* Downers Grove, Ill.: InterVarsity, 1986.

*Surin, Kenneth. *Theology and the Problem of Evil.* New York: Blackwell, 1986. A scholarly study of theodicy. Divides theodicies into the more theoretically oriented and the more practical theodicies.

Swartley, Willard M. *Homosexuality: Biblical Interpretation and Moral Discernment.* Scottdale, Penn.: Herald, 2003.

———. *Slavery, Sabbath, War & Women: Case Studies in Biblical Interpretation.* Scottdale, Penn.: Herald, 1983.

Tate, Marvin E. "Satan in the Old Testament." *Review & Expositor* 89 (1992): 461-74.

Thiel, John E. *God, Evil, and Innocent Suffering: A Theological Reflection.* New York: Crossroad, 2002.

Thomas, Elizabeth Marshall. *The Hidden Life of Dogs.* New York: Pocket Books, 1995.

Thomas, L. Eugene, and Susan E. Eisenhandler, eds. *Religion, Belief, and Spirituality in Late Life.* New York: Springer, 1999.

Thomasma, David C. *Human Life in the Balance.* Louisville: Westminster John Knox, 1990.

Thomason, Bill. *God on Trial: The Book of Job and Human Suffering.* Collegeville, Minn.: Liturgical, 1997.

*Tiessen, Terrance. *Providence & Prayer.* Downers Grove, Ill.: InterVarsity, 2000. A scholarly study of several models for understanding how God relates to the world, including Calvinism, open theism, and process theology.

Tilley, Terrence W. *The Evils of Theodicy.* Washington, D.C.: Georgetown University Press, 1991.

Tillich, Paul. *Dynamics of Faith.* New York: Harper & Row, 1958.

Toole, David C. "Divine Ecology and the Apocalypse: A Theological Description of Natural Disasters and the Environmental Crisis." *Theology Today* 55 (1999): 547-61.

Towner, W. Sibley. *How God Deals with Evil.* Philadelphia: Westminster, 1976.

Trible, Phyllis. *God and the Rhetoric of Sexuality.* Overtures to Biblical Theology. Philadelphia: Fortress, 1978.

———. *Texts of Terror: Literary-Feminist Readings of Biblical Narratives*. Overtures to Biblical Theology. Philadelphia: Fortress, 1984.

Trull, Audra, and Joe Trull, eds. *Putting Women in Their Place: Moving Beyond Gender Stereotypes in Church and Home*. Macon, Ga.: Smyth & Helwys, 2003.

Trull, Joe. *Walking in the Way: An Introduction to Christian Ethics*. Nashville: Broadman & Holman, 1997.

Tuck, William Powell. *Getting Past the Pain: Making Sense of Life's Darkness*. Macon, Ga.: Peake Road, 1997.

*Tupper, E. Frank. *A Scandalous Providence: The Jesus Story of the Compassion of God*. Macon, Ga.: Mercer University Press, 1995. One of the best academic studies of God's providence. Prompted in part by his wife's struggle with cancer. Focuses on the New Testament especially.

Turnage, Mac N., and Anne Shaw Turnage. *Grace Keeps You Going: Spiritual Wisdom from Cancer Survivors*. Louisville: Westminster John Knox, 2001.

Van Leeuwen, Raymond C. "Breeding Stock or Lords of Creation?" *Christianity Today* (11 November 1991): 36-37.

Verhey, Allen. *Remembering Jesus: Christian Community, Scripture, and the Moral Life*. Grand Rapids, Mich.: Eerdmans, 2002.

Vieth, Richard F. *Holy Power, Human Pain*. Bloomington, Ind.: Meyer Stone, 1988.

Wakefield, Dan *Expect a Miracle: The Miraculous Things that Happen to Ordinary People*. San Francisco: HarperSanFrancisco, 1995.

Walls, Jerry L. *Heaven: The Logic of Eternal Joy*. Oxford: Oxford University Press, 2002.

Weatherhead, Leslie D. *Why Do Men Suffer?* 7th ed. London: Student Christian Movement Press, 1947.

———. *The Will of God*. New York: Abingdon-Cokesbury, 1944.

Webb, Stephen. *Good Eating*. Grand Rapids, Mich.: Brazos, 2001.

———. *On God and Dogs: A Christian Theology of Compassion for Animals*. New York: Oxford University Press, 1998.

Weems, Renita J. *Battered Love: Marriage, Sex, and Violence in the Hebrew Prophets*. Minneapolis: Fortress, 1995.

Weinandy, Thomas G. *Does God Suffer?* Notre Dame: University of Notre Dame Press, 2000.

Welty, Eudora, and Ronald A. Sharp, eds. *The Norton Book of Friendship.* New York: Norton, 1991.

Wennberg, Robert N. *God, Humans, and Animals: An Invitation to Enlarge Our Moral Universe.* Grand Rapids, Mich.: Eerdmans, 2003.

———. *Terminal Choices: Euthanasia, Suicide, and the Right to Die.* Grand Rapids, Mich.: Eerdmans, 1989.

Wesley, John. "The General Deliverance." Pages 436-50 in *The Works of John Wesley, Volume 2.* Edited by Albert C. Outler. Nashville: Abingdon, 1985.

White, Lynn. "The Historical Roots of Our Ecological Crisis." Pages 15-31 in *Ecology and Religion in History.* Edited by David Spring and Eileen Spring. New York: Harper & Row, 1974.

*Wiesel, Elie. *Night.* Translated by Stella Rodway. New York: Avon, 1969. A moving account by a Jewish survivor of the Holocaust.

Wiersbe, Warren. *From Worry to Worship: Studies in Habakkuk.* Wheaton, Ill.: Victor, 1983.

Willard, Dallas. *The Divine Conspiracy: Rediscovering Our Hidden Life in God.* San Francisco: HarperSanFrancisco, 1998.

Willimon, William H. *The Service of God: How Worship and Ethics Are Related.* Nashville: Abingdon, 1983.

Wilson, A. N. *C. S. Lewis: A Biography.* New York: W. W. Norton, 1990.

Wiseman, Donald J. *1 & 2 Kings.* Tyndale Old Testament Commentaries. Downers Grove, Ill.: InterVarsity, 1993.

*Wolterstorff, Nicholas. *Lament for a Son.* Grand Rapids, Mich.: Eerdmans, 1987. Reflections by a Christian professor emeritus of philosophical theology at Yale Divinity School about his son's accidental death.

"Women's Leadership in the Church" [theme issue]. *Review & Expositor* 95 (1998).

Wood, John A. *Perspectives on War in the Bible.* Macon, Ga.: Mercer University Press, 1998.

Woods, B. W. *Christians in Pain.* Grand Rapids, Mich.: Baker, 1974.

Wright, N. T. *The Resurrection of the Son of God.* Minneapolis: Fortress, 2003.

Yancey, Philip. *Disappointment with God: Three Questions No One Asks Aloud.* Grand Rapids, Mich.: Zondervan, 1988.

Yoder, John H. *What Would You Do?* Scottdale, Penn.: Herald, 1983.

*Young, Frances. *Face to Face: A Narrative Essay in the Theology of Suffering.* Edinburgh: T&T Clark, 1990. A Christian theologian and ordained minister reflects on her son being born brain damaged (microcephalic).

INDEX OF AUTHORS AND SUBJECTS

INDEX OF SCRIPTURE REFERENCES